The Christian Initiation Series

GUIDE FOR
SPONSORS

FOURTH EDITION

Ron Lewinski

LITURGY
TRAINING
PUBLICATIONS

Nihil Obstat
D. Todd Williamson
Censor Deputatus
March 4, 2008

Imprimatur
Reverend John F. Canary, STL, DMin
Vicar General
Archdiocese of Chicago
March 5, 2008

GUIDE FOR SPONSORS, FOURTH EDITION © 2008, 1993, 1987, 1980 Archdiocese of Chicago: Liturgy Training Publications, 1800 North Hermitage Avenue, Chicago IL 60622; 1-800-933-1800, fax 1-800-933-7094, e-mail orders@ltp.org. All rights reserved. See our Web site at www.LTP.org.

Photos on pages viii, 14, and 56 © John Zich; on pages 20, 38, and 46 © Bill and Peggy Wittman; and on page 32 © St. James Cathedral.

Printed in the United States of America.

Library of Congress Control Number: 2008923099

ISBN 978-1-56854-658-2

ECIGS4

Table of Contents

Dear Godparent or Sponsor,

You have been chosen to be a godparent for someone who is preparing for Baptism or a sponsor for someone who is preparing for reception into the full communion of the Roman Catholic Church. What a wonderful opportunity and humbling invitation! You may be asking yourself whether you are worthy or qualified. Although you may be committed to your faith, you may wonder if your understanding and practice of the faith is something you will be able to communicate and share with another. Remember what Saint Paul wrote to the Corinthians: "We have this treasure in clay jars, so that it may be made clear that this extraordinary power belongs to God and does not come from us" (2 Corinthians 4:7). Keeping these words in mind may keep you from becoming too anxious about being a worthy sponsor. Saint Paul's words may also help you to avoid taking too much credit for what God will accomplish through you.

Being a sponsor is like being a trusted friend or mentor. You share what you can. Your faith becomes transparent in the simple and natural process of accompanying another on a spiritual journey. You offer support and counsel as you are able, and to the extent that it is needed or desired. Each relationship between a sponsor and a catechumen or candidate is unique. Each catechumen or candidate has a distinct history, a unique relationship with God, and a personality that must be respected.

As a sponsor, you accompany a catechumen through a formation process that reaches its climax in the initiation sacraments of Baptism, Confirmation, and Eucharist at the Easter Vigil. The Church also refers to your role as a "godparent." If you are accompanying a candidate who is a baptized Christian preparing for the Rite of Reception into the Full Communion with the Roman Catholic Church, the rite of reception may be celebrated at any point during the year, sometimes at the Easter Vigil.

Sponsors establish an enduring relationship with the catechumen or candidate through the sacramental rites that are celebrated and the natural bonds that grow throughout the formation process. Therefore, there needs to be an openness on the part of the sponsor to a relationship that God will use for the benefit of the candidate or catechumen.

This book is provided to assist you in your role as a sponsor. It will offer you some background and support as a resource for how you might best fulfill your responsibilities. The catechumenal ministry in your parish will introduce you to some of the specific expectations for being a sponsor in your community. Be aware that no guide or manual could spell out every aspect of what might be expected in your role, nor could it anticipate every possible scenario. Ultimately, it is the Holy Spirit who will give you the gifts needed to be a positive and effective influence on the life of another. In your preparation for assuming this special ministry in the Church, ask the Holy Spirit to guide and direct your efforts. And don't be surprised if the Spirit has a plan in mind for calling you to a deeper conversion and commitment to the Church through this whole process. God's grace is always at work among us. God be with you!

Father Ron Lewinski

The Prayer of a Godparent or Sponsor

God of all ages,
you send your Holy Spirit
to touch the hearts of people
so that they may believe in you
and in Jesus, whom you sent to save us.

Look kindly on all catechumens and candidates
as they listen to your voice.
Open their hearts to your life-giving Spirit
and bring to fulfillment the good work
you have begun in them.

As I accept the call to accompany N. on his/her journey of faith,
make me an instrument of your love and grace.
Teach me to reverence what is holy
in the one I am called to sponsor
and to be patient with what I do not understand.
Deepen my faith in the Gospel
and help me to pass it on by word and example.
When N. is hesitant or afraid,
let me offer encouragement.
When N. feels weak or confused,
let me be a source of strength and reassurance.
When N. arrives at new insights
and noticeably grows in faith,
let me affirm the gifts I see.

I humbly accept the ministry of sponsor
and pray that you will continue to guide me and sustain me
in fulfilling my role in this special ministry
to which I have been called.

I praise you through Christ our Lord.

Amen.

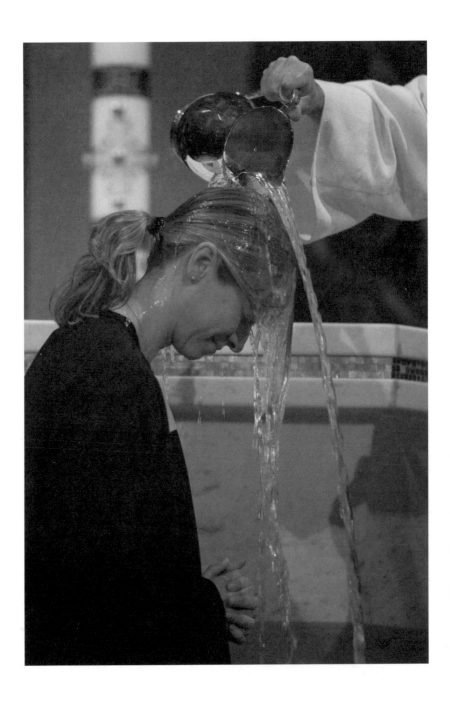

Chapter One

The Christian Initiation of Adults

Have you witnessed an adult Baptism at the solemn celebration of the Easter Vigil? What a joyful occasion it is to baptize new members into Christ's body on this night when we celebrate the Resurrection of the Lord and his victory over sin and death! The meaning and impact of the Easter mystery comes alive in a very special way as we celebrate the sacraments of initiation: Baptism, Confirmation, and Eucharist. The liturgy of the Easter Vigil, including the initiation of new members, has the power to stir up within us the grace of our Baptism and our participation in the life-giving death and Resurrection of Jesus.

As you've witnessed the Baptism of adults or the reception of baptized Christians into the full communion of the Catholic Church, have you ever wondered how they arrived at this point? What led them to Baptism and the desire to share in the Eucharist? What did they have to do to prepare for Baptism or reception into full communion with the Catholic Church? How long did their preparation take? Who was involved in the process? These are some of the questions this *Guide for Sponsors* will attempt to answer for you. As a sponsor, you will learn firsthand what the process of becoming a Christian involves and what is required of an already baptized Christian who desires to become a Roman Catholic.

Five Key Components

Becoming a Christian or professing one's faith in the Catholic Church is an all-encompassing process that engages the whole person. It includes these key components: conversion, community, prayer/ritual, catechesis, and formation for mission.

Conversion Is the Heart of Initiation

The word *conversion* has many meanings. Put most simply, it means change: a move from one way of seeing life and living to another. In this move, something is gained, but something else is let go. That letting go makes conversion difficult and sometimes even painful.

When people talk about someone "converting to Catholicism," they usually mean that a baptized Protestant has decided to become a Roman Catholic. The kind of conversion we are talking about here, however, goes much deeper than a transfer of Church membership. What we are discussing is a change of attitude, values, priorities, and behavior. And the standard for this change is nothing less than the teaching of Jesus. The conversion we are describing means believing firmly in Jesus Christ as Lord and accepting everything Jesus stands for as a model for one's life.

This kind of conversion doesn't happen easily, nor does it come about in a flash. When we make a choice to believe in the one God, Father, Son, and Holy Spirit, it may take a long time, even a lifetime, to reshape our lives accordingly. This is important to remember when you are sponsoring a catechumen or candidate. We cannot expect everyone to reach our ideal of a converted Christian life within the short span of the catechumenal process. Nor would it be fair to expect everyone to progress at the same pace and to reach the same depth of faith. For those who are being received into full communion with the Church, we presume that they are converted to Christ Jesus. They may have a very strong faith and an active prayer life. Nevertheless, conversion is a lifelong process. And so there is always room for growth as we stretch to become more deeply committed to Christ.

As you read this, you may begin to wonder whether you are truly converted to Christ Jesus and the kingdom he preached. It's natural to feel that way. That's why the Church's preaching and celebration of the sacraments always calls us to an ongoing conversion of life. From season to season and feast to feast, we encounter the mystery of Christ, which challenges us to deeper faith. Our transformation continues daily.

Conversion to Jesus Christ is no easy thing, especially when much of society is at odds with Gospel values. Frequently, the world's values are so effectively marketed that we need all the help we can get to put on the mind of Christ. The sponsor's ministry is crucial in helping new Christians learn to follow in the way of Christ.

Community

The process of becoming a Christian involves the whole community. The very meaning of Christian initiation implies initiation into a body of believers, the mystical body of Christ. Once we are baptized, we are joined to Christ and his Church. We come to faith through the witness and support, teaching, prayer, and encouragement of others. As faith is shared with us, we come to a deeper understanding and appreciation for how faith is lived. We grow in the awareness of how the Holy Spirit is at work among us. The strength and solidarity of the Christian community enables us to do the work of Christ together in a way that we could not do alone. The purpose of community is more than just a provision for organizational unity. The heart of our living in communion reflects our grounding in the Trinity, the perfect communion of love and unity.

As a sponsor, you will be a direct link from the parish community to the person you sponsor. You will be able to pass on the tradition and values, customs, and spirit of the community to the person you sponsor. What is most important is that you will give witness to the living Christ by simply sharing your experience as a Catholic Christian that is ultimately grounded in your relationship with the Lord. Your faith and your love for the Church will naturally spill over into the life of the individual you are sponsoring.

If you are sponsoring someone who is preparing for Baptism, the role you assume is traditionally referred to as a godparent. If you are accompanying someone who is a baptized Christian preparing for reception into the full communion with the Catholic Church, the title of sponsor is appropriate. In this book, we will use the term "sponsor" to refer to both godparents and sponsors.

Prayer/Ritual

It's important to acknowledge that the process of becoming a Christian or that of a baptized adult joining the Catholic Church is not an academic exercise. It's not just a matter of learning "about" Jesus Christ but meeting him and establishing a relationship with him. Prayer leads us into communion with God. Ultimately, it is God who takes the initiative in calling us into communion with him. Jesus said, "You did not choose me but I chose you" (John 15:16). Prayer and ritual is our response to God's call or invitation. We leave ourselves open in prayer to the Holy Spirit's guidance and direction. Saint Paul says, "Likewise the Spirit helps us in our weakness; for we do not know how to pray as we ought" (Romans 8:26).

All the members of the community have a responsibility to pray for those who are making the journey of faith that ultimately leads them to the Lord's table. As a sponsor, you have a special calling to keep the one you sponsor in your prayers throughout the process.

We are blessed as Catholics with a rich tradition of prayer and liturgical rituals. Among the forms and styles of prayer, many are practiced universally. Others may be more common in particular cultures or ethnic groups. In the process of sponsoring, you will have the opportunity, along with the one you sponsor, to explore some of the Church's prayer traditions. Some of these prayer practices may be new to you, or you may discover new insights or a better appreciation for a form or method of prayer. It will be important to remain open to different prayer experiences, so that you will not only have the opportunity to grow in your practice of prayer but model for the one you sponsor an openness that we would hope to see in them.

In addition to teaching others how to pray, the process of becoming a Christian and a member of the Church is marked by ritual steps along the way that celebrate the grace of God at work within those who are making this journey of faith. These liturgical rituals, the communal prayer of the Church, remind us that it is not by our human efforts alone that an individual's conversion and commitment to Christ comes about but by the power of God's acting among us.

Catechesis

In his great commission to his apostles, Jesus entrusted the continuation of his mission to the Church so that the Good News of salvation would be announced to all the nations (see Matthew 28:16–20). At the heart of this commission is proclaiming Jesus Christ himself and all that Jesus taught. The Gospel that the apostles handed on is the same Gospel that we treasure as the foundation of our faith today. The word *catechesis* refers to the essential ministry of the Church to proclaim the Gospel and the teachings of the Church that are grounded in the teaching of Jesus. The purpose of catechesis is not simply acquiring religious information but to lead people "to enter the mystery of Christ, to encounter him, and to discover themselves and the meaning of their lives in him" (*National Directory for Catechesis,* #19B).

The process in which you will be involved will include a very significant catechetical component. You are not being asked to be a catechist, one who formally teaches the faith. As a sponsor, however, you will be able to share how you have come to integrate the faith and doctrines of the Church into your life. Do not be anxious about this. Accept the fact that the Church presumes that we are all committed to lifelong catechesis. Even if you were blessed with a solid Catholic upbringing, the place in life you find yourself in today will raise new questions and give rise to new insights about the faith that you were unaware of in earlier years. That should give you a hint that catechesis is more than just learning quick answers to frequently asked questions about Catholicism. The *National Directory for Catechesis* quotes Pope John Paul II's apostolic exhortation *On Catechesis in Our Time:* "The definitive aim of catechesis is to put people not only in touch but in communion, in intimacy, with Jesus Christ: only he can lead us to the love of the Father in the Spirit and make us share in the life of the Holy Trinity" (#19B).

Catechesis helps us to integrate the scriptures and the teachings of Jesus and his Church in such a way that our values and our outlook on life are shaped by our beliefs. The greatest challenge to catechesis will be the culture in which we live. In a society where individualism, relativism, materialism, and religious indifference are rampant, the message of Jesus and the teaching of the Church will be a countercultural message. Catechesis will call us to a deeper conversion, for we will have to make a conscious and deliberate choice about what values, what morals, what fundamental truths we will follow. Through the process of catechesis, our identity is formed as disciples of Jesus and as members of his Church. As a sponsor, you can expect that there will be some difficult points along the way when the one you are sponsoring may have to struggle with a change in belief, values, and lifestyle prompted by what he or she is experiencing in catechesis.

Just as we Catholics have a rich tradition in prayer, we also have a wealth of teaching and doctrine that enlightens our faith. Some fundamental Catholic teachings ought to be known and understood by every Catholic. Unfortunately, it's all too common to find Catholics today who do not know the basics of their Catholic faith. A thorough catechesis will provide these basics and give Catholics a common language and the fundamental teachings of the Church upon which all Catholic Christians build their lives.

A great deal of diversity in the religious background or spiritual awareness is found among those who have asked to be baptized or to be received into the Catholic Church. Do not presume that everyone in your group comes without faith or has never been catechized in the fundamentals of the Christian tradition. It's not uncommon that Catholic sponsors and catechists are inspired by an inquirer's or candidate's personal relationship with God. Allow yourself to be surprised by what you can learn from the individual you sponsor. Remember that the Holy Spirit moves freely and touches the lives of all who open their hearts.

Formation for Mission

To be a Christian is to be a disciple in mission. By virtue of our Baptism, we are all called to spread the Good News and to further the kingdom of God. Joined to Christ and his Church like a vine and its branches, we share in the Church's mission in the world. Our vocation is to transform society by the values of the Gospel. Beginning with Christian family life as the place where disciples and missionaries are formed, Christians are called to live their faith in the midst of the world. The works of charity and justice are not optional side interests for Christians but integral to discipleship. Human labor becomes an expression of our sharing in the creative power of God. The Creator holds us responsible as stewards of all that has been divinely created.

Preparing others for mission in the world needs also to be part of our total formation in faith. While the parish is home to our practice of the faith, as Catholics our vision is always being stretched to include a more catholic or universal vision that puts us in solidarity with our brothers and sisters around the globe.

You may be asked to introduce the person you sponsor to some of the ways in which your parish or the larger Church reaches out in mission to others. The Church makes a difference in the world by its firm stand on social issues and its affirmative action in various sectors of society. Each Christian is called to put faith into action given one's gifts and abilities and the needs and opportunities that present themselves. You may find that, as a sponsor, this journey of faith in which you are participating will open up new doors to exercise your missionary vocation.

Placing These Key Components into a Structure: The Rite of Christian Initiation of Adults

How does the Church take the components of conversion, community, prayer/ritual, catechesis, and formation for mission and provide a structure where all of these components work together in harmony? The *Rite of Christian Initiation of Adults* (RCIA) is the Church's ritual process for calling adults to conversion and preparing them for Baptism, Confirmation, and Eucharist. All of the key components that we have addressed above are brought together in the *Rite of Christian Initiation of Adults* in such a way that Catholic communities around the world are provided with a common vision and plan for forming new Christians. This rite is intended primarily for those who are preparing for Baptism. However, the spirit and wisdom of this rite also serves as a paradigm for the continuing efforts of the Church in the ongoing formation of all its members. At the heart of the RCIA is the universal call to holiness through ongoing conversion and a lifelong catechesis. Pastoral adaptations are provided in the rite for baptized adults who are preparing for reception into the full communion of the Roman Catholic Church. Some accommodations for ministry to the baptized will need to be made with care and sensitivity, always respecting the baptismal status and religious background of the candidate. Any confusion must be avoided that would treat the baptized in the same way as the unbaptized. It would be inappropriate to celebrate rites that presume that an individual has not already been claimed by Christ in Baptism or to offer prayers that imply a lack of belief in Jesus Christ.

Those who come seeking Christ and initiation into the Church through Baptism are initially called "inquirers." When they are ready to formally commit themselves to the process that is outlined in the *Rite of Christian Initiation of Adults* and the community finds them to be ready, they become catechumens. Later, at the beginning of Lent when they are formally called to the Easter sacraments, they are the elect. Adults who are preparing for reception into the full communion are candidates.

The Stages of the Initiation Process

This brief outline of the periods in the process of Christian initiation as prescribed in the *Rite of Christian Initiation of Adults* is provided to help you understand the purpose and dynamic of the order of Christian initiation. The framework provides room for adaptations that respect both the backgrounds of the candidates and catechumens, and the nature of the local community. The catechumenate team in your community can explain how each of these periods takes shape within your parish.

I. PERIOD OF INQUIRY: The first period of the process is known as the period of inquiry, or precatechumenate. It is a time for evangelization. The basic Gospel message is proclaimed, and inquirers reflect on their lives in its light. This is a good time for inquirers to have questions answered that they may have had for years about the Church, its beliefs, and practices. Even those who already believe in the Gospel of Jesus Christ can find this a time to hear the message anew and move to a deeper conversion of mind and heart.

During this period, some inquirers may choose not to pursue initiation, either because they feel the time is not right for them, or because they feel they are not ready to make the Catholic Church their spiritual home. The Church respects the decision of each inquirer.

II. PERIOD OF THE CATECHUMENATE: The unbaptized who profess their faith in Jesus Christ and desire to enter the Church are accepted as catechumens at the Rite of Acceptance into the Order of Catechumens. To say that the catechumens belong to an "order" in the

Church means that they have a particular status within the Church that is recognized in canon law (Church law). The baptized faithful form another order of the Church, the order of the laity, and the ordained ministers constitute still another order, the clergy. Those who belong to the order of catechumens are considered part of the household of Christ. Although they are still unbaptized, the Church embraces them with a mother's love and nourishes them with the word of God.

During the period of the catechumenate, much of the catechesis, or teaching, takes place. With the help of a sponsor and other members of the parish, the catechumens experience the Church as a community of the faithful. They explore the community's spirit, its work, its prayer, its creed, and its mission.

The initial conversion of the catechumens is deepened as they discover the tremendous love of God and become convinced of the power of God in their lives and in the life of the community. Persons may remain catechumens from a few months to a number of years.

Baptized adults preparing for reception into full communion and uncatechized Catholics preparing to complete their initiation may join the catechumens during this period, if it is helpful to their formation. The optional Rite of Welcoming the Candidates formally acknowledges commitment to the formation process and desire for Confirmation and Eucharist.

III. PERIOD OF PURIFICATION AND ENLIGHTENMENT: Catechumens who are ready for Baptism are invited to celebrate the Rite of Election at the beginning of Lent. Ordinarily, the Bishop presides over this rite at the cathedral or another central location. His involvement is a clear indication that the initiation of new Christians goes far beyond initiating new members into the local parish. To be ready for Baptism means that the catechumens have undergone a conversion of mind and heart and have developed a sufficient acquaintance with Christian teaching and a spirit of faith and charity.

Once the catechumens have celebrated the Rite of Election, they are referred to as the elect. By calling them elect, we are reminded that it is the Lord who has invited them into a life of faith and who, through the community of the Church, has chosen, or "elected," them to be counted among the baptized.

Lent is the time of final preparation for initiation. Through the scrutinies—rites celebrated on the Third, Fourth, and Fifth Sundays of Lent—the community assists the catechumens in strengthening all that is good in them and prays to remove all that is harmful or sinful in their lives. By reflecting with the elect on the Lenten scriptures, by passing on to the elect its practice of faith (as symbolized in the Creed) and its practice of prayer (as symbolized by the Lord's Prayer), and by observing the traditional disciplines of fasting and works of charity, the community guides the elect as they journey together toward Easter.

Candidates preparing for reception into full communion may be invited to celebrate the call to continuing conversion at the beginning of Lent. They are not included in the scrutinies and exorcisms. However, parishes may celebrate a penitential rite with them. With the catechumens and the baptized faithful, the candidates enter into the spirit of Lent, reflecting more deeply on their own Baptism, performing works of charity and penance. They use the Forty Days of Lent as a spiritual retreat in preparation for the Easter sacraments.

IV. SACRAMENTS OF INITIATION: The sacraments of Baptism, Confirmation, and Eucharist are celebrated at the Easter Vigil. Ordinarily, candidates for reception into full communion will make their profession of faith, be confirmed, and begin to participate in the Eucharist at other appropriate times during the year when they are deemed ready. For pastoral reasons, however, people will be received into full communion at the Easter Vigil. The Easter Vigil liturgy is, of course, the high point of the liturgical year for Catholics. While those who are to be baptized at the Vigil will certainly take a prominent role in the liturgy, it is important to remember that the true focus of the Vigil is on Christ Jesus, dead and risen, present among us. The whole Church is renewed this night in the light of Christ's Resurrection. That is why the entire assembly solemnly renews its baptismal vows at the Easter Vigil.

V. PERIOD OF MYSTAGOGY: The period of 50 days from Easter Sunday to Pentecost helps to unfold the meaning of the Easter mystery. This festive season of mystagogy (post-baptismal catechesis), leads new members and the whole Church to penetrate the deeper meaning of the Easter sacraments. It is a time for new members to find their home in the community and to consider how they will share in the mission of the Church through Christian service. In some dioceses, the bishop meets with the newly initiated during this time to celebrate the Eucharist. This period is a reminder to everyone that the process of spiritual growth is not completed with the celebration of the sacraments of initiation. Pastorally speaking, it would be wise to extend this mystagogy period for at least a year. Ultimately, it is a lifelong task.

A Spirituality of Baptism

Underlying this ritual process of Christian initiation is a rich spirituality on what it means to be a baptized Christian. For many Christians, Baptism may mean becoming a member of the Church. Indeed, it is. But our initiation into the Church as the body of Christ has enormous implications for our identity as Christians. When we are baptized, we are immersed into the saving death and Resurrection of Jesus Christ in such a way that our old self is said to die, and we emerge from the waters of Baptism as a new creation. Saint Paul described this mystery powerfully when he said, "Do you not know that all of us who have been baptized into Christ Jesus were baptized into his death? Therefore we have been buried with him by baptism into death, so that, just as Christ was raised from the dead by the glory of the Father, so we too might walk in newness of life" (Romans 6:3–4). By dying and rising with Christ in Baptism all our sins are forgiven, original sin and all personal sin, as well as all punishment for sin (see the *Catechism of the Catholic Church* [CCC], #1263).

Born anew in Christ Jesus we are joined to him in such an intimate way that Saint Paul could say, "It is no longer I that live, but Christ who lives in me" (Galatians 2:20). What this means is that by being members of the body of Christ we become partakers of his divine life. Our lives are taken up into the mystery of the Trinity. Even in this life we can regard ourselves as citizens of the kingdom of God. Once God claims us in Baptism as sons and daughters, nothing can undo that adoption. The seal of Baptism is the promise of eternal life. If we remain faithful to our Baptism, we can depart from this life with the hope of sharing fully in the Resurrection of Christ. The words we hear in the Eucharistic Prayer when we gather for a funeral bridges the font of Baptism to our departure from this life:

Welcome into your kingdom our departed brothers and sisters,
and all who have left this world in your friendship.
There we hope to share in your glory
when every tear will be wiped away.
On that day we shall see you, our God, as you are.

—*Eucharistic Prayer III*

To be joined to Christ in Baptism also means that we are joined to the Church, since Christ is inseparable from the Church of which he is the head. Baptized Christians are expected to live in communion with one another, striving always for the unity for which Jesus prayed to his Father when he said, "As you, Father, are in me and I am in you, may they also be in us" (John 17:21). The Church is far more than an institution with a hierarchical structure. As members of the Church, we are the living stones that form the temple of God (see 1 Corinthians 3:16–17). This makes the Church a sacrament in the world, a sign that reveals the living presence of the Lord in the midst of the world. All the baptized are bound together in a profound communion with the Trinity that forms the foundation for what it means to be members of the Church. The institutional and hierarchical structures of the Church serve this communion of the baptized.

We should not overlook the obvious fact that in Baptism we take on the name of Jesus. Once baptized we call ourselves "Christian." To bear the name of Christ is also to share in his role as "priest, prophet and king" (CCC, #1268). To share in the common priesthood of all believers means that by virtue of our Baptism we are called to offer praise and thanksgiving to God through Jesus Christ. We have a right and a duty to offer prayers of supplication for the needs of the world. Because we share in the priesthood of Jesus, we do not come to the eucharistic table as spectators but as active participants joining ourselves to Christ in his offering to the Father (CCC, #1273). Our baptismal priesthood sets us on a path that charges us to sanctify the world in the name of Jesus.

To share in the role of Christ the prophet means that we must not keep our faith to ourselves but profess what we believe before all. Baptism commissions us to be missionaries, to "proclaim the mighty acts of him who called [us] out of darkness into his marvelous light" (1 Peter 2:9). What this means practically is that we may often find ourselves in a culture with values and practices that are incompatible with the way of Jesus. Our baptismal vocation calls us to be prophetic by not giving in to popular opinion or societal pressure when we are faced with what is contrary to the Gospel.

We call Christ our king because he rules the universe. His reign transcends all space and time. Through Baptism we are citizens of his kingdom and are mandated to further his reign by our Christian influence in the world. Our mission in the world is to transform society by the values that are inherent in the teaching of Jesus and which form the hallmarks of his kingdom. The preface of the Mass for the solemnity of Our Lord Jesus Christ the King describes Christ's eternal and universal kingdom as:

> a kingdom of truth and life,
> a kingdom of holiness and grace,
> a kingdom of justice, love, and peace.

Our Baptism, then, is more than just a "rite for church membership." It is a sacrament of regeneration, adoption, and identification with Christ. It is the doorway to a new life, a life that will never end. Whether we are newly baptized or baptized long ago, we should reflect often on the power and mystery of the sacrament, renewing it daily through prayer and good works.

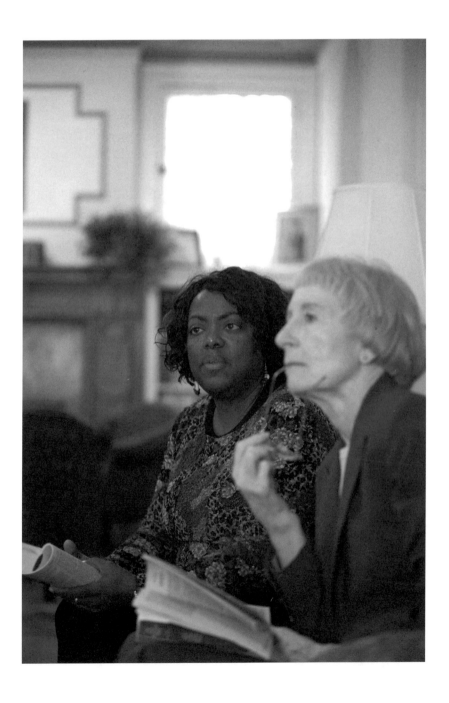

Chapter Two

What Does It Mean to Be a Sponsor?

The Church wishes to share its beliefs, its way of life, its values, its prayer, and its apostolic work with those who have expressed a desire to become Catholic Christians. Because this living tradition of the Church is all-inclusive of life, passing on this tradition of faith may take a long time. Those who have been Catholics from birth often take their Catholic upbringing and Catholic identity for granted. Our Catholic identity presumes a firm Christian foundation in a personal relationship with Jesus Christ. If we were reared in a Christian home, it was probably our parents who first introduced us to the living God and our Savior, Jesus Christ. Our families nurtured our gradual conversion to the Lord by day-to-day living, prayer, and good works. Upon this foundation, others along with our parents were able to build up our faith in the Catholic tradition. We cannot presume that every inquirer, catechumen, or candidate has had the benefit of a family-centered upbringing in the Christian faith, and obviously not in Catholicism. It is the role of the sponsor then, together with other members of the parish community, to create a milieu that will be conducive for the dynamics of conversion and passing on our faith tradition.

Receiving the Church's tradition is not like taking a class and passing the test. The tradition of the Church is a living one; it presumes that we are living the tradition that we hand on to others. It also means that what we pass on is integrated into the life of the inquirer, catechumen, or candidate. Unlike the mere exchange of information, handing on the living tradition of faith transforms lives, choices, attitudes, values, and relationships. This is the process of conversion that gradually reshapes or reorients our lives. You will play a special role in the life of the one you sponsor, as you will be a direct link for the individual to the living tradition of the Church. You will not be alone in this responsibility, for it takes the whole community to raise a Christian.

In the more immediate circle that surrounds the one you sponsor you will find catechists, catechumenate team members, pastoral staff, clergy, and other representatives of the parish community sharing their time and gifts in the creation of a seedbed where conversion, formation, and strong faith-building can occur.

Sponsors Represent the Catholic Community

Although the entire community is responsible for sharing its faith and assisting catechumens and candidates on their journey of faith, it is impractical for a large group to minister personally to each catechumen or candidate. That's why you are important. You may be a relative or friend of the one you sponsor. That will give you the advantage of knowing firsthand some of the individual's background, questions, motivation, fears, and expectations. Or the parish ministry team might have chosen you to assume the role of sponsor for an individual. In either case, as a sponsor you represent the Church to the catechumen or candidate. By your friendly support, you will help the individual feel welcome and at home in the Church. The one you sponsor will catch the spirit of the Church from you. Your positive approach to the Church and a hospitable attitude toward a catechumen or candidate will make a lasting impression. It will be helpful if you are able to introduce the catechumen or candidate to other parishioners, to the activities of the parish, and to the organizations of the community. At some point, you will be asked to share your assessment of the catechumen or candidate's progress. You can assist the pastoral team and catechumenate leadership by noting any issues, misunderstandings, or hesitations on the part of the one you sponsor. Whether you are a relative or friend, or appointed from the parish to be a sponsor, you will be expected to exercise your role with trust, respect, and confidentiality.

One of your primary responsibilities will be to accompany your candidate in the celebration of the various liturgical rites. The questions that are asked of the godparents in the Rite of Election, for example, offer some insight into what you should be attentive to in sponsoring an individual. The presider asks, "Have they faithfully listened to God's word proclaimed by the Church? Have they responded to that word and begun to walk in God's presence? Have they shared the company of their Christian brothers and sisters and joined with them in prayer?" (See RCIA, #131B.) The questions that may be asked of those who are sponsors for individuals preparing for reception into full communion are similar: "Have they faithfully listened to the apostles' instruction proclaimed by the Church? Have they come to a deeper appreciation of their baptism, in which they were joined to Christ and his Church? Have they reflected sufficiently on the traditions of the Church, which is their heritage, and joined their brothers and sisters in prayer? Have they advanced in a life of love and service of others?" Being a sponsor or godparent, then, is not just an honorary title or position. It is a relationship with a serious spiritual responsibility. The community will look to you to offer your insights and affirmation of the one you sponsor.

Sponsors Are Companions and Guides

Being a sponsor means that you serve as a companion and a guide. As a companion, the sponsor must be available to the individual. If you are a relative or friend, that availability may be more easily achieved. However, assure the catechumen or candidate of your willingness to help whenever there is need. Let him or her know when and how you can be reached. The help that you can offer will be support when there is hesitation, understanding when there is doubt, or comfort when there is inner conflict. As a sponsor, be a trustworthy companion upon whom a catechumen or candidate can trust, turn to, and talk things over.

Occasionally, the catechumen or candidate may need a gentle challenge from you when effort or enthusiasm wanes. Even a good sense of humor can be helpful. As a guide, you may have to remind yourself at times that this journey of faith does not depend entirely upon you. The Spirit is the first and most effective guide in the process. Keep a healthy and realistic perspective on life and the overall purpose of the catechumenal process. The way of the Lord, not your way or anyone else's, is the path for this journey, "for we do not proclaim ourselves; we proclaim Jesus Christ as Lord and ourselves as your slaves for Jesus' sake" (2 Corinthians 4:5).

A sponsor is not a catechist. You are not responsible for formally imparting Church teachings. That is the catechist's role. Nevertheless, the person you sponsor will likely ask you questions and seek your opinion. Honesty is best. Don't feel threatened or inadequate if you do not have a ready answer for every question. Rely on the help of the catechists and clergy. Your willingness to try to find an answer or resolve an issue will be good modeling. Two excellent resources you can rely on for what the Church teaches are the *Catechism of the Catholic Church* and the *United States Catholic Catechism for Adults.*

Sponsors Are Mentors

Catechumens and candidates learn what being a Catholic Christian is all about from many people, but in a special way from their sponsors. The constant challenge for a sponsor is to be open to growth in faith and to putting into practice what that faith requires.

In his book, *Mentoring: The Ministry of Spiritual Kinship* (Notre Dame: Ave Maria Press, 1990), Edward C. Sellner describes a spiritual mentor as a teacher, a sponsor, a host and guide, an exemplar, a counselor, and a facilitator of the other person's dream (p. 25). That sounds like a lot to expect of any person. But relax. Nobody expects you to be perfect. A sponsor who can admit limitations and who continually tries to grow is an excellent model.

A mentor's influence is often subtler than that of a teacher. You don't need outlines or lesson plans to be a sponsor. Your encouragement and advice based on your experience will go a long way in the art of sponsoring. It's good to trust the way you live out your faith on a daily basis. The one you sponsor will catch more from you than you realize.

Your catechumenate team is available to assist in your role as sponsor. They can help you grow to be more confident in your faith so that you can be a positive and effective influence on others. Trust their judgment and assume your ministry with confidence. Welcome the opportunities that the parish may offer for training sponsors. Know your strengths and use them wisely. Rely on the help of the Holy Spirit.

You may discover that your involvement as a sponsor may be a valuable time of reflection and renewal for your journey of ongoing conversion and communion with the Church. The more you are aware of the ways your faith is continually growing, the more you will appreciate the catechumen or candidate's journey of faith.

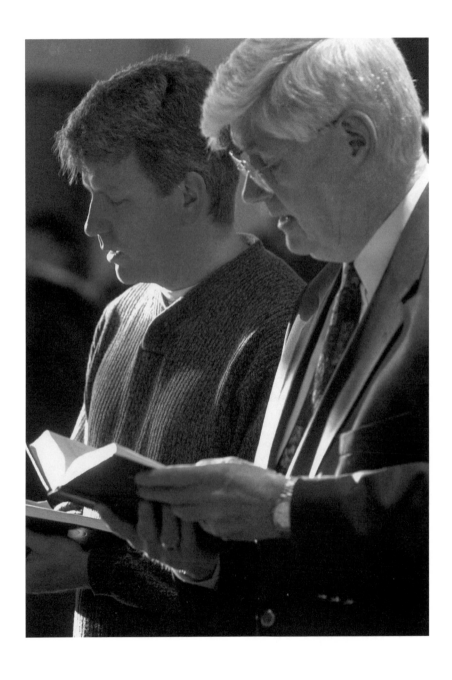

Chapter Three

Traits of an Effective Sponsor

Each community will have its way of helping sponsors fulfill their responsibilities. But all sponsors should strive to develop the following traits.

A Sponsor Prays

A sponsor humbly recognizes that he or she is an instrument whom God uses to touch the life of a catechumen or candidate. Prayer properly disposes a sponsor for this special ministry. In prayer, the sponsor can come to a greater awareness of his or her Baptism and the faith he or she will hand on.

As a sponsor, you may be asked to introduce a catechumen or candidate to some of the many forms of prayer in the Church. Keep the person you sponsor in your prayers and ask God for the wisdom and guidance to be the best sponsor that you can be. If you have a healthy prayer life, the catechumen or candidate will learn how to pray from your example. Anyone can teach different styles of prayer, but only a person who prays can convey the life and spirit behind the words and gestures.

This ministry may inspire you to deepen your prayer life. Begin by allowing yourself enough time for prayer. As simple as that may so nd, you may find it difficult to put that into practice. As the pace of life increases, often the first thing we drop is our prayer time, as if it were a luxury we could do without. Finding the right time and maybe even the right place for prayer is not easy for busy people, but we must be committed to regular prayer. We cannot afford not to be.

SOURCES OF PRAYER: Many sources can help us grow in prayer. The scriptures are a firm foundation for prayer. Spend time in silence with a few lines from scripture, reflecting on the message and allowing a prayer to flow freely from your heart. The Sunday scriptures provide the most suitable structure for this style of prayer. When the catechumenate meets after dismissal from the Liturgy of the Word, there is even more reason for sponsors to use the Lectionary as their prayer book. By doing so, they will be all the more in tune with the catechumens who use the Lectionary as their catechism.

The psalms are a rich source of prayer. As a faithful Jew, Jesus prayed the psalms daily. We sing the psalms at Mass and use them in most of our liturgical services. They form the basis for the Church's official daily prayer, the Liturgy of the Hours. Become better acquainted with the psalms. They reflect the full gamut of human emotions. They can become a good foundation for your prayer.

An often overlooked source of prayer is found in the very experience of life. The people we meet, the places we visit, our successes and failures, and everything that fills our memories can be the subject of reflection and prayer. Sponsors also can draw from the experience of the catechumenate as a springboard to prayer. As you listen to the one you sponsor, you will be left in awe and wonder at times. On those occasions, entrust yourself to the Holy Spirit in a prayer of praise, realizing that you have witnessed the Spirit at work in your midst.

For help with understanding the power and dynamics of prayer, refer to Part IV of the *Catechism of the Catholic Church,* which is devoted to Christian prayer.

Chapter six of this book contains some traditional Catholic prayers to use alone or with the person you are sponsoring. Catholic bookstores also can help you search out resources for prayer.

Silence

Prayer does not require a lot of words. In fact, much of our prayer time may be spent in silence. The Lord continually speaks to us, but we usually need more silence and stillness in our lives to hear the Lord's voice clearly. If our minds are filled with distractions, if we are busy finding words, or if we are fidgeting, it may be difficult to hear the message the Lord has for us. Every Christian, and certainly every sponsor, should strive for the quiet and stillness in which to hear and experience the Lord. Do not grow discouraged if you are new to making silent prayer and meditation a regular part of your day. Begin by committing yourself to a reasonable amount of time, increasing the time spent in silence as you become more comfortable with praying in this way.

COMMUNAL PRAYER AND LITURGY: The catechumenate staff undoubtedly will provide some opportunities for sponsors to pray together. You may not have had much opportunity previously for praying in a small group. The occasions of praying together will deepen your faith and broaden your experience of prayer. You will learn different styles of prayer and the language and structure for prayer. As you become more comfortable and more accustomed to group prayer, especially more spontaneous prayer, you will be better prepared to help others in the art of praying.

Along with private and group prayer, let the liturgy of the Church be the foundation for all your prayer and your constant source of spiritual nourishment and direction. Consider using some of the prayers from the Church's rites for personal prayer and reflection. Spend time focusing on the signs and symbols of the liturgy and their meaning in your life. Consider how you can use a gesture such as the Sign of the Cross more deliberately and with greater devotion. Allow your imagination to take you beyond what you see to a deeper level of meaning. Through the process of the Rite of Christian Initiation of Adults, you will develop a greater appreciation for the rhythm of the Church's life as you observe the fasts and feasts and seasons of the liturgical year.

The Church's liturgy is very often what attracts people to Catholicism. Observing the celebration of the liturgy, catechumens and candidates often become curious about why we do what we do and say what we say. We have a rich tradition of worship to share. But interest will grow into a desire to pray with us only when we have made the Church's prayer life our own. We have to model for the catechumens and candidates the Church's ideal of full, conscious, and active participation.

Finally, as you strive to deepen your prayer life, don't forget that you can learn a great deal from the catechumens and candidates. By careful listening, sponsors can discover new dimensions of prayer. Catechumens or candidates have much to teach us. Many come to us with mature experience in prayer. Sometimes the very simplicity or sincerity of their prayer can awaken within us a deeper awareness of God's work among us.

A Sponsor Listens

Sponsors are usually excited about sharing their thoughts and experiences of being a Catholic. They want the catechumen or candidate to know more about the Church and the parish. In that enthusiasm, however, is a temptation to talk more than we listen. It's a poor assumption to think that just because we are the Catholics and the ones leading this process that the catechumens or candidates have little to say, or that we have little to learn from them. It's imperative that we commit ourselves to listening with respect to the catechumen's or candidate's perspective. The goal is to provide a comfortable climate that allows an inquirer, catechumen, or candidate to ask any question without feeling foolish.

Each person comes with a unique story. That life story is like the Gospel stories that reveal the living Christ. We have to learn how to listen well to the stories of others, or we will fail to recognize Christ working in them. Of course, we cannot expect catechumens or candidates to tell their whole life story in one sitting. Trust must be built. For some people, it takes a long time to feel comfortable enough to share private thoughts or personal stories. Privacy also should be respected. Some things are best not shared publicly in a group setting. These faith formation settings are not group therapy sessions for the troubled in mind or spirit. These faith-based sessions should elicit from the participants whatever they feel free to share that is relevant in their quest for a deeper spiritual life.

Good listening can create the right climate for sharing between a sponsor and his or her catechumen or candidate. Listening is not just a matter of not talking. Good listeners put themselves completely in the presence of the speaker, giving the speaker their undivided attention. They are not preoccupied with getting a response ready while they are supposed to be listening. They not only hear the speaker's words, but they also try to understand what the speaker wants to communicate.

Good listeners catch the feelings and emotions that often lie below the spoken words. They are not so quick to offer solutions or give answers. Instead, they offer assurance that the other is being heard and understood. Sponsors who are good listeners can be of assistance to the initiation team by sharing with the catechists what the catechumens and candidates need. The questions, comments, and doubts of catechumens and candidates help to set the agenda for catechetical sessions and further spiritual formation.

In their first meetings with us, catechumens and candidates will begin to perceive whether they are going to be heard. They will judge how interested we are in them by the way we listen to what they say and don't say. Listening well is the best way to express our welcome and concern for catechumens and candidates.

A Sponsor Is Respectful

Closely related to listening is respect. Sponsors should learn not only to listen well but also to honor what they hear. Because the background of a catechumen or candidate may differ greatly from the sponsor's, there may be a temptation to judge or to point out differences. Sometimes the religious ideas, values, or priorities of a catechumen or candidate may strike a sponsor as immature, wrong, or odd, and the sponsor may lose interest or even fail to see good in the person. Sponsors need to respect and try to understand the cultural values or customs of the one they are sponsoring. If a catechumen's or candidate's viewpoints differ from Catholic teaching, a sponsor may feel threatened, defensive, or even argumentative. Most often, a discussion of religious differences can be managed more appropriately in catechetical sessions. This does not mean that a sponsor should never discuss religious differences or even challenge a catechumen's or candidate's viewpoint. But it is important that the sponsor first learn to understand and value the candidate's religious background through genuine interest and openness.

Candidates who have a Christian background occasionally come to the Catholic Church with some prejudice, suspicion, or misinformation. They may have heard stories about Catholics that they question but that still keep them wondering. Our love and respect will allow a candidate to feel comfortable and trusting enough to talk this over without feeling embarrassed or anxious about how we may respond.

Many candidates preparing for reception into full communion come to the Catholic Church with wonderful memories of the Church to which they previously belonged. They may recall their family's participation in a Church community, their introduction to the Bible, the fellowship of their former congregation, the kindness of a minister, maybe the memory of their Baptism. While they may be interested in becoming Catholic, they understandably do not want to lose or dismiss the good they remember.

By respecting the Christian roots of the candidates and acknowledging that they are not beginning all over again as Christians, sponsors can reassure candidates that they do not have to forget or regret their roots. A sponsor who respects the Christian experience of a candidate will be better able to build a bridge from past to future.

A sponsor's interest and respect for a catechumen's or candidate's religious background may at times demand some further study. If, for example, one is sponsoring someone who was Buddhist, the sponsor should seek out more information about the fundamental religious beliefs and practices of Buddhism in order to appreciate more clearly the person's position. Catechists can assist sponsors in obtaining this kind of information.

At times, what we may initially perceive as a major religious difference is merely a language difference. Becoming familiar with the terminology of other faiths can be helpful in understanding the background of catechumens and candidates.

At other times, a significant difference in the way in which we perceive the world, God, and salvation may be apparent. It will take a great deal of patience and careful listening to identify the genuine differences in the way one thinks, the assumptions made about God, or the ultimate values by which one lives.

A sponsor's understanding of and respect for a person's ethnic background, cultural heritage, values, and beliefs are the foundation for communication and a productive relationship.

A Sponsor Serves as a Bridge

It is hard to imagine how catechumens and candidates can ever feel at home in the Catholic Church if they do not become acquainted with some of the people, places, and traditions of Catholicism. Consider the many times you have entered a new situation, whether it was a neighborhood, a party, a school, a job, or an organization. What made you feel at home? It was probably getting acquainted with some of the people, with the work, or the rules or procedures of an organization. When someone introduces us to others, shows us the layout of the building, and explains the operation of things, we are no longer strangers.

As a sponsor you are a bridge between the catechumen or candidate and the Church. You have the opportunity to acquaint him or her with some of the people in your parish or community. Make sure the catechumen or candidate knows the pastoral staff and the people to turn to during formation. Introduce key people in the parish gradually, so that the newcomer may begin to see how the parish operates. Through these simple actions, your catechumen or candidate will begin to feel at home with Catholic values and customs. If you are a family member of the catechumen or candidate, you will want to introduce him or her to the religious customs of your family from table grace to those associated with the major feasts and seasons.

We Catholics take much for granted: the language we speak, the feasts we observe, the rites we celebrate, the ways we pray, the calendar we follow, the history we claim as our heritage. A sponsor should not presume that catechumens or candidates are familiar with these and other Catholic traditions or be surprised when they ask questions about them.

Adults who express interest in the Catholic Church frequently feel like strangers in the community. Not only are the people new; so are the customs and practices. Some catechumens and candidates may even be reluctant to attend liturgical services because they are not sure they will know what to do, and they do not want to be embarrassed. Even something as common to us as the Lord's Prayer or the Sign of the Cross should not be taken for granted. As a sponsor, you can help by gradually acquainting a catechumen or candidate with things that are authentically Catholic or, better still, by accompanying them to religious services so they can comfortably rely on your companionship and guidance.

Because we may take so much for granted as Catholics and are enthused about sharing the essentials of our faith and tradition, the questions and concerns of catechumens and candidates may sometimes seem unimportant. We may want to share our faith in the Eucharist, but they may be more concerned about why people use holy water when they enter the Church. The sponsor may be interested in talking about the sacraments, but the catechumen may want to know what to do at a Catholic funeral. Whatever the questions may be, if they are of interest to a catechumen or candidate, they should be addressed if he or she is going to feel at home with us.

Once they are better acquainted with Catholicism from the outside, the catechumens and candidates will be better prepared to examine the inner life of the Catholic community. A sponsor's patience and willingness to be a bridge, to introduce catechumens and candidates to the many facets of Catholic life, plays a big part in the welcoming process.

A Sponsor Respects the Candidate's Freedom

A sponsor can hold on too tightly. One of the most valuable traits in a sponsor is to respect the freedom of the catechumen or candidate.

In our enthusiasm to greet inquirers, we run the risk of leaving them unfree to probe and choose. This is especially true in the initial stages. We should not presume in our first meetings with inquirers that they are fully committed to becoming Christians or joining the Catholic Church. In welcoming them, we must respect their right to discern whether they feel called to Baptism or full communion with the Church.

There is a subtle art to warmly reaching out to inquirers while leaving them free to depart without feeling they will offend us. Our respect for them must allow them to choose which way is for them.

It may be that you will be a companion to a person who will choose to take another course. You may wonder whether you did something wrong. But the fact that an inquirer, candidate, or catechumen would feel free to pull back from the initial journey is a sign that, as a sponsor, you did not impose artificial controls. At the same time, someone who expresses doubt about Baptism or pursuing membership in the Catholic Church may need to be encouraged. The sponsor should not hesitate to offer such encouragement without forcing the initiation sacraments or the Catholic way of life. If you are related to the one you are sponsoring or a close friend, be aware of the pressure that that relationship may add for going along with the process. Let your catechumen or candidate know that you and other family members love them and that your relationship is not dependent on whether he or she becomes a Catholic.

Some catechumens and candidates need more time than others. Everyone accepted into the order of catechumens at the same time will not necessarily be ready for initiation at the same time. Catechumens and candidates should feel free to take as much time as needed. Some may end their involvement in the formation process to return another year. When there is a serious question about a person's motivation or progress, consult with the coordinator of the catechumenate or the pastoral staff. They will be able to assist you in offering the best help to the catechumen or candidate.

A gracious welcome, one that leaves the person free, is easier to give when you are secure in your life as a Catholic. You will not then be seeking to impose your piety on the catechumen or candidate. For example, you may have a great devotion to a particular saint or enjoy some special prayers, but it would be inappropriate to expect the candidate to adopt that same piety. Or you may be enthused about charismatic prayer, Marriage Encounter, or Cursillo. All of this is part of the Catholic picture. But it would be out of place to expect a catechumen or candidate to participate in a Cursillo or prayer group as if it were a requirement for Christian discipleship. Sponsors should feel free to share their personal devotional practices, but they should not make catechumens or candidates feel obliged to adopt them.

A Sponsor Lives in the World with Hope

While Christian initiation is a spiritual process, the goal of Christian initiation is to prepare men and women for living in the world as disciples of Jesus. The ultimate purpose of the catechumenal process is to help the newly initiated feel not only welcome in the Church but confident in their ability to live their faith in the modern world. Christians are not called to live in the pews, but rather in the world of work, family, social concerns, and business.

The values of the world frequently conflict with the values that Jesus taught. Living in the modern world can be confusing and stressful. We are confronted daily by the bad news of war and poverty, prejudice and hatred, greed and corruption. How does one live as a disciple of Jesus in this world? How do we discern what is good and what is evil, what is true and what is false?

While we may be tempted to retreat into the safety of the church building, we know that we are called to live in the world and—with the help of God—to transform the world into the kingdom of God. The key is hope.

An effective sponsor is one who strives to be in touch with the world as it is, both the good and the bad, and who chooses to live in hope. Hope gives meaning in the face of discouragement. Hope is not a naive optimism, but rather a belief in the power and wisdom of God to transform all things. Hope arises from the conviction that no matter how dark and gloomy the forecast, Jesus is Lord and ultimately will triumph over it all as he triumphed over death. By living in hope, the sponsor fosters in the catechumen or candidate an essential virtue of Christian life.

As you reflect on all the traits of a good sponsor, you may feel overwhelmed or unqualified for your role as a sponsor. Just remember that we are all in the process of becoming mature Christians. Use this opportunity to grow in your faith and in your relationship with the Church. Together with the one you sponsor, trust in the guidance of the Holy Spirit and walk confidently on the path of faith that lies before you.

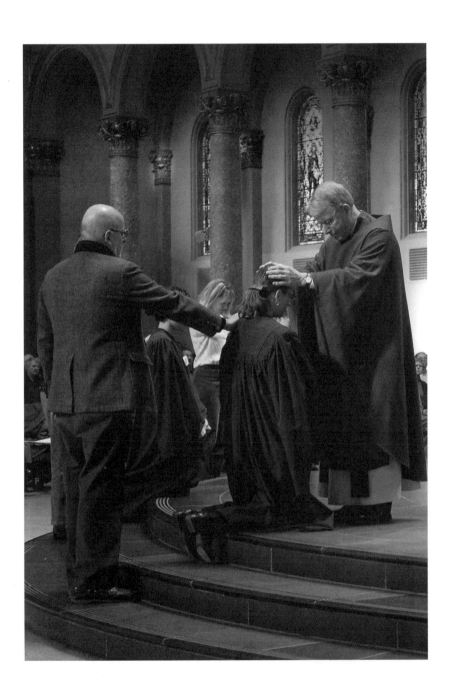

Chapter Four
Sponsor's Checklist

The following is a list of some things you can do as a sponsor. Add to this list your ideas of ways you can be helpful to a catechumen or candidate. Consult with the catechumenate team for further suggestions.

- The sponsor is expected to accompany the candidate in the liturgical rites of the initiation process.

- Take some time at the beginning of the formation process to sit down with your catechumen or candidate and coordinate your appointment books with the liturgical calendar and the catechumenate team schedule. Help the catechumen or candidate mark the Sunday Mass times, meetings, liturgical seasons, fasts, and feasts. Keep the one you sponsor informed about any modifications in schedule. Whether or not he or she will be baptized at the Easter Vigil, be sure that the most important event of the liturgical year, the Paschal Triduum (Holy Thursday evening through Easter Sunday), is the first thing written on both of your calendars. Find out from your team the times of services and special activities. Be sure to mark your calendar for the important dates when the special rites will be celebrated: Rite of Acceptance into the Order of Catechumens, the Rite of Election, the Scrutinies, Holy Saturday morning, the Vigil.

- Pray daily for all inquirers, catechumens, candidates, elect, and sponsors and pastoral team members.

- Attend meetings and sessions with your catechumen or candidate as directed by the parish catechumenate team.

- Greet your catechumen or candidate when he or she arrives for a meeting.

- Make sure he or she feels welcome and has a place to sit. Your hospitality, especially when things are new, is very important.

• Call your catechumen or candidate frequently. When there is a meeting, call to see if a ride is needed or if you might go together. If a meeting is missed, a phone call the next day will reassure the person you sponsor of your interest.

• Invite your catechumen or candidate to other communal prayer opportunities besides the Mass. Be confident in sharing your beliefs about prayer.

• If you are related to the catechumen or candidate you are sponsoring, use the opportunity within the family to share experiences of faith and Catholic tradition.

• If you see your catechumen or candidate at Mass or another church function, introduce him or her to other parishioners, especially to parish leaders.

• Invite your catechumen or candidate for coffee after Mass or a meeting. Invite another sponsor and candidate or catechumen along, if that would be more comfortable.

• Be direct in asking how you can be most helpful. Be clear about expectations.

• Take your catechumen or candidate on a tour of the church. Show and explain the worship area. Allow sufficient time for getting acquainted with the different objects and artifacts and answering any questions. The sacristan can be of assistance to you.

• Introduce your catechumen or candidate to a good bookstore where Catholic reading material can be obtained.

• Acquaint the catechumen or candidate with the diocesan newspaper and other Catholic periodicals.

• Make a trip with your catechumen or candidate to the cathedral, the principal church of the diocese. Point out the bishop's chair (*cathedra* in Greek), from which we get the word "cathedral." Many cathedrals have guides or pamphlets to assist those who visit the building. While there, point out any other significant or historical buildings in the area associated with the local Church.

- If you sense that a catechumen or candidate had a difficult time understanding what was said or experienced at a group session, ask if you can help. Be sensitive to other personal concerns. Be supportive and helpful to the extent that it is welcomed.

- When a date has been set for the catechumen's Baptism, you may wish to volunteer to provide the baptismal garment or candle. Consult with the catechumenate team.

- Invite the catechumen or candidate and his or her family to dinner with your family if that seems appropriate.

- With your catechumen or candidate, plan to visit one or two churches in the diocese that are significantly different from your parish church. If your church is a contemporary building, visit an older one. If your church is suburban, visit an urban or rural church. Perhaps you could visit the church where your family has its roots. A visit to an Eastern Catholic church may prove interesting.

- If your catechumen or candidate has strong roots in another Christian tradition, offer to learn some of his or her cherished prayers.

- Arrange to visit one of the social agencies in the diocese or special ministry sites to witness the church at work. If possible, plan your visit so that you both can volunteer a few hours or a day's time assisting in the work. The site might be a nursing home, an orphanage, a center run by a parish community or religious organization, a Catholic Worker House, a school for exceptional children, a soup line, one of the agencies or centers of Catholic Charities, or a prison. Be sure to spend some time after your visit discussing your experience.

- Invite the catechumen or candidate to a parish function other than the liturgy, such as a pastoral council meeting, a parish play, or a potluck supper. Keep a journal of your thoughts and questions. Share these, if appropriate, with one of the team members or in your group meetings with sponsors.

- Be prepared to share Catholic customs associated with wakes and funerals, weddings, the practice of Christian stewardship, the support of the missions, prayers before meals, and so on.

- After Baptism or Reception into Full Communion, continue to follow through with your relationship. Sometimes it will be weeks or months later that the newly baptized or newly received will appreciate the opportunity to reflect on the experience and perhaps have insights or questions to share. A sponsor's interest and friendship can help settle any feeling of letdown after the initial exuberant feelings that come with Baptism or reception into the Church.

- Make a point of observing the anniversary of the day the person you were sponsoring was baptized or received into full communion.

- Trust the Lord! Be yourself. Stay interested in the catechumen or candidate, and your support will come across naturally. Keep a good sense of humor. Although our ministry is serious, it should not be joyless. Be ready to laugh and socialize with a catechumen or candidate as well as to pray and study. Remember that although God has brought the catechumen or candidate to this turning point in life, God also has led you into this relationship. Be thankful for the opportunity to grow deeper in your faith.

10. A sponsor accompanies any candidate seeking admission as a catechumen. Sponsors are persons who have known and assisted the candidates and stand as witnesses to the candidates' moral character, faith, and intention. It may happen that it is not the sponsor for the rite of acceptance and the period of the catechumenate but another person who serves as godparent for the periods of purification and enlightenment and of mystagogy.
11. Their godparents (for each a godmother or godfather, or both) accompany the candidates on the day of election, at the celebration of the sacraments of initiation, and during the period of mystgogy. Godparents are chosen by the candidates on the basis of example, good qualities, and friendship, delegated by the local Christian community, and approved by the priest. It is the responsibility of godparents to show the candidates how to practice the Gospel in personal and social life, to sustain the candidates in moments of hesitancy and anxiety, to bear witness, and to guide the candidates' progress in the baptismal life. Chosen before the candidates' election, godparents fulfill this office publicly from the day of the rite of election, when they give testimony to the community about the candidates. They continue to be important during the time after reception of the sacraments when the neophytes need to be assisted so that they remain true to their baptismal promises.

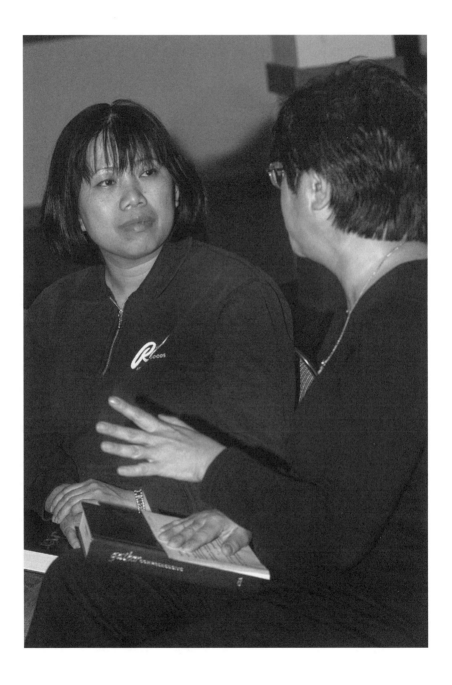

Chapter Five

Questions and Issues

This chapter presents some of the questions and issues sponsors frequently raise or are addressed to the sponsors. In addition to these notes, remember that your catechumenate team or pastoral staff is always ready to assist you.

1. I don't feel qualified or prepared to be a sponsor.

Sometimes sponsors have the impression that they are supposed to know everything about the Church and its teachings and to have answers for any questions that may arise. Remember, sponsors are not catechists, so you aren't being asked to assume responsibility for formal catechesis or teaching. Catechumens and candidates may pose questions that will challenge you. Rather than being intimidated by a question, take advantage of the opportunity to explore the matter. It's good modeling to show catechumens and candidates that a mature Catholic Christian need not have all the answers to every question that could be asked about the faith. Catechumens or candidates will learn that our spiritual growth does not end with initiation or reception into full communion. We are all "on the way."

2. What do I do if the catechumen or candidate I sponsor is shy or appears unresponsive?

Some catechumens and candidates may be shy and share little in group discussions. If you are an extrovert, you may feel they are unresponsive. Try not to interpret this behavior prematurely. Give the one you sponsor time to become comfortable with you and the group. Even if you have known the catechumen or candidate for a long time or are related to him or her, this is a new relationship that seeks sharing at a different level. As the individual comes to trust you, he or she will share more about him- or herself. Offer positive support when that happens.

3. How much that a catechumen or candidate tells me has to be kept confidential?

The catechumen or candidate always should feel free to speak with a sponsor in confidence. At no point may that confidence be betrayed. If a serious matter arises (such as a situation that might require professional counseling), encourage the catechumen or candidate to seek help. Ask the catechumen's or candidate's permission to consult a member of the pastoral staff.

The catechumen or candidate needs to understand that a sponsor is expected to give testimony to the catechumenate team concerning the individual's development. Nevertheless, the sponsor must not betray the catechumen's or candidate's confidence by sharing anything that is meant to be kept private.

4. My candidate cannot be received into the Church this Easter because of some marriage issue. I don't understand.

Before one can be fully initiated into the Catholic Church, an individual must be free of all impediments as listed in Church law, because some of these issues would prevent one from receiving the sacraments. Whether a person is baptized or unbaptized, if that person has been married and divorced, the first marriage may be an impediment to contracting another marriage. If the person has entered into another marriage, the first marriage (or all previous marriages, if there are more than one) may have to be annulled or dissolved by the Catholic Church before the sacraments of initiation can be celebrated.

If such a situation occurs with someone you are sponsoring, you are not expected to handle, or even to understand, all the details. That is for the pastoral staff of the parish. If you are interested in learning more about the process, the staff can explain it or help you find materials to read.

Your role is to support and encourage the catechumen or candidate. A person in this situation may feel judged, rejected, disappointed, or frustrated. The candidate may not understand how and why Catholic marriage laws affect a marriage that took place outside the Catholic Church. Your understanding, patience, and compassion will help the one you sponsor and will deepen the bond between you.

5. The person I sponsor doesn't come regularly to the catechumenate sessions. What should I do?

When a catechumen or candidate misses a session without notice, the sponsor may call the next day to tell the person that he or she was missed and to see if anything is wrong. If the person's absence develops into a pattern, the sponsor may need to ask the catechumen or candidate why he or she is not coming to the sessions. Before this, however, consult with the pastoral staff.

6. The candidate I am sponsoring is having a hard time accepting the sacrament of Penance. What can I say?

The fears catechumens or candidates express about the sacrament of Penance often stem from stories, real or exaggerated, heard from Catholics. It is important that you share your positive experience of the sacrament. Invite the catechumen or candidate you are sponsoring to a communal celebration of reconciliation at your parish, if one is scheduled. Talk about the experience afterward. Show the catechumen or candidate the reconciliation chapel. The catechists will teach the catechumens and candidates about the sacrament, but your encouragement, stories, and positive attitude will do much to allay fears and promote acceptance and understanding of the sacrament. If there is a question of why one is required to confess sins to a priest, you can point out that the sacraments are celebrations of the Church in which we encounter the living Christ. In the sacrament of Penance, the priest confessor acts in the person of Christ and in the person of the Church, exercising the ministry Jesus gave to his Church to forgive sins.

7. Sometimes I feel that the catechumens and candidates are not receiving enough of the content of the Catholic faith.

The Rite of Christian Initiation of Adults prescribes a thorough catechesis for all who are being prepared for Christian initiation. The essential teachings of the Church need to be presented in such a way that catechumens are given a solid foundation upon which they can continue to build. Our Catholic tradition is rich and full, and so it is difficult to teach everything possible. What is important is that we offer catechumens the tools and discipline by which they can continue to grow in their faith. Furthermore, the faith of the Church is not just about information and facts, but a full picture of what it means to be a faithful disciple of Jesus in the Catholic way of life. The goal of catechesis is more than just learning "about" the faith. Effective catechesis aims to integrate the teaching of Christ and his Church into the fabric of life. Candidates being prepared for reception into full communion will not necessarily need as much catechesis as the unbaptized. For this reason, your parish may have separate groups for catechesis: one for catechumens and another for candidates. Those who are already baptized may have a strong faith background, including a familiarity with scripture and an active prayer life. Candidates may appreciate hearing more about the differences between Catholic teachings and the beliefs from the faith community in which they were raised. Sponsors who have serious questions or doubts about Catholic teachings would be wise to seek clarification from the catechumenate team or pastoral staff outside the formal session. In this way, the catechumens or candidates will not be confused by the discussion, and undue time will not be given to an issue that may not be a problem for others.

8. Why do we use a Lectionary instead of a catechism?

In many communities the Lectionary (the book containing the scripture readings for Mass) is the primary catechetical book. Although it is not laid out like a catechism, the fundamentals of our Catholic Christian faith emerge from the scriptures. Trained catechists are able to hand on the doctrinal traditions of the Church as it unfolds week by week through the scriptures of our public worship. The advantage of using the Lectionary as the source for catechesis is that the catechumens and candidates can be helped in seeing how the Church's teachings are grounded in the word of God. Using the Lectionary also gives a lifelong learning method that they can use to continue their study of the faith and their growth in the way of Jesus.

9. Why are the catechumens dismissed after the Liturgy of the Word?

When we dismiss catechumens from the Liturgy of the Word, we send them forth to continue their prayer and reflection on God's word. We are not expelling them. Because they are not yet able to participate in the Eucharist with the faithful, they are led to another space where they can be nourished by the real presence of Christ revealed in his word. The dismissal of the catechumens reminds the assembly of its privilege to celebrate Eucharist, and it invites the catechumens to make the dismissal a joyful fast as their hunger for the Eucharist grows. Ordinarily, candidates are not dismissed after the Liturgy of the Word at Mass. By virtue of their Baptism, they are already Christians and called to worship. Because they are not in full communion with the Church, however, they are not yet able to receive Holy Communion. Nevertheless, the baptized already belong to the Church. Their Baptism should not be overlooked by treating them in the same fashion as we would the unbaptized.

10. Why can't all who are already baptized receive Holy Communion in the Catholic Church?

The Catholic Church teaches that the Eucharist is a sign of the reality of faith, life, and worship. Even though a common bond exists among all Christians because of Baptism, the sad divisions in Christianity have broken the unity that Christ desires for his Church. The Roman Catholic Church's discipline ordinarily is not to admit to Holy Communion members of those churches with whom it is not fully united. When unity is restored, the sign of Holy Communion will be a true reflection of our unity in Christ.

11. Why do Catholics pray to saints and place so much importance on Mary?

Catholics do not worship the saints. We honor or venerate the saints, but we reserve our worship and adoration to God alone. We look to the saints as our friends and ask them to pray or intercede for us. Most Christians will ask someone to remember them in prayer. So why wouldn't we ask our friends, the saints, to pray for us? Our devotion to the saints is a testimony to our belief in everlasting life. Because we believe the saints live with God, we ask them to intercede for us. Because Mary is the mother of Jesus and thus the Mother of God, she holds a unique place in our hearts. Who could be closer to the Lord than Mary? Catholics regard Mary as their mother, too, and so praying to Mary is natural for Catholics.

Chapter Six
A Selection of Catholic Prayers

Sponsors can be helpful in introducing catechumens and candidates to some of the traditional Catholic prayers. A few of these traditional prayers are provided in this chapter. When the one you are sponsoring looks to you for help in learning traditional Catholic prayers, you may wish to refer to this section. In addition to these prayers, you may also refer to the psalms and any of the traditional prayers of the Mass. These few selections do not exhaust the rich repertoire of prayers that are part of our Catholic heritage. The parish pastoral staff can direct you to other sources and offer suggestions on praying spontaneously from the heart.

In addition to the words of these prayers, be aware of how the Catholic tradition of prayer also includes gesture and posture. When we make the Sign of the Cross, for example, we sign our bodies with the cross of Jesus. When we pray the Lord's Prayer, we may stand and hold our hands outstretched and open, or we may fold our hands in a gesture that points to heaven. In our penitential prayers we may kneel or bow. Gesture and posture can integrate our whole selves into our prayer.

Sign of the Cross

As the words are spoken, the Sign of the Cross is made by touching the forehead, the chest, the left shoulder, and finally the right shoulder with the right hand. The hands are then folded together.

In the name of the Father,
and of the Son
and of the Holy Spirit. Amen.

The Lord's Prayer

Our Father, who art in heaven,
hallowed be thy name;
thy kingdom come;
thy will be done on earth as it is in heaven.
Give us this day our daily bread;
and forgive us our trespasses
as we forgive those who trespass against us;
and lead us not into temptation,
but deliver us from evil.
Amen.

Hail Mary

Hail Mary, full of grace,
the Lord is with you!
Blessed are you among women,
and blessed is the fruit of your womb, Jesus.
Holy Mary, mother of God,
pray for us sinners,
now and at the hour of our death.
Amen.

Glory Be

Glory be to the Father
and to the Son
and to the Holy Spirit,
as it was in the beginning
is now, and ever shall be,
world without end.
Amen.

Nicene Creed

Some wording in the Nicene Creed will change with the promulgation of the third typical edition of the Roman Missal.

We believe in one God,
the Father, the Almighty,
maker of heaven and earth,
of all that is seen and unseen.
We believe in one Lord, Jesus Christ,
the only Son of God,
eternally begotten of the Father,
God from God, Light from Light,
true God from true God,
begotten, not made, one in Being with the Father.
Through him all things were made.
For us and for our salvation
he came down from heaven:
By the power of the Holy Spirit
he was born of the Virgin Mary, and became man.
For our sake he was crucified under Pontius Pilate;
he suffered, died and was buried.
On the third day he rose again
in fulfillment of the scriptures;
he ascended into heaven
and is seated at the right hand of the Father.
He will come again in glory to judge the living
and the dead, and his kingdom will have no end.
We believe in the Holy Spirit,
the Lord, the giver of life,
who proceeds from the Father and the Son.
With the Father and the Son he is worshipped and glorified.
He has spoken through the prophets.
We believe in one holy catholic and apostolic church.
We acknowledge one baptism for the forgiveness of sins.
We look for the resurrection of the dead,
and the life of the world to come.
Amen.

Apostles' Creed

Some wording in the Apostles' Creed will change with the promulgation of the third typical edition of the Roman Missal.

I believe in God, the Father almighty,
creator of heaven and earth.
I believe in Jesus Christ, his only Son, our Lord.
He was conceived by the power of the Holy Spirit
and born of the Virgin Mary.
He suffered under Pontius Pilate,
was crucified, died and was buried.
He descended to the dead.
On the third day he rose again.
He ascended into heaven,
and is seated at the right hand of the Father.
He will come again to judge the living and the dead.
I believe in the Holy Spirit,
the holy catholic church,
the communion of saints,
the forgiveness of sins,
the resurrection of the body
and the life everlasting.
Amen.

Penitential Prayers

These prayers can be used at the end of the day or in the celebration of the sacrament of Penance.

Act of Contrition

My God,
I am sorry for my sins with all my heart.
In choosing to do wrong
and failing to do good,
I have sinned against you,
whom I should love above all things.

I firmly intend, with your help,
to do penance,
to sin no more
and to avoid whatever leads me to sin.
Our Savior Jesus Christ
suffered and died for us.
In his name, my God, have mercy.

Confiteor

This prayer is used at Mass and can also be used as a private prayer of contrition. Some wording in the Confiteor will change with the promulgation of the third typical edition of the Roman Missal.

I confess to almighty God,
and to you, my brothers and sisters,
that I have sinned though my own fault,
in my thoughts and in my words,
in what I have done,
and in what I have failed to do;
and I ask blessed Mary, ever virgin,
all the angels and saints,
and you, my brothers and sisters,
to pray for me to the Lord our God.

A Brief Penitential Prayer

Father, I have sinned against you
and am not worthy to be called your son.
Be merciful to me, a sinner.

Blessing before Meals

Bless us, O Lord, and these thy gifts which we are about to receive from thy bounty through Christ our Lord. Amen.

Prayer at Work

Lord,
may everything we do
begin with your inspiration
and continue with your help
so that all our prayers and works
may begin in you
and by you be happily ended.
We ask this through Christ our Lord.
Amen.

Prayer for the Dead

This may be prayed with two voices.

V. Eternal rest grant unto him/her, O Lord.
R. And let perpetual light shine upon him/her.
V. May he rest in peace.
R. Amen.
V. May his/her soul and all the souls of all the faithful departed,
through the mercy of God, rest in peace.
R. Amen.

Prayer to the Holy Spirit

Come, Holy Spirit,
fill the hearts of your faithful
and kindle in them the fire of your love.
Send forth your Spirit
and they shall be created.
And you will renew the face of the earth.
Lord, by the light of the Holy Spirit,
you have taught the hearts of your faithful.
In the same Spirit,
help us to relish what is right
and always rejoice in your consolation.
We ask this through Christ our Lord.
Amen.

Jesus Prayer

This is prayed as mantra, repeated several times with the same rhythm.

Lord, Jesus Christ, Son of God, have mercy on me a sinner.

Hail, Holy Queen

Hail, Holy Queen, Mother of Mercy,
our life, our sweetness, and our hope.
To thee do we cry,
poor banished children of Eve;
to thee do we send up our sighs,
mourning and weeping in this valley of tears.
Turn then, most gracious advocate,
thine eyes of mercy toward us,
and after this exile
show unto us the blessed fruit of thy womb, Jesus.
O clement, O loving,
O sweet Virgin Mary.

Marian Anthem for the Easter Season

Queen of heaven, rejoice, alleluia.
The Son whom you merited to bear, alleluia,
has risen as he said, alleluia.
Pray for us to God, alleluia
Rejoice and be glad, O Virgin Mary, alleluia!
For the Lord has truly risen, alleluia.
Let us pray:
O God, through the resurrection of your Son, our Lord Jesus Christ,
did vouchsafe to give joy to the world; grant, we beseech you, that
through his Mother, the Virgin Mary, we may obtain the joys of
everlasting life. Through the same Christ our Lord. Amen.

The Angelus

This is traditionally prayed at noon and may be prayed with two voices.

V. The angel of God declared unto Mary,
R. And she conceived of the Holy Spirit.
Hail, Mary . . . .
V. Behold the handmaid of the Lord:
R. Be it done unto me according to thy word.
Hail, Mary . . . .
V. And the Word was made flesh
R. and dwelt among us.
Hail, Mary . . . .
V. Pray for us, O holy Mother of God,
R. That we may be made worthy of the promises of Christ.
V. Let us pray: Pour forth, we beseech thee, O Lord, thy grace into our hearts; that we, to whom the Incarnation of Christ, thy Son, was made known by the message of an angel, may by his Passion and Cross be brought to the glory of his Resurrection. We ask this through Christ our Lord.
R. Amen.

The Rosary

The Rosary may be prayed alone or with others. It combines traditional prayers with meditations on some of the central mysteries of the faith. Pope John Paul II taught us that the Rosary is one way for us to contemplate the face of Christ.

To Pray the Rosary

- Make the sign of the cross.

- Recite the Apostles' Creed.

- Recite one Our Father, three Hail Marys and one Glory Be.

- Begin each decade of the Rosary by meditating on one of the mysteries. On the large bead recite the Lord's Prayer. On the ten small beads recite ten Hail Marys. Then pray the Glory Be.

- Conclude with the Hail Holy Queen or the Marian Anthem for the Easter season.

The Mysteries of the Rosary

Joyful Mysteries *(on Mondays and Saturdays)*
1. The annunciation of the angel Gabriel to the Virgin Mary (Luke 1:30–36)
2. The visitation of Mary to Elizabeth (Luke 1:39–45)
3. The Nativity of our Lord Jesus Christ (Luke 2:6–7)
4. The presentation of Jesus in the Temple (Luke 2:29–32)
5. The finding of Jesus in the Temple (Luke 2:48–52)

Sorrowful Mysteries (on Tuesdays, Fridays, and Sundays in Lent)
1. The agony of Jesus in the garden (Matthew 26:38–39)
2. The scourging of Jesus (John 19:1)
3. The crowning of Jesus with thorns (Mark 15:16–17)
4. The carrying of the cross (John 19:17)
5. The Crucifixion and death of the Lord (John 19:28–30)

Glorious Mysteries (on Wednesdays and Sundays outside Lent)
1. The Resurrection of Jesus (Mark 16:6–8)
2. The Ascension of Jesus (Acts 1:10–11)
3. The descent of the Holy Spirit on the apostles (Acts 2:1–4)
4. The assumption of Mary into heaven (Song of Songs 2:3–6)
5. The coronation of the Blessed Virgin Mary (Luke 1:51–54)

The Luminous Mysteries (on Thursdays)
1. The Baptism at the Jordan (Matthew 3:1–17)
2. The miracle at Cana (John 2:1–12)
3. The proclamation of the kingdom and the call to conversion (Mark 1:15)
4. The Transfiguration (Luke 9: 28–36)
5. The institution of the Eucharist (John 13:1–11 or Matthew 26:26–29)

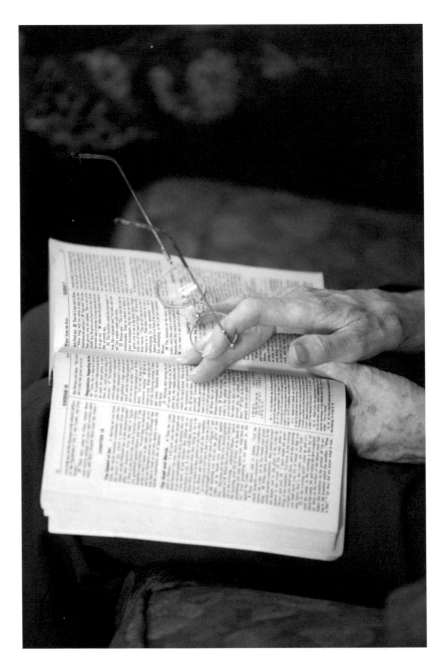

Chapter Seven

A Sponsor's Time for Reflection and Prayer

The initiation process is a rich source of prayer and spiritual growth for sponsors. The transitions from one stage to the next are particularly ripe moments for prayer and reflection. This brief outline for the reflective prayer of a sponsor is based on the journey of a catechumen. Candidates may parallel these stages, but will not necessarily follow the full cycle of a catechumen's preparation. Nevertheless, what follows here can be adapted if your journey is alongside a candidate preparing for reception into full communion.

This pattern of prayer can be repeated at various times. For each of these reflective meditations, find a quiet, comfortable space. Try to put aside the distractions of the day. Begin each meditation by sitting quietly for a few minutes. Open your mind and heart to the presence of God within you. As you proceed with the meditation you may find it helpful to write some of your thoughts and reflections. You may want to return to these thoughts later as a catalyst for other times of prayer.

During the Inquiry Period

Prayer

Lord,
grant that I may be attentive
to your presence
and generous in responding
to what you ask of me.

Word of God

Romans 10:9–18
Confess with your lips that Jesus is Lord.
or
Isaiah 61:1–3
He has sent me to bring glad tidings to the lowly.

Questions to Ponder in Prayer

- The inquirers have come in search of God to inquire about the Church, its beliefs, and practices. They come with questions about life, its meaning, and its purpose. What do I bring of myself to this inquiry period? What is the good news that I have to share?

- Who in my life has preached good news to me? Who has been a voice of hope for me? What were the circumstances in which I received hope and Good News? What have I heard or seen in the inquirers that challenges my attitudes, values, and faith? What have I experienced in the midst of the inquiry that leaves me in awe?

- With God's help I will support the inquirers and witness as best as I can to the faith that gives me life. For what do I give thanks to God? What do I ask of God at this stage?

Prayer

Make me to know your ways, O Lord;
    teach me your paths.
Lead me in your truth and teach me,
    for you are the God of my salvation.
(Psalm 25:4–5)

During the Catechumenate Period

Prayer

My soul languishes for your salvation;
   I hope in your word.
Your word is a lamp to my feet.
   and a light to my path.
(Psalm 119:81, 105)

Word of God

1 Corinthians 1:18–25
We preach Christ crucified.
or
2 Corinthians 4:1–2, 5–7
We preach Jesus as Lord, with ourselves as your servants for Jesus' sake.
or
Mark 1:14–15
Reform your lives and believe in the Gospel!

Questions to Ponder in Prayer

- During the catechumenate period, the catechumens and candidates are invited to grow in their relationship with the living God. What does my relationship with God look like? What would I say to others about my belief in Jesus? In the Holy Spirit?

- The Christian life is an ongoing conversion process. In what way might I still need to change to be converted more deeply?

- What have I heard or seen in the catechumens or candidates that challenges my attitudes, values, and faith? What have I experienced in the catechumenate that leaves me in awe?

- As a Catholic, what do I value most about the Church? How did I come to value this?

• With God's help I will support the catechumens and candidates and witness as best as I can to the faith that gives me life. For what do I give thanks to God? What do I ask of God at this stage?

Prayer

But as for me, I will look to the Lord,
    I will wait for the God of my salvation;
    my God will hear me!
(Micah 7:7)

During the Period of Purification and Enlightenment

Prayer

Lord God,
during these forty days of Lent,
help us to understand the meaning
of your Son's death and Resurrection,
and teach us to reflect it in our lives.
(adapted from the Roman Missal)

Word of God

Philippians 3:8–14
I wish to know Christ and the power flowing from his Resurrection.
or
2 Timothy 1:8–10
God has saved us and called us to be holy.
or
Matthew 16:24–27
Take up your cross and follow in my footsteps.

Questions to Ponder in Prayer

- In the Rite of Election, the catechumens celebrated their being chosen or elected by God. In what way do I feel called or chosen by God?

- The way of Jesus is also the way of the cross. How have I experienced the cross in my life? How have I experienced Christ's Resurrection?

- What do I hear or see in the elect or the candidates that challenges my attitudes, values, and faith? In what way has my relationship with the elect and candidates left me in awe?

- What are the sins in my life? How can I use this Lent to rid myself of sin? What are the evils and falsehoods that tempt me?

- As I approach the renewal of baptismal vows at the Easter Vigil, how has the meaning and appreciation for Baptism changed in my life?

- With God's help I will support the elect and candidates and witness as best as I can to the faith that gives me life. For what do I give thanks to God? What do I ask of God at this stage?

Prayer

As the deer longs for flowing streams,
    so my soul longs for you, O God.
My soul thirsts for God,
    for the living God.
(Psalm 42:1–2)

During the Period of Mystagogy

Prayer

Alleluia!
Praise the LORD!
Praise the LORD, O my soul!

I will praise the LORD as long as I live;
    I will sing praises to my God all my life long.
(Psalm 146:1–2)

Word of God

Romans 6:3–11
Through Baptism into his death we were buried with him.
or
Acts 4:32–35
The community was of one heart and one mind.

Questions to Ponder in Prayer

- The celebration of the Triduum is a celebration of the Passover of the Lord. In what way have I joined the Lord in his Passover?

- Christ is risen! In what ways have I seen the risen Lord?

- At each celebration of the Eucharist, the Lord invites us to share ever more deeply in his dying and rising. How might I see in the Eucharist the opportunity to renew my Baptism?

- What do I hear or see in the newly initiated that challenges my attitudes, values, and faith? In what way has their initiation left me in awe?

- With God's help I will support the newly initiated as they take their place in the community. For what do I give thanks to God? What do I ask of God at this stage?

Prayer

I will give you thanks, O LORD, with my whole heart;
before the gods I sing your praise.
(Psalm 138:1)

Glossary

BAPTISMAL FONT: A large vessel that holds the water used in the Baptism of adults and children, either by immersion or infusion (pouring). The baptismal font usually is located in a place of prominence that clearly conveys the importance of Baptism in the life of the Christian community.

CANDIDATE: An individual who is preparing to become a Catholic. The term often is used to denote a person baptized in another Christian tradition who is preparing for reception into the full communion of the Roman Catholic Church.

CANON LAW: The body of Church law that governs Church practice and protects the rights and privileges of individuals and community.

CATECHESIS: The instruction and spiritual formation of catechumens who are preparing for Baptism and for baptized Christians who seek full communion with the Catholic Church. Through catechesis, the Church passes on its faith and leads men and women to a deeper conversion and relationship to Jesus Christ. The catechesis for the unbaptized is ordinarily more extensive than is necessary for those who are already baptized.

CATECHUMEN: An unbaptized person who is seeking initiation into the Church and who has been accepted into the order of catechumens.

CATECHUMENATE: The process by which the Catholic Church brings unbaptized children of catechetical age and adults to Christian initiation. Also, the period of time during which an unbaptized person prepares for Christian initiation. For pastoral reasons, baptized adults who are preparing for reception into the full communion of the Catholic Church may be included in the catechumenate gatherings for at least some portion of the catechesis.

CHRISM: A combination of oil and sweet balsam or perfume that is mixed and consecrated by the bishop and used to anoint newly baptized people and newly ordained priests and bishops. Chrism is also used in the consecration of churches and altars, in the Baptism rite for infants, and in the sacrament of Confirmation.

DOCTRINE: The official teachings of the Church.

ELECT: Catechumens who have been found ready by the faith community to take part in the next celebration of the sacraments of initiation.

ELECTION, RITE OF: The ritual celebration in which catechumens who are considered ready to take part in the next celebration of the sacraments of initiation are called to the Easter sacraments. The celebration of the Rite of Election ordinarily takes place at the beginning of Lent. In this rite, the bishop or his delegate declares in the name of the Church that the catechumens who are presented are ready and chosen for the sacraments at Easter. During this celebration, the names of the elect are written in the Book of the Elect.

ENLIGHTENMENT: The period of Lent during which the elect are involved in the final stage of preparation for celebrating the rites of initiation. Synonyms are illumination and purification.

ENROLLMENT: The rite of inscribing into the Book of the Elect the names of those catechumens elected to take part in the next celebration of the sacraments of initiation. See election.

EPHPHETHA: The rite in which the presider touches the ears and the mouth of the elect and prays that they be open to hear and proclaim the word of God in faith. It may be celebrated as part of the preparation rites on Holy Saturday.

EXORCISMS: Prayers for the deliverance from the powers of evil and falsehood and for an openness to the gifts of the Lord, especially the Holy Spirit. Exorcisms are part of the rites of scrutiny.

EVANGELIZATION: The activity by which the Church proclaims the Gospel in word or in deed, inviting a response of faith and conversion in Jesus Christ.

FASTING: A form of sacrifice by which individuals join themselves with the suffering and death of Jesus by forgoing food for a specific period of time. On Ash Wednesday and Good Friday, Catholics who are in good health and between the ages of 18 and 59 (see canon 1252) are obliged to fast in a modified way: one full meal and two other small meals may be eaten, and no food is eaten between meals. Many Christians fast from Holy Thursday evening until after the Easter Vigil in anticipation of the celebration of the Lord's Resurrection.

GODPARENT: The person who accompanies the catechumen during the rites and periods of election, initiation, and mystagogy. This person may be selected by the catechumen with the approval of the pastor and catechumenal team or assigned to an individual by the community. Being a godparent is a lifelong relationship that is sealed in the sacraments of initiation. One cannot change a godparent at a later date.

IMMERSION: A way of baptizing in which the person is partially or entirely submerged in the baptismal water.

INFUSION: A way of baptizing in which water is poured over the head of the person.

INITIATION, CHRISTIAN: The process by which a person enters the faith life of the Church through a thorough catechesis and spiritual formation and the sacraments of Baptism, Confirmation, and Eucharist. The process extends from the person's first inquiry through the completion of mystagogy.

INQUIRERS: Persons who are at an initial stage of seeking to learn what the Church and its faith and practices are all about.

LECTIONARY: A book containing the assigned scripture readings for the celebration of the Mass and the sacraments.

LECTIONARY-BASED CATECHESIS: A catechetical method for learning the foundation of faith and doctrine by study of and reflection on the scriptures as they are arranged for the liturgy over a three-year cycle.

LITURGY OF THE HOURS: The official liturgical prayer of the Church consisting of psalms, scriptural prayers, songs, and readings for the morning, daytime, evening, and nighttime of each day.

MAGISTERIUM: The official teaching office of the Church as it is exercised by the Pope in communion with all the bishops of the Church.

MISSAL: The book that contains the prayers spoken or sung by the presider at the eucharistic celebration.

MYSTAGOGY: The period of time following initiation, usually the Easter season, which centers on catechesis in the meaning and experience of the mysteries of baptismal faith. Mystagogy may continue for a full year.

NEOPHYTE: A newly baptized person who is in the final period of Christian initiation, mystagogy.

OIL OF CATECHUMENS: The blessed oil used in anointing catechumens as a sign of their need for and God's offer of strength in overcoming all opposition to the faith they will profess throughout their lives.

PASCHAL CANDLE: The large candle lighted each year from the new fire ignited and blessed at the Easter Vigil. From this light, representing the risen Lord who destroys the darkness of sin, the newly baptized light their candles.

PASCHAL TRIDUUM: The Three Days from Holy Thursday evening through Easter Sunday evening during which Christians celebrate the Passover of Israel from slavery to freedom, the Passover of Jesus Christ from death to life, our own Passover in Christ from sin to grace, from darkness to light.

PERIODS: Times of growth in the initiation process: 1) inquiry, or precatechumenate; 2) catechumenate; 3) purification and enlightenment; 4) mystagogy.

POSTBAPTISMAL: After Baptism.

PRECATECHUMENATE: The period of inquiry prior to acceptance into the order of catechumens; the time of initial evangelization.

PRESENTATIONS: The rites during the period of purification and enlightenment through which the Church passes on to the elect the Creed and the Lord's Prayer, the most cherished documents of the Church, and the traditions they represent: the way Christians believe and the way Christians pray.

PURIFICATION: See enlightenment.

RECONCILIATION ROOM: A place for the celebration of the sacrament of Penance. A reconciliation room is set up so that penitents may meet face to face with the priest or confess anonymously from behind a screen. This room is sometimes called a reconciliation chapel or a confessional.

SCRUTINIES: Rites celebrated with the elect, usually at the Sunday liturgy on the Third, Fourth, and Fifth Sundays of Lent, petitioning for the spirit of repentance, an awareness of temptation, an understanding of sin, and the experience of the true freedom of the children of God.

SPONSORS: Those persons who accompany the inquirers when they seek acceptance into the order of catechumens and who remain with them as companions on the way to Baptism or reception into full communion. Ordinarily, the one who sponsors a catechumen is known as a godparent.

Notes

Notes

———

Notes

Notes

Notes

Graffiti

811.54

Jackson
Acts of Mi

18.75

JAN 30 198

AUG 2 3

811.54

Jackson
Acts of Mind

18.75

54,541

DATE	ISSUED TO
JAN 30 1984	
AUG 2 3 1989	11276
	10,681 Please Renew

TETON COUNTY LIBRARY
320 King Street
Box 1629   Phone 733-2164
Jackson, Wyo. 83001

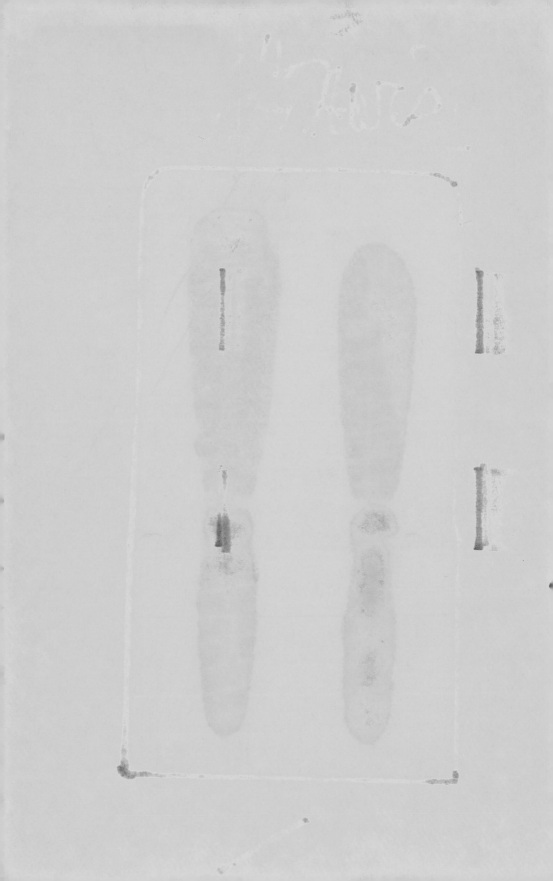

ACTS *of* MIND

CONVERSATIONS WITH
CONTEMPORARY POETS

by Richard Jackson

THE UNIVERSITY OF ALABAMA PRESS

Library of Congress Cataloging in Publication Data

Jackson, Richard, 1946–
  Acts of mind.

  Bibliography: p.
  Includes index.
  1. Poets, American—20th century—Interviews.
2. American poetry—20th century—History and
criticism—Addresses, essays, lectures. 3. Poetics—
Addresses, essays, lectures. I. Title.
PS325.J3   811′.54′09   82-4767
ISBN 0-8173-0122-4   AACR2

for Marg and Amy

Contents

ACTS *of* MIND

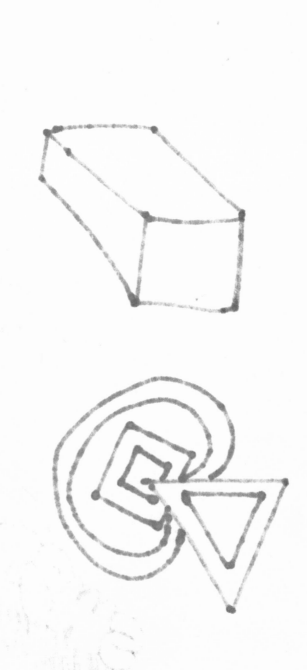

Stanley Plumly, 1979

The Path of Saying

POETRY MISCELLANY: Hans-George Gadamer, a student of Heidegger w
work has become influential in recent years, writes, "The meaning of a
surpasses its author not occasionally, but always." That is, there is alw
what Keats would call a "fine excess." Gadamer calls this excess the "cir
of the unexpressed" or the "infinity of the unsaid." He suggests—and here
the application to poetry—that the primary motive of a text is not to infor
but to evoke. Language, Heidegger had said, can show or designate, eve
or simply enumerate, and it does so by "withholding" something fundam
tal, by its inability to express all, its inability to be infinite. What
withholding does is to evoke a sense of Being, a sense of what it means t
The language of poetry, for Heidegger and Gadamer, is thus a w
presencing Being. I think that your poems work in a similar way. The
that first comes to mind is "Peppergrass," with its focus on the nothing
is a presence, on anonymity (in one poem your father is "anonymous")
kind of universality. The poem ends by evoking an unnameable sens
"Being"—

> We were the windmills where the wind came from,
> nothing, nothing you could name,
> blowing the lights out, one by one.

talking about language—what it expresses and what evades
vocative power of poetry, about this sense of presencing (of
unnameable, the ineffable. Your poem "Wildflower" that
ntaeus also exemplifies some of these issues.

LUMLY: In a new poem, "Summer Celestial," which may turn
itle for my next book, I go to the center of a circle that is the
first stanza. I am preparing in that stanza for the next six that
nding a place in the landscape, a center, where I can divest
e burdens of the everyday. The process is a difficult one—it is a
ith long lines. It is a process of finding a language in which I
t lose myself, become anonymous, change my face among
me, I suppose, that is the secret of poetry. Poetry holds a kind of
I enter—I think you called it a presence. That is why I feel that
how conversational or colloquial or at ease the language may seem
itself, it has about it, in a good poem, a whole different feel, a
al nature that distinguishes it from everyday discourse. I don't
imply formal or metaphoric senses. I am trying to describe an
lity. I hear voices in those poems.

MISCELLANY: In a way this bringing to presence can be described
you use in your essay "Sentimental Forms." You talk in that essay
how James Wright's best poems allow him to "identify with the
s of emotion." You use critical terms in discussing Wordsworth that
d have been unheard-of not long ago— "a kind of buoyancy, a kind of
rosity, a kind of conviction." This Heideggerian or Gadamerian lan-
ge searches for special qualities and is part of a revaluation within criti-
m that has come to us from European criticism.

STANLEY PLUMLY: It is a language that is very useful to me. I don't think it
jargon, as some people contend, but an important way of looking at
ms. I could explicate in the traditional way at the drop of a line, but I
nk we are past that. I think we have to begin to deal with the issue of
ces. I think we have to get rid of the mysticism that has surrounded
es. I think the issue is one that we can talk about in practical and
table ways. I think a good critic of poetry is one who tries to discover
et's particular language what he is saying about his sources, how well
identifying them. The good critic should talk about the language the
is using to communicate those sources, or even to communicate with
sources. Those sources are what the poem's language comes from.
are totemic resources, and those resources have faces on them—not
consciousnesses but human faces. For example, what I like about
Wright is the way he is vulnerable to the past, the real past—he
to shine through. But it is not that everyday past, as I mentioned
that presence; I mean, he's not an Ohio poet, he's a river poet.
its various ways, is the source for him.

POETRY MISCELLANY: Heidegger says that as readers and listeners we must "have an experience with language." We must listen not so much to what is said as to the "path" a saying has taken.

STANLEY PLUMLY: I don't remember the exact etymology of "craft," but it suggests the way craft can "empower," the way it refers to "the way" and even "the means of the way," the way of the way. It invites, it brings, it implicates a whole world, a social world. This, for instance, is the depth and width of poetry that Wordsworth wrote, and I suppose that was what the Romantic movement was about. What Wordsworth really invented was a way of constructing out of the line and out of the bind that pure lyricism gets us into. For Wordsworth there is always a reason for carrying one line to the next.

POETRY MISCELLANY: There's a strong narrative base in his poems and an increasingly stronger narrative base in your more recent poems. Even the title *Lyrical Ballads*, a contradiction in terms, suggests the infusion of narrative into the lyric.

STANLEY PLUMLY: Yes, poems are first of all spoken. That is, you have to identify a speaker, the narrator. He or she provides a point of view to the story. We haven't been paying enough attention to this fictive part of poetry. A lot of our recent poetry contains fine lyricism, but remains very dead on the page. I think we have to remember that poetry has a vertical dimension. There is a rhythm of thought, the speed with which it moves down the page. In prose the rhythm never halts—a printer decides on the line breaks. But poetry goes up and down the page—that is "the way" we were just talking about. And the way has to have a reason, a point of view, that human rather than lyrically mystical saying, an empowering.

First, it is not a form of escapism; it's more philosophical, I guess. The expression is that "someone has a calling." I take that to heart, take it literally. When I sit down to the materials of a poem, I do feel taken out of myself. I am listening to that calling. I am going, as it were, somewhere else. It seems to be a phenomenological process I can't fully understand, but the only way for me to write anymore is, to use Stevens's word, be "transported." For me to stay in my body, so to speak, would be to foster an anxiety, a sadness, a burden, a weight.

It is important that this whole experience be seen as a process, a natural process, a process of mortality, death. Out-of-body travel is the process of imagination. I have to clarify imagination, though, because I think the word is abused today. For me that transport works alongside a force of gravity, a sense of being tied to the body. That is why the process can be associated with mortality and death. Out-of-body travel moves through a world of real furniture and that furniture holds the body to its mortality. The whole process becomes threatening too, then. But the poems are not about the furniture—they are not "mother" poems or "father" poems or "animal" poems—the poems are processes, travels out of the dark. I think the last book is the book of a visionary who wants to live with human beings, a person who is concerned with the terrestrial matters that reside within the bubble of the celestial.

POETRY MISCELLANY: I think of the apocalyptic lines that end "Insomnia"—

> some shape of yourself at the center of the sun,
> wings spread,
> the body rising from fire,
> from body, from infinite dead weight,
> lifting to life the whole new day,
> to be burned alive till dark.

Existence here is always in a state of transition, both ever ending and ever beginning.

STANLEY PLUMLY: Yes, that phoenix figure. W. C. Field's advice for insomnia is to get plenty of sleep. I have never been able to manage that cure. If I had to identify a particular state of being, a place where I live, a time of day that frightens me most, it would be that time we refer to when we treat insomnia. And yet the part of the day I love is dusk, the time of very special light, of moving from one light to another. It gives a fullness, a joy. And it is a time for dreams—my poems have the ambience of dreams, and many are announced as dreams. Insomnia, dusk, even dawn, dreams—all these things are sources for me for a kind of transcendence. They are processes, means of travel.

POETRY MISCELLANY: Your books have always been organized in very careful structures that illustrate "the way" that we talked about earlier. In *Giraffe*, the three sections go from an external view, a scratching of the surface as the giraffe itself does, to the movement in "Heron" which is internal, a movement "down those long flights," and finally a sense of interpenetration, of transcendence as you call it, in the last section. In *Out-of-the-Body Travel* the movement is more complicated; it begins by assuming what is learned in the first two. There is an interpenetration or sharing of images from one poem to another, like the image of the girl in the iron lung. And it seems that your lines have had to get longer, and the poems, too, to carry this meaning.

STANLEY PLUMLY: Well, yes, the first two books are what I consider apprentice books, at least spiritually. I think I'm working more toward amplifying material, not tightening it. And if we are not quite sure of where we stand in one poem, it will be amplified later on. There is a kind of residual ambiguity. There is a single speaker in *Out-of-the-Body Travel*, but he is involved with several other people who try to represent themselves.

This creates part of the texture of interpenetration, I guess. And, yes, the lines keep getting longer. They are more filled up—the sense of one body filling another body. I guess that for me the more I can put into those poems, the more I can divest of myself. The fuller those poems are, the more empty I am, and relieved. I don't want that to sound confessional and therapeutic in a reductive way, though.

POETRY MISCELLANY: Many of the things we've been discussing—interpenetration, association of images, "out-of-body travel"—inform a complex sense of time, of the moment, the now. The moment is never confined to a "here and now." If we go back to *In the Outer Dark*, we find a poem like "Rilkean Autumn," where you say, "today, thought, in the held moment, / sucked to a single drop, / still wags at the lip of the top." Another is "October Tree," where you acknowledge "the movement / in all still things." What this tension leads to in the book is exemplified in "January at Saddler's Mill," where the "paddle-wheel is a stilled clock" and where, in that stillness of time—from it—"all around us single trees aspire to a touch / beyond all possible sense of reach." Time becomes spatialized in that book, a kind of measure of the threshold between inner and outer darks.

In *Giraffe*, the now becomes more "phenomenological"—or Heideggerian. In "Fungo," one of your most complex poems, there is a sense of simultaneous approach and waiting (Heidegger's "anticipating resolution") around a moment that is not at all stilled as in the first book— "as if this moment / were in perpetual motion." This leads in the end to a very Heideggerian sense of time—

> I think about now
> the way one thinks
> about the future,
> how the mind, all alone,
> makes it up in order to deal
> with what is coming.   ["One of Us," 51]

Finally, in *Out-of-the-Body Travel*, the sense of time is most dynamic—there's a fluid sense of passage of intervals, of durations—that sense that "Recovery is memory" ("For Esther"), which interpenetrates several time schemes. Do you feel a more complex sense of time evolving that better effects your out-of-body travel?

STANLEY PLUMLY: Right. The first book is preoccupied with space because I can't get out. It's also the most locally contemporary—I am the age of the speaker. *Giraffe* is also contemporary, but it is organized in a more linear way—I grow through time. In the last book there's a Bergsonian sense, to use the big terms, that all time is one time. But that time has to be dealt with, it has to be organized, has to be sequenced. Otherwise we are left only with uncertainty. We have to hold time in a pattern, even though we change the pattern from day to day. This is the source of our narratives. They don't quite stop, they defer to the next poem in a way we were talking about earlier. The patterns, the narratives, change from poem to poem. The whole book tries to contain these different patterns and relate them, to be as expansive as it can in containing, ordering time.

Now, this relation between poems is very important. A story becomes interrupted and the speaker tries again in the next poem. One poem leads to another. Perhaps what I am saying is that I have become my own parent by being able to arrange time. I stand at the moment of epiphany alongside the narrator. I let him suffer through, then figure a way out. Perhaps what I'm saying is that I'm not there, at least not then. Perhaps this sense of time gives me not so much a subjective relation to my origin, as I have often thought, but an objective position. This may account for the "temperature" in the poems—neither hot nor cold, but moving toward a kind of lower-case sublime, at least a synthesis.

Miller Williams, 1979

The Sanctioned Babel

POETRY MISCELLANY: In all your poems, however free they seem, there is a careful control of the line. Let's begin by talking about that basic unit, the line, about a theory of the line.

MILLER WILLIAMS: The line is very important to me. I like the five-stress line as a base, but I like to have it broken into twos and threes for sense, breath, conversational tone, pacing. If you take a poem like "The Caterpillar" or "Let Me Tell You," you can usually take adjacent lines and put them together into five-stress lines. I suppose, then, that almost all my poetry could be read as blank verse. But I hope that some interest is created when you realize that you are not moving through quite those blank verse rhythms. I hope that there's a tension between the sense of free verse and the sense of blank verse and that this creates a richness of texture. At least it seems to give me an opportunity to control pacing and meaning better than the squared blank verse base itself.

I agree with Conrad Aiken's 1917 review of *Prufrock and Other Poems*. He talked in that review about T. S. Eliot's fragmented blank verse, about Eliot's concealment of iambic pentameter. He suggested that this technique might be followed profitably in American poetry, and I think he's been proven right. And I think some of our best poetry has not only done that but has added "scattered" rhyme—full and slant rhymes that don't just occur at line breaks, but at more random intervals, unexpected places.

POETRY MISCELLANY: Your poems have a very physical texture to them—not just by the metaphors and images you use, but through the sense of one level of discourse colliding with another, a sense of the abrasions and cuts in language. This is one way your lines form units. Could we relate this physicality of language to the use of sudden shifts and cuts, to a sense of surprise?

MILLER WILLIAMS: There ought to be continual surprise. I think a line should be a little poem; that is, I like for something interesting to happen in each line. The line break should not be arbitrary. I like a line to be a rhythmical unit and yet not be fully resolved in a rhythmical sense. When we say, "shave and a haircut, six bits," the phrase "shave and a haircut" is not a *resolved*, though it is clearly a rhythmical unit. We don't say "shave and a" as a satisfying unit.

I like a line to cause the reader to ask a kind of question and then have the question answered at the beginning of the next line. This creates a sense of forward motion. In the very simple terms of our small example, then, the line asks, "Shave and a haircut, what about it?" or "Shave and a haircut, how much?"

This forward motion is also carried by the sounds. When I write, I write out loud. It's very important to me how the consonants click off against one another and how the vowels move into one another and out again. I also like the sounds of a line to move in an interesting and logical way through the mouth. For instance, let's take the line, "Whose woods these are I think I know." You start with the center of sound just in front of your lips, and then it moves back low in your mouth, rocks up to the top of the soft palate, back down along the tongue, and finally out to the beginning point. There's an interesting sound migration there. It's like rocking back and forth on a rocking chair.

When the line does these things we've been discussing, I think a poem is going to have a sense of richness and texture. We can't make every line do all these things—it would be like eating fudge that's too rich. We couldn't deal with it. But maybe every line should strive to do these things.

POETRY MISCELLANY: Roland Barthes talks about the physicality of language, relating it to what we might call the poem of pure play. He says, "The text of pleasure is a sanctioned Babel." You could also relate this "sanctioned Babel," I think, to your sense of irony—the way your poems lie "halfway" between the serious and the parodic, the objective and the subjective, the cold and the pathetic—the way one side of these dualities undercuts the other.

MILLER WILLIAMS: I think of most of my poems as having a touch of dark, hopefully ironic humor about them. I think there are many smooth and well-crafted poems that fail because of a lack of ironic vision. By the ironic vision, I mean that view of the world in which we see that all human statements contain their own contradiction and all human acts the seeds of their own defeat. Our acts, whether art works, marriages, governments, whatever, are bound to fail because they are built upon the fallacious assumption that we can do what we set out to do, or that we can say what we mean to say. It's not important, for instance, that a husband and wife tell each other what they mean to tell each other precisely, successfully. It's important that they know they can't. It's important that when we set out to build the tower of Babel, and we don't get what we want, we find a way to live with what we get. I think this gives us a means to sanity.

POETRY MISCELLANY: I'm reminded of your lines: "None of which facts we have gotten our words around, / not having understood them, words or facts. / We have been sure and courageous and skillfully wrong." There's a suspicion about language throughout your poetry, isn't there? And a suspicion about poetry itself?

MILLER WILLIAMS: Oh, yes. I'm concerned with our essential inability to know where we are at any given time, or to know what we're saying. Perhaps this is a poetic or humanistic version of the Heisenberg principle — the uncertainty principle. The thing we have to remember as poets is that we never get our words right. This is at least true in poetry. A Latin friend of mine once said that poetry is all "como si fuera" — it's all "as if it were." It's the same in our lives. We live life as if it were what we wanted; we read a poem as if it got to the truth of our lives. It never does, but the poet fails only because we all fail.

POETRY MISCELLANY: "Think of Judas That He Did Love Jesus" is particularly interesting in the context we have been developing. In that poem you provide various versions of Judas that undercut each other. This deconstructive strategy seems basic to all stories. In fact, you say, "These are the stories of Judas that fill the spaces / inside the story of Judas. Look quickly / behind the words you have heard and uncover creatures / looking the other way with words in their hands." There are always these "ghosts," *traces* that undermine history, story, gospel, conversation, perhaps even the poem. A question, maybe, of words and the Word. This raises the question of representation. Your poem "Cabbala," where there is a sense of a reality behind the dream behind the reality, raises the question in a more dramatic way.

MILLER WILLIAMS: Anything that we say in a poem has got to mean more than it would mean outside the poem, or the poem is not working. Poetry is an act of language that goes beyond the merely representational or the conversationally meaningful. The Judas poem tests out the implications of the fact that Jesus must have known what was going to happen, that he had to have someone there to betray him for the story's sake. This changes the usual view of Judas and so subverts the world order that the story represents.

But I want to say something about the suggestion in "Cabbala" that I question the objectively comprehensible universe. I don't mean to suggest utter chaos. I may seem to call into question an objective reality, but at the same time I write in a narrative framework filled with the furniture of this world. So when I question the reality of that furniture, I have to do this by building poems in which I assume that very reality. You have to start some place. What gets called into question is not the world itself but our ideas about it, our orderings of it.

POETRY MISCELLANY: Precisely. And this explains the strong visual quality in your poems, doesn't it?

MILLER WILLIAMS: Well, I don't usually like poems that are purely contemplative. I like a poem to be a little short story. I'm reminded that Donald Justice sometimes says to his writing students when they show him a poem— "film it." It's occurred to me lately that a lot of my poems are cinematic—a kind of panning, zooming in and out.

POETRY MISCELLANY: Well, there's another dimension besides this spatial, visual sense. I mean a sense of time. Of course, there's the man in "Notes from the Agent on Earth" who in a kind of Einsteinian universe invents a time machine to go back to his own childhood and kills the child and so has never lived to go back in the first place. We always see ourselves, you go on to say in the poem, standing in the past and talking to the people there. I suppose that raises the question of when and where we actually are. In "The House in the Vacant Lot," presence is seen as an absence, a ghost. And you give time a mythic dimension in "July 20, 1969"—as we go out to the moon, advancing technologically, we also retreat into a primitive past where the moon was worshiped.

MILLER WILLIAMS: You're the first person who's mentioned that—and I think it's important. I do play with time a great deal. I don't know if my concern for time is part of an aesthetic or philosophical position, but it is at least a problem in psychology. I can begin by saying that my concern with time originates with the uncertainty we were talking about before. We don't really know where we are in time or space; perhaps this is not *now* just as this is not *here*. Robert Penn Warren is another poet very much concerned with time, but our two concerns with it are like opposite sides of the same coin. For him, time is an unseen presence, but very real, that haunts his characters. I'm dealing with the problem of how we perceive time, and whether it can exist in a line or any sense of a "now" and a "to come." I think you're right in pointing to Einstein, and I'd point to Michelson and Morley, who also told us a lot about the illusory nature of time.

It may be that I'm using time as a synecdoche, then, as part of the illusory nature of the world. But in a poem you can't say everything is an illusion or there would be nothing to say. You have to find a particular something that's an illusion—time in this case—and let it represent the illusory nature of our perceptions, if not the world itself. I don't know precisely what I'm doing with time, but it intrigues me. I think I might come to say, though, that I do use time as a kind of synecdoche. I've never thought of that before.

POETRY MISCELLANY: I wonder how much this sense of time can be related to the Calvinistic context of a poem like "Notes from the Agent on Earth," where you emphasize the terror of knowing how mortal we are. What makes us "human / ...is a cold hand that reaches from under the bed" and closes on our ankles, the recognition that we may cross our hands on our chests when we sleep as we will in the coffin. And as you've been suggesting, this is part of the larger problem of just not knowing what will happen next. Perhaps, as you say in "How a Sparrow Was Caught in My Trap," the "darkness in our hearts is not what we think, / We ask how this could happen. We pretend. / The darkness in our hearts is that we know." What we know is a darkness.

MILLER WILLIAMS: The statement is ironic, of course. We know something, but the poem never says *what* we know. There is in all of us a secret darkness of the heart. It's a secret because none of us knows what is there, precisely. This is related, certainly, to Calvinism, and I think those who live in the Bible belt are more aware of it than other people. There's a certain guilt associated with this secret. Ultimately, I think my use of this religious background, and it is a strong background, is metaphoric. It doesn't finally matter what we call the source of our guilt, a godhead or whatever. Dealing with guilt requires me to deal with some sort of God-presence because that's the simplest way to introduce the question. We need a god for our guilt.

Still, I don't think I can talk very long about my poems in religious or Calvinistic terms because I think that if there is a pervasive statement in my poems, it is a humanistic one. A sense of guilt is a sense of isolation, and it's the sense of isolation that makes inevitable our sense of mortality, our sense of loss, our uncertainty about where and when we are, the consciousness of our illusions. Because of this isolation we try to build bridges between each other. This is what a poem does. This is a humanistic attitude, not a religious one. Perhaps the tone is colored by a religious background, but finally the important thing is the human being. My priorities are horizontal, not vertical.

POETRY MISCELLANY: There's another aspect to this, related to your translating, which of course you do a lot of, and which you teach. I mean that the translator has to be able, as Keats says of the poet, to fill in for some other body; perhaps he has to have the same degree of "negative capability," too — the ability to live in uncertainty and doubt. The translator has to bridge the gap between cultures, doesn't he?

MILLER WILLIAMS: To me the role of the translator is very close to that of a spiritualist medium. When I'm translating I want the poet to be able to speak through me. I want to know his work well enough so that I move from metaphor to metaphor at his pace, to vibrate as it were with him so that I can look at something and respond to it as he would. I want to create the poem that he would have created had English been his language. When we talk about the translator's humility, we're not talking about piousness, or even a humble deference, but the kind of humility that causes one actor to be quiet backstage when another one is working. Part of the humility is the awareness of the inability to say all we want to say, to say enough of what the original poet said. There's an essential futility, the futility of an act we can't help trying to perform. It's part of the terror of any writing, but also its motive.

Mark Strand, 1979

Untelling the Hour

POETRY MISCELLANY: In "Notes on the Craft of Poetry" (*Antaeus*), you mention that poems seem to have a tautological existence: "A poem is itself and is the act by which it is born; it is self-referential and is not necessarily preceded by any known order." This, you say, provides what Stevens calls a motive for metaphor—"Perhaps the poem is ultimately a metaphor for something unknown, its working out a means of recovery. It may be that the relation of the absent origin is what is necessary for the continued life of the poem as *inexhaustible artifact*." In fact, the man in your poem "Inside the Story" faces the impossibility of achieving an absent origin in a dream. He cannot fully remember the experience, and toward the end, "He stood in the absence of what he had known / and waited, and when he woke / the room was empty."

MARK STRAND: I think when I talk about the absent origin I mean the mystery that is entailed in the making of anything and that is preserved even after the thing is made. I believe that we never know what the source of a poem is ultimately. Part of a good poem is the discovery of this, and that moment of discovery is a moment of loss. We discover that we can never really go back, as the writer can never get back to the original story in "The Untelling." To a certain extent, the act of writing is itself a metaphor for the way we relate to the hidden sources of our own lives. A truly exciting poem has something evasive or mysterious at the core, and it succeeds in suggesting to us that the core is essential to our being. But that core's absence reminds us of how precariously we exist in the universe that evades us, that is always beyond us. If poetry makes our existence important to us, it is because it suggests this totality, this open-enddness. The poem is the infinitive.

POETRY MISCELLANY: Later in that essay you write: "Poems must exist not only in language, but beyond it." I suppose this has been a constant in your poetry. Several years ago in an interview you said that poems deal with "identifiable states of mind that are at the same time elusive." This sort of situation occurs as recently as "From the Long Sad Party," a poem of evasive references; "Somebody" is always saying "Something" about "Something."

MARK STRAND: One wouldn't write poems if there wasn't something, a remainder that is beyond the grasp of the previous poem. There is always something beyond the power of language to name. So much of our experience is nonverbal and can't be fitted into the categories of language which we have that we must realize that any attempt to capture experience is highly provisional—hence the self-mockery in many of my own poems. I would like to be able to describe just what it is that's so wonderful about getting between two freshly ironed, clean sheets on a cold winter day with maybe two blankets on top. Or what it's like to be isolated on a North Atlantic island with nothing but sky and not a single light. But the experience would remain largely ineffable in language.

POETRY MISCELLANY: There is that sort of evasiveness in your haunting line, "You lie under the weather of stones." It seems to fall naturally into the end of "Elegy for My Father" and yet is startling and powerful. But it remains ineffable.

MARK STRAND: Well, yes, the line may be vague—it's about the graveyard and the gray, opaque air of Nova Scotia in January. It's vague enough so that people might find something challenging and even attractive in it. You never know whether your audience will understand and sympathize with what you had in mind—but then why should they because you didn't have anything in mind when you thought it. You thought of *it*. What I mean is, after I wrote the line you refer to I decided that it suggested the color of Nova Scotia air, but I didn't plan the line as a representation of any vision that I had. The line came in a purely verbal fashion, but afterward I've been able to learn from it. I'm writing a poem now about my mother, and in the course of the poem all she does is smoke a cigarette behind the house in Nova Scotia, but there are other images that seem almost irrelevant. Perhaps I'm beginning to understand in some oblique way, by the verbal associations, something about how I've never been able to understand her. All these things originate, I guess I'm saying, in some lost region.

POETRY MISCELLANY: The last section of "Elegy for My Father" is a section of retrievals—the repetitions of "nobody" and "nothing" that balance off statements like "And nothing comes back." There's a balancing of the fact that the year is "over" and the fact of the "new year" beginning.

MARK STRAND: I suppose that rhetorical strategy of repetition which is inherent in poetry is a way of preserving something. Perhaps we could say that these rhetorical forms are forms by which we retain the representation of loss which is in some ways a compensation for an actual loss.

POETRY MISCELLANY: I wonder in what sense rhetoric provides the writer with a fictive identity.

MARK STRAND: Well, I think that if you're as deeply alienated as I am or as I believe I am that you're at some loss to know if the life you have is yours because you have it or because you *say* you have it. There is something more real about my representations of my life that culminate as poems than in the everydayness of my living. I suppose that it means I'm unable to vouch for the authenticity of my experience on its own terms and must have it fortified in poems.

POETRY MISCELLANY: That's an interesting distinction between the life in art and the real life. You've certainly constructed a style which a self can inhabit. And you certainly are more of a stylist than most contemporary poets. I wonder, as your career progresses, about fidelity to that style.

MARK STRAND: Yes, I believe I'm a stylist. I would like to escape, perhaps into something else I'm not yet aware of—one feels constrained, feels a certain tyranny of the past. In some ways, the writing of prose has liberated me. It is an area I really don't know that much about. I write as naturally as possible and make my own rules. I don't mean that I don't read other prose, but I don't study it so closely as I did poetry when I began writing poems.

POETRY MISCELLANY: The lines of your poems have become more full, obviously, in your later books. But then, even in poetry, your basic unit has always seemed to be the sentence, hasn't it?

MARK STRAND: That's true. The sentences in my first book are so simple I really couldn't manage anything very complex. The sentence is very important in free verse because with no specific measure it is difficult to tell what is stressed or not—you need a larger rhythmical unit. Your phrasing in the sentence takes on a great significance, and even line breaks become absorbed in a larger movement. I don't mean to say that the line is not important at all, only that it is part of a larger unit. In a longer line you gain a kind of creative energy toward the end. There's a horizontal thrust, like in prose, rather than a vertical one. The longer line also allows for incremental build-up of complex units, for a progression through parallel structures. Now, though, I'm freer to write a greater variety of sentences in the prose that I'm doing than I ever was, especially in the earlier poems.

POETRY MISCELLANY: That sense of style, at least in the poems, establishes a decorum that presides over the tone.

MARK STRAND: Perhaps that decorum, or taste, prevents me from making awful errors and exercising bad judgment in my poetry. But it perhaps prevents me from being a more important and better poet than I might be because I don't ever allow my poems to get away from me. I wish somehow that I were able to let go a little more and find myself more frequently in a terrain that I know very little about, a terrain in which there would be no rhetorical way out. I'm not sure whether I'm just fantasizing and whether I wouldn't hate being so lost, too. Maybe we just like to create other, more daring selves.

POETRY MISCELLANY: Actually, the notion of the Other is central in your work. I'm reminded as I read your poems and as I read *The Monument* of Kierkegaard in *Diary of a Seducer*: "Everything is symbol; I myself am a myth about myself, for is it not as a myth that I hasten to this meeting?" That missing self in "Keeping Things Whole" is this Other. The Other predominates *Darker* and *Reasons for Moving* and *The Monument*, and it surfaces in the other books, too. Jacques Lacan, among modern thinkers, has perhaps made the most out of this phenomenon, locating the Other in language and in the unconscious.

MARK STRAND: Though I find Lacan unnecessarily obscure, I would certainly agree that the Other is really a part of myself, my unconscious. It is a part of me that I live with but don't really know except when it chooses to reveal itself to me, usually at inopportune moments when I'm least expecting it. I am not often able to receive or even deal with the truth that the Other reveals to me. The best I can do is make poems like "The Mailman" about the figure who is the courier between the realm of the Other and the part of me that's the writer of messages. I guess that one of the most extreme forms of this concern for the Other occurs in "My Life by Somebody Else." There's always a sense in which we live a couple of lives even on the surface, in our consciousness. Our selves can be the foreign and the near, the social and the personal, etc. This is another dimension to the problem entirely.

POETRY MISCELLANY: It would seem that this sense of the Other informs your striking use of pronouns.

MARK STRAND: I've thought of myself as "we," as "you," as "I," as "he"— I've put myself in all of the pronouns. However the pronoun in my poems has always been closer to myself than the pronoun in my prose. I've just written a story, "True Loves," in which the character is completely unrelated to me. One of the problems we've gotten ourselves into today is thinking that the poet or the writer is always speaking about himself. Most poets today want themselves to be very present in their poems. I find Stevens very refreshing for his refusal to do this—the living personality is not an issue there; the personality the poetry has is in the language, the style. You know, there's an enormous amount of fakery involved in writing despite the belief in sincerity and honesty in poetry that we have today. We lie all the time—not in essential matters, maybe, but in the overemphasis we give to some words, in our phrasing. This isn't often picked up by critics. Somehow we have come to live in an age where everything is a document.

POETRY MISCELLANY: It's ironic, then, isn't it, that *The Monument* is a document. Like the poem, "The Untelling," it confronts the question of textual referentiality. So the author says to his translator, whoever that will be, "This work has allowed you to exist, yet this work exists because you are translating it." The text becomes, as you suggest, a means of self-creation as a function of the Other: "Consider how often we are given to invent ourselves; maybe once, but even so we say we are another, another entirely similar."

MARK STRAND: Yes, *The Monument* is a document, but whose document it is we're not certain, and whose evidence it presents we're not certain. The real translator is the one I've invented who is myself and who has also created me. He is myself, my immortal self, my projection. The book itself anticipates his translation of it. I actually wrote it very quickly, keeping crude notes, then changing everything later on. I decided I wanted it to have fifty-two sections, ironically, like "Song of Myself," and I wanted the language to get wilder at the end. I wanted a stereo effect between the quotations and the text; the quotations are part of the fabric of the text. The relation between them and the text is sometimes close, sometimes very distant. The irony is that the quotes get the last word, that the words of the so-called original writer are lost in the quotes. When you think that their lives, which are what they write, are completed by quotations, the commentaries from someone else, then it can be comic vision of our elaborate concern for the "author." In a way, the thing is an elaborate conceit, an elaborate joke at my own expense. There was a terrific release in doing it.

POETRY MISCELLANY: *The Monument* points toward a future, and I would describe your sense of time as futural, too. In "Breath," you say, "by being both here and beyond / I am becoming a horizon." The moment, as a horizon, seems dear to you, as in "Snowfall," where you describe "the fall of moments into moments."

MARK STRAND: We live in a world, in America, where the past is done away with quickly. We fasten ourselves to the now. This isn't the case in Europe, where there is a sense of the verticality and connectedness of time. But still, the now is very important. It is created again and again as we create ourselves. The most penetrating revelations we have are of the now, where there is an instantaneous and heightened perception in which everything takes on a certain clarity. And the now is so transitory—this sense of transitoriness is at the heart of Ashbery's poems. So there is an elusiveness about the now that generates a great sadness in his poems, and in mine, too, in a different way. We want to have the present without having to eulogize the previous present. If we can retain a sense of the past at the same time we are aware of our moments, then we can occupy a horizon as we move from one now to the next. By looking to the future in this context, we give some sort of meaning to our lives.

POETRY MISCELLANY: In what way are these horizons fictions in Stevens's sense? How does a fiction differ from myth? Is there any possibility for myth today? I ask these questions because all that we have been talking about this afternoon seems to point to a loss of myths and the rise of fictions.

MARK STRAND: I don't think a poet can develop a mythology today. Myth is absolutely representative and suggests something cosmic, eternal, or at least something beyond the moment. We don't have anything that stable in our world today. Fictions are much more concerned with the specific, with the now; they are much more modest. We have to live with a supreme fiction, as Stevens says, and realize that it must constantly be remade. Stevens can never get back to that origin he's looking for in "Notes Toward a Supreme Fiction." We can only keep "untelling" the origin and in that way compensate for its loss.

Charles Simic, 1978

The Domain of the Marvelous Prey

POETRY MISCELLANY: In the Introduction to *Another Republic* you make the distinction between mythological and historical writing, and in doing so you describe a form of "phenomenological interrogation" in which there is an "elaborate narrative which tells the story of its own formation." In your essay "Composition" in a recent issue of *NLH* you talk about how in moving from the "origin" of the poem to the language of the poem, one moves from a "simultaneous" and timeless world to a finite world of linear time. The poem, at least the mythical poem, becomes a "myth of origins" or a "place where origins are allowed to think." Could you elaborate on your notion of the mythic, of the movement from the timelessness of a mythic impulse into the language of the poem?

CHARLES SIMIC: I used to think the way to introduce mythic consciousness into poetry would be to study texts from various mythic traditions, both Western and non-Western. By cataloging the archetypal structures one would, I thought, understand how to cast one's own poems. The problem with that approach is that one makes a false separation between form and content. If you look at a Navaho myth you can intellectually deduce its form, but the content, and the deeper psychological impetus for that content, would be missing. Unless you were a Navaho living when the myth was set, you could only provide a generalized content. I began to realize that these structures would be imposed from the outside, and so there would necessarily be something foreign about the way they came to my poems. There was something mechanical and unsatisfying in trying to fit an experience into a deliberate mythic structure.

It occurred to me that mythical consciousness, the kind that is still present in our world, is to be found in language. The first examples for me were idiomatic expressions using the impersonal "it" in an expression like "it goes without saying." Here you have an ambiguity at the core of the expression that points to something nameless. The "it" is both minimal and all-inclusive. "It" can open up to whatever is beyond, can include all the other "its." This is a mythical situation; you eventually hear the little drama of the expression as its possibilities unfold. There's another aspect, too, as in idiomatic and figurative expressions. Take the expression, "counting bats in his belfry." Here you get the kind of "place" you referred to in the question; somebody has a head that is really a belfry, and it has bats in it, and he's counting them. It's a bizarre predicament which can be dramatized by taking the line literally and ignoring the figurative intention. The first poems in this direction were the Riddles, where I tried to follow a literal logic in a figurative and metaphoric world and then to pick up and dramatize the forces, the meanings that were created. So the mythic, then, occurs where something is transformed—the familiar is made strange, made miraculous, and it can generate a story line, a plot, a destiny.

POETRY MISCELLANY: Could we discuss the notion of place further? Sometimes it seems to be associated with origins, sometimes with ends. In "Return to a Place Lit by a Glass of Milk," you say, "The sea is a room far back in time / Lit by the headlights of a passing car. / A glass of milk glows on the table. / Only you can reach it for me now." On the other hand, "Euclid Avenue" seems poised to move in the opposite direction. There your "dark thoughts" are "laid out / in a straight line. / An abstract street," and the struggle to "retrieve" a "language / as old as rain," a "beginning," becomes a striving for "a place / known as infinity" and then "a place known / as infinity." The poem ends by pointing toward a language which is "endlessly screeching." How, then, would you describe a poetic place?

CHARLES SIMIC: As a first step, the place exists in the psyche. The place is never really physically there, and you keep moving toward it, or you keep circling it. What happens is a process of circling around, pointing at, saying something about, even turning away from the "place."

"Euclid Avenue" is a little different from the kinds of poems I described before. I had an idea, an abstraction, a generally accepted law. What could be more vigorous and austere than Euclidean geometry? The poem was an attempt, like those other poems that deal with figures, to humanize an abstraction, to invest something personal in it. One of the ways that seemed possible was to assume that each geometric figure tells a different kind of story. That is, there could be stories that go on a straight line to infinity;

there could be circular stories. Triangular stories start out and try to retrace their own steps but can't get back to their beginnings so they end up at some distance from the beginning before they return to it; by that time they've traced a strange figure. There's a comic aspect to all this. My favorite is "The Point," the story which takes one step and then immediately has a kind of regret. It's horrified at the whiteness of the page. In these poems, then, a meaning would be unraveled around the logic of a particular geometric figure.

What we have been talking about relates to a wish I have always had, both conscious and unconscious, to place myself in a verbally impossible situation. The aim is to abbreviate myself to some sort of minimal equation and then to work my way out of that. Many of the poems have that sort of predicament: somebody is there as an "it," a geometric point. This is the essence, there's nothing around it except empty space. Here is where he locates himself, and now he has to do something out of that, tell a story, establish a place, a time.

POETRY MISCELLANY: For Heidegger, in the "The Origin of the Work of Art," a genuine beginning is always "a leap...a head start, in which everything to come is already leaped over." It is a flash, the details and horizons of which will later be explored as time. This exploratory process leads him to remark in another essay ("What Are Poets For") that this "anticipation" is linked with a "holding back"—a concept I think we can link to what Paul Ricoeur calls "suspicion," which he says characterizes modern thought. The poet, for Heidegger, exists in a state of betweenness. As you say in "Ode," "between the premonition / and the event // the small lovely realm / of the possible." Suspicion for Ricoeur and, we might add, for Heidegger involves "the possibility of signifying another thing than what one believes was signified." It involves what you call in "Negative Capability and Its Children" a "maintaining oneself in the face of that multiplicity." What I am trying to suggest is that there is always a suspicion about what is leaped over, about origins, about the language we use to embrace them. In its most radical form, as you say in "The Prisoner" it suggests "the suspicion / That we do not exist." Can we talk about an ontological suspicion, a holding back, an emphasis on the uncertainty about the poem's space?

CHARLES SIMIC: Suspicion is the voice because language is not mine. I'm one of those who believes that there is something that precedes language. The usual view is that there is some kind of equivalence between thought and language, that if you can't verbalize it you can't think it. I've always felt that there is a state that precedes verbalization, a complexity of experience that consists of things not yet brought to consciousness, not yet existing as language but as some sort of inner pressure. Any verbal act includes a selection, a conceptualization, a narrowing down. Let's say someone has the experience of walking around in a swamp at night, sees things he wouldn't see in another place or in the daytime, perhaps feels fear, confusion. Now, he would have to be seriously deluded to believe that when he sits down to render all this that he can equal its complexity. Since what he writes doesn't equal the experience, there's this suspicion which becomes a voice, a voice that asks, "What have I experienced?" But let's say he begins to write and arrives at an acceptable equation. The problem is then with a language that is larger than his uses for it. On the one hand, it's not specific enough to carry all of his experiences, but on the other hand, it contains echoes and resonances he never suspected before he began to write about the experience. So he starts hearing two things. He hears what recreates his swamp experience, but also other things that are unexpected, that point to a different subject matter, to a different development. Here he has to make some sort of choice. I find that in my own poems I tend to abandon the original cause or the visible aspects of the original cause and follow wherever the poem leads. That's why my poems often seem impersonal. It is not clear who the "I" is. It doesn't seem necessary for me to equate that "I" with myself. I follow the logic of the algebraic equation of words on the page which is unfolding, moving in some direction.

POETRY MISCELLANY: You mentioned that you sometimes abandon the visible origin. Perhaps at the heart of this suspicion is a sense that the origin is an absence, a loss. "Language," says Michel Foucault, "always seems to be inhabited by the other, the elsewhere, the distant; it is hollowed by absence." This absence is like Freud's "novel" of the dream—an abyss. Your own metaphors suggest such notions as silence, invisibility. For example, there is often a sense of things fading, as the end of "Nursery Rhyme," where you "see a blur, a speck, meagre, receding / Our lives trailing in its wake." In "Poem," you say, "The invisible is precisely that / which no one remembers." Finally, the poem "Eraser" seems to talk about this—there is a "summons" motivated by the flight of a "marvelous prey." The erasing is a means to "recover a state of pure expectancy," to recover traces of what seems absent, the hollowness, the cleared place—"Only the rubbings only the endless patience / As the clearing appears / the clearing which is there / Without my even having to look / The domain of the marvelous prey."

CHARLES SIMIC: I've always felt that inside each of us there is profound anonymity. Sometimes I think that when you go deep inside, you meet everyone else on a sort of common ground—or you meet nobody. But whatever you meet, it is not yours though you enclose it. We are the container, and this nothingness is what we enclose. This is where Heidegger is very interesting to me. He describes the division between the world as nothing, as what he calls the "open," and any act of conceptualizing which restores the world in a particular way. Many of his texts are longings to experience that anonymity, the condition where we don't have an "I" yet. It is as if we were in a room from which, paradoxically, we were absent.

Everything is seen from the perspective of that absence. I suppose, in some ways, this is a mystical vision that brings to me a sense of the universe as an anonymous presence. The force of that sometimes frightens me, sometimes delights me.

POETRY MISCELLANY: I think this is related to your sense of "poverty." I think, too, of Stevens's "The greatest poverty is not to live in a physical world."

CHARLES SIMIC: Yet, that anonymity for me is physical. It's not exactly nothing. And poverty is both a lack of imagination and real poverty—an empty plate, no money. What I've always tried to do in these metaphysical excursions is to remember the predicament of that "I." I dislike flights of imagination that leave behind the human condition. It delights me to remember this "I" who might be trying to figure out some incredible abstract proposition about the nature of the universe, this "I" who has holes in his socks, perhaps. It is Thoreau's notion, I guess, of keeping an allegiance to the soil, to our everydayness in the same instant as we experience the transcendental.

POETRY MISCELLANY: So that there is always a duality in the poem's reality? As you say in "Stone," one can find "the star charts / on the inner walls" of the stone?

CHARLES SIMIC: Yes, the whole notion of truth does not reside in finely formulated metaphysical propositions or visionary passages. They may be seductive, but that kind of suspicion we talked about earlier always enters. Some poems of mine that I didn't publish were like that. What seemed to be a brilliant series of propositions about some abstract problem eventually seemed empty and arbitrary. What was missing was a test of the presence of the human being who accepts the responsibility of those visions. There is a constant dialectic in my poetry between a longing to take off on abstract flights and my concrete, physical needs. One has to consider the life of the world: the historical dimension, the horrifying history of our age. All that intrudes into poems.

POETRY MISCELLANY: In the context of the notions we have been discussing—language, origins, suspicion, absence, poetic reality—can we examine the nature of metaphor? I think of Heidegger's notion that the poet's intimacy with the world "occurs through the creation of a world and its ascent, and likewise through the destruction of a world and its decline." If classical metaphor is based on substitution, is modern metaphor based on a shattering of structures of language? In "The Point," you talk about the nothingness that is inside the story that has halted as "whatever / Is destroyed // Each time / It is named."

CHARLES SIMIC: On one level metaphor is naming, however provisional and temporary the name is. Metaphor has interested me more as a way of knowledge, a way of grasping something. I like to take a metaphor and look at it, then do something like what I do with idiomatic expressions—discover a kind of mythic structure, use the metaphor as a way to discover something about the nature of reality. You have to accept the metaphor's premises and follow its logic. Take the expression, "a bladeless knife without a handle," where you have a figurative proposition which doesn't mean anything. Yet by simply saying the expression, it exists somehow. Looking at the expression, you realize it is possible to construct a poem around it, but a poem that would follow the logic of a world where there are bladeless knives without handles. You couldn't have ordinary tables and chairs around it. The other objects would have to have some distortion to accommodate themselves to that new world. So the poem becomes a statement about a kind of reality with a logic of its own. That little cosmos is there and yet it isn't. It almost seems to cancel itself. That brings us back to Heidegger and the suspicion of utterance. You really can say anything and make it exist; existence is saying, speaking.

POETRY MISCELLANY: It also brings us to the role of chance and the irrational. In "Elementary Cosmogony," you talk about the relation of the "invisible" and the "submission to chance," and in "Ode" there is that crucial "fall of the dice." On a linguistic level, and also in terms of the ideas of history and mythology we mentioned earlier, we might remember Nietzsche's definition: "The entire history of a 'thing,' an organ, a custom can...be a continuous sign-chain of ever new interpretations and adaptations whose causes do not even have to be related to one another but, on the contrary, in some cases succeed and alternate with one another in a purely chance fashion." I suppose one paradigmatic example is "Charon's Cosmology," where the two sides of the river become interchangeable. The result of all this is a subversion of teleology. What role does chance play in the composition of your poems or in the vision they suggest?

CHARLES SIMIC: I think chance is tied to metaphor—semblances seem to come out of our unconscious by chance, though there are arguments about this. But there is also a mechanical operation, say, as when someone cuts out words and puts them in a hat and then picks them out as a way of beginning to write. The curious thing for me has been that the original material may be provided by a random operation, but the moment we look at it there is no longer chance because what we select as examples of chance is something that signifies, even if it paradoxically signifies chance. I have used this, then, only as a tool to liberate and engage my imagination. I suppose it is like saying that I can't make metaphors without having some language there to begin with; I make metaphors by moving language around. Beyond that, I don't have a view of the universe that contains chance. Antonin Artaud says, "Chance is myself." What we call chance is for him the "I" who enters a scene.

POETRY MISCELLANY: How does chance affect what constitutes meaning?

Lacan, following Freud, talks about the endless "sliding" of signifiers over signifieds, the two sets never really meeting except at mythical *points de capiton*. Traditional meaning is, for him, inaccessible; "but what can be done is to pin one signifier to another signifier and see what happens. But in this case something new is invariably produced... in other words, the surging forth of new signification." At what point would this process stop? What are the limits of language? What is the poet's responsibility here? When, as you say in "Unintelligible Terms," does the poem match its silence, its "remote," chancy "hush" that reveals an "expanding immensity"? Can it? Should it?

CHARLES SIMIC: Theoretically, it would be that place where it seems possible for that other, the reader, to absorb and reexperience the terms of the poem. Now, there are poems where I can be quite aware I have done just that, but there are also poems where I know nothing. I am surprised and puzzled at what is happening, and yet it seems extremely interesting and important. The crucial thing, in either case, is for the poem to have access. I'm interested in how poems open. Once the poem is made available, you have a choice of either fulfilling or frustrating the reader's expectations. It has always seemed more interesting for me to frustrate those expectations. I like to compare the experience of the poem to someone who comes upon a corner and doesn't know what he will encounter next when he turns the corner. One way to establish this sort of suspense is by dialectic. Ivor Winters says a poem is a statement, but it seems to me that in a statement nothing happens. I conceive of the poem as having a more dramatic form that embroils the reader in its action and takes him some place. It sets in motion a number of possibilities, doubts, suspicions, frustrations, contradictions.

POETRY MISCELLANY: The notions of chance, the play of possible meanings, the sense of language going on by itself that we have discussed lead to what Foucault and Jacques Derrida call a fundamental absence—the absence of the author. How would you define the author? Nietzsche says in the *Genealogy of Morals*, "'the doer' is merely a fiction added to the deed— the deed is everything." How would you react to this?

CHARLES SIMIC: I would agree, though Foucault sees the death as a kind of "erasure" of the author, and I see it more as a physical death in the sense that there is a confrontation between myself and the universe, something large and inhuman against which I feel small. But I don't think the author is ever absent. The simple act of selectivity from the vast possibilities of language and experience introduces the author. Except that for me there is no *one* "I." "I" is many. "I" is an organizing principle, a necessary fiction, etc. Actually, I'd put more emphasis on consciousness: That which witnesses but has no need of a pronoun. Of course, consciousness has many degrees, and each degree has a world (as an ontology) appropriate to itself. So, perhaps, the seeming absence of the author is the description of one of its manifestations, in this case an increase of consciousness at the expense of the subject? It's a possibility.

Jean Valentine, 1980

The Hallowing of the Everyday

POETRY MISCELLANY: Your poetry is unique in the way it presents itself; it seems to be based upon fragments, shifts in perspective, traces, frayings. As you say in "Twenty Days' Journey," it is a world of things "almost visible," of "The blown away footstep / in the snow." Could we begin by talking about the nature of the vision, this world, where often, it seems, "it was like touching the center and therefore losing it, emptying it of what you might have been able to hold on to" ("February 9th"). It seems a world of deferrals, discontinuities, differences, gaps.

JEAN VALENTINE: I can only respond to your first sentence here, very simply: that when I'm most attentive, these "fragments," etc., are very often what I sense and feel; they are how I "get" this time and place and the currents of my private and public life and the lives around me. To try to clarify this—not to compare—I think of, for instance, Paul Klee's painting, certain newspaper photos or documentary film scenes, or certain intricately plotted mysteries.

In "The Lives Around Me" I include the work of someone like Huub Oosterhuis (you quote next from my version of his long poem *Twenty Days' Journey,* made with the Dutch poet Judith Herzberg). To try a version of this poem, I had to feel very close to it. There are still mysteries in the poem for me, but I make out this much: a vision of both personal and worldwide suffering of loss and anguish, in which a personal and/or an Everyman "I" undertakes a journey: a journey in search of God, who is both present and absent in the poem, and who also suffers loss and anguish. (I should say clearly here that I haven't had the chance to talk with either Herzberg or Oosterhuis about this, and I could be very far off.) The experience of that journey is something I could only have known or approached at all through Oosterhuis's poem: but to return to your question, the poem seems fragmented as its subject seems to demand.

Your second quotation, from "February 9th" (from *The Messenger*) came to me in a letter from a friend and spoke wonderfully to me of one negative side of naming: I think Robert Coles said this somewhere, though I can't remember his exact words: "Name it, and it is so." Just the opposite, of course, of the creating or the hallowing powers of naming, this would be the destructive use of language to lie, to deny, to erase life. In the quotation, it would be the violent or intrusive use of touch.

POETRY MISCELLANY: Your sense of time seems predicated upon this same fragmentary vision. For example, "This Minute" portrays the moment as being continually undercut as the filmstrip keeps running again and again, presencing future, present, and past in the one moment. Or take "Here Now," where "The sky is the same changing / colors as the farthest snow"— here the moment gets defined by all the possibilities that range beyond it. Could you sketch out, then, how you feel time is at work in the poems as a theme, as a principle of structuring?

JEAN VALENTINE: I don't think the use of time in "This Minute" is trying to do anything more than to present a nightmare, in which time does not move naturally, historically, but is fixed, distorted.

About how time is at work in the poems in general, again I can only say simply that this awareness of past and present and future "in the one moment" seems to me how time is experienced, when one is most alive, most attentive—except perhaps for extraordinary moments when only the present is there.

I don't really see time as a "theme" in my own poems, except in the most ordinary and universal ways. As a "principle of structuring"—our thoughts do range all over time, and in lots of poems I am trying to catch the way someone might think, or "think out loud" in a quiet talk with some close friend, or say in a letter.

POETRY MISCELLANY: In the context of this fragmentary vision, it often seems that the processes of writing, collecting, locating, comparing, absenting become themselves part of the subject of the poems. That is, there often seems a way in which the process itself is the subject, not the fact of the finished poem. I perceive a sense that the poem is always emerging, even in its last line—this holds especially true for the poems in *The Messenger*. I think of Stevens's ideal that all poems comprise or refer to an ideal, always unwritten poem. Do you have this sense of your work? I think of the last poem in *The Messenger* that is also a sort of collecting of images from earlier in the book.

JEAN VALENTINE: If this "sense that the poem is always emerging" is working successfully, that is, if the poem is accessible, I'd be very content. I have this wish, right now anyhow, to catch our experience "on the fly," so to speak: a pull against the poem as a sort of finished, well-wrought statement—much as I admire and love that kind of poem by certain other poets.

Yes, like Stevens, I certainly do imagine how one is writing along underneath some one "ideal, always unwritten poem" all one's life—I like very much Anne Sexton's notion that this ideal poem is being written by everyone all the time, a sort of communal poem being written by all the poets alive. Though with Stevens again, I would imagine this poem as "an ideal, always unwritten." Being "written after," maybe.

In the last poem in *The Messenger*, "March 21st," I'm sure there are images collected that I wasn't conscious of; but in that piece I was consciously trying to bring in sense-echoes from the various sections of the sequence, "Solitudes," trying to get to a moment of gathering-in, there.

POETRY MISCELLANY: There is a double movement in the poems—in "Sanctuary," for instance, there is a "scattering of life" that is counterpointed by the movement along "the thread you have to keep finding, over again, to / follow it back to life." Could you describe your sense of this movement? It seems as if the farther you go out into things, into the world, the more you find yourself intact; an escape from the self to find the self. In psychology, at least that of Jacques Lacan, this movement tends to suggest an otherness we seek; we always seek to know ourselves in, identify with, the Other, a double.

JEAN VALENTINE: What you say is very good, and it ought to be included. But I have nothing to add because you really answer it yourself.

POETRY MISCELLANY: How do you see yourself figured in the poems? In other words, what is the relationship between you and your voices, narrators? Sometimes your perspective changes in a single poem, such as "Susan's Photograph," where you are razor, wrist, photographer, the friend, and so on. Ultimately, then, this is a question about voice, its varieties and modulations, about the ways you throw yourself, aspects of your self that are real or imagined, into the poems.

JEAN VALENTINE: One thing I feel sure of about the use of the self is that while there are poems that may use the "I" with very little of the "real self" in them, there are *no* poems that present the "real self" precisely, "as is," as one would try to in, say, an autobiography.

I think "the relationship between me and my voices, narrators," is the common one: I am trying to move into an other, into others; to move out of the private self into an imagination of everyone's history, into the public world. This is what I most *want* to do—maybe what every lyric poet most wants to do. This effort in no way means to exclude the eccentric, but to enlarge what is human. (Here Emily Dickinson and Whitman both come to mind and the wonderful southern poet of our own time, Eleanor Ross Taylor.)

POETRY MISCELLANY: What is the nature of the "messenger"? It seems a sort of metamorphic entity. I think, for example, of "Beka, 14," where you tell the girl that the messenger is like her brother,

> like the penguin
> who sits on the nest of pebbles, and the one
> who brings home pebbles, to the nest's edge in his beak,
> one at a time, and also like the one
> who is lying there, warm, who is going to break out soon:
>
> becoming yourself; the messenger is growing....

I think also of "Turn (2): After Years," where the name of the absent friend is presenced at the end by uttering the two words "other" and "thou" almost as if to bring them together, as if to presence the absent other, to bring the messenger close. Could we talk, then, about the "messenger" and the "you"?

JEAN VALENTINE: Yes, in "Beka, 14," the messenger is a metamorphic figure: I tried to use the changing figures as messengers coming, gradually, to call the fourteen-year-old child to her adult life, including, at the end of the poem, her leaving home to go her own way. A series of callings. Whether the "messenger" is thought of as internal (as it becomes, halfway through this particular poem), or as an external figure, doesn't matter, I don't think: what matters to me in the poem is the figuring of the person's coming into possession of his or her own strongest desires—something which Father William F. Lynch, S.J., writes so clearly and so healingly of in his book *Images of Hope*.

In "Turn (2): After Years," I hadn't thought consciously of a messenger figure, but I do feel the absent friend "present at the end" of the poem, yes. The two words *Other* and *thou* are trying to express closeness and the redemption of a harmful past. In this way, the poem is (maybe like many poems) part recognition and part talk, real or imagined, to another person.

POETRY MISCELLANY: Your poems, especially in *The Messenger*, defy paraphrase perhaps as well as any I know. Yet there is a certain "path of saying," as Heidegger calls it, that can be followed in poems. For him, this sort of movement is an undercurrent or underplot that must be participated in and that goes below the surface of the words. It is something like a "gesture" of language. I think that all the things we have been talking about so far are the elements of this underplot. Could you speak to how this works in poems or something like it that you might have experienced?

JEAN VALENTINE: I like Heidegger's notion and his phrase for it. I'm more familiar with the process you bring up here as a teacher than in my own writing: to try to *hear* a poem with students, rather than to encourage a kind of structured puzzling out of the poet's "meaning," which ends up being reductive. But this can be a tricky business, because in the poems I most value, there *is* meaning, and very precise meaning, at that.

POETRY MISCELLANY: Barthes called texts "infinite ciphers" because for him their ultimate meanings were unresolvable, unfathomable. Would you say that a poem should strive for this (from your own point of view), and that the techniques of fragmentation, shifting perspectives, and so on that we discussed earlier are means of achieving the character of an infinite cipher? How much of what goes on beyond the words is the poet aware of? to what extent?

JEAN VALENTINE: I haven't read Barthes, but from what you tell me here, I'd go on with my last sentence, in the previous question, to disagree with his idea of a poem as an "infinite cipher," etc. For myself, I'd always want a poem to have mystery, yes, but also to be very clear. That tension matters as much as anything to me in a poem—as much as the music of its language, say.

As to how aware the poet is of "what goes on beyond the words," I just don't know. Sometimes a reader will see a lot in a poem of mine that I never say; but I do always hope absolutely that what I *did* see will be very clear, very precise. And when a reader misses what I'm up to, well, then I know I've missed getting it down.

More and more, I revere poets who are both simple and endlessly resonant with meaning: Elizabeth Bishop, Tomas Transtroömer, to think of just a couple. Their poems remind me of a phrase of Frost's, about thought being "a feat of association." And their thought is always grounded in the real: there's a real bridge, a real gas station, and so forth.

POETRY MISCELLANY: Barthes also talked about literature's subversive activity. That is, for him, literature subverts by undermining the ordinary ways we perceive and think about the world. For him, as for, say, Susan Sontag, literature ought to be unsettling. It ought to provide new categories of thought. Do you see anything like this working in your own poems? Your "ordinary things," to steal one of your titles, become very extraordinary in your poems.

JEAN VALENTINE: "New categories of thought"—well, the writing we remember does bring us something new, does in that sense trouble our sleeping selves, keep us from settling down in whatever we thought last year, or last month; and that's one thing writing seems to be for, yes.

But my wish in using the title "Ordinary Things" was not so much to be ironic as to look as attentively as I could at the ordinary, at the sort of feelings and events that are part of everyone's daily life in this time and place. It was a high ambition which I still have (and which many writers must have): an attempt at what Martin Buber calls "the hallowing of the everyday."

A. R. Ammons, 1978

Event: Corrective: Cure

POETRY MISCELLANY: In "Pray Without Ceasing," you talk about "tensions sprung free / into event." And "Saliences" talks about the "one event that / creates present time / in the multi-variable / scope." The "event" and "eventuality" figure prominently in "Essay on Poetics," too. It seems to me this is a useful way to begin responding to your poems—they have the character of "events"—they use "events" as opposed to concepts or abstract ideas. Even words like "suasion," "salience," "periphery" must be described in terms of "events" from which they emerge. In fact, on one level "events" are modes of emergence of meaning, experience, perception, aren't they? Could you begin to "weave" some further descriptions of the nature of events?

A. R. AMMONS: Not only is the finished poem about an event, but the making of it is an event as well. I am probably externalizing a sense of forces and events from an interior recognition of things that are happening; probably externalizing them onto the environment and then onto analogous situations in the environment. The emergence of the poem is often unexpected, though the poet may be under durance of heavy tension—those interior forces. There's a certain undefined anxiety before the poet recognizes that two or three things come together in the mind that create an unexpected conjunction which is integrated and expressive at the same time. The poet consequently feels the release of himself into this "event."

Another reason the "event" is interesting to me is that it can be so manifold. We can talk about sand on the beach, a flock of swallows flying in so many directions and yet seeming to assume a single shape. The result of this manifold dimension is that an "event" has the capacity to criticize given mental forms, conventional thinking, any kind of narrowness, any sort of insistence on the truth of a particular point of view. The event in its power and unexpectedness is more material to be considered against the too narrow symmetry of a previous definition. What I try to do in my poems, essentially, is to resist my own obsessions and others', to dissolve those obsessions to some extent, and to replace them with a more complex, easy-going, tolerant mental scope. I appreciate the tiny event that in its many-sidedness can be so staggering as to dissolve bigger forces.

POETRY MISCELLANY: The notion of "event" might also be related to your feeling for the moment, the now. This raises the larger issue of time. In "One: Many" you talk about how you "tried to summarize / a moment's events," which becomes an enormous if not impossible task. One thing always leads to another. There is always a pressure from within the moment to expand—as in *Sphere,* where you talk about the "moment of consciousness" which is a participation with what moves past and through a moment, and this leads to radiations and expansions in subsequent sections. In section 67 you say, "the purpose of the motion of a poem is to bring the focused, / awakened mind to no-motion, to a still contemplation of the whole motion" of the poem. So the moment seems to contain both motion and rest, many and one. Hegel describes this coalescence as one between the action of a whirl and the consciousness of a repose. The moment sometimes becomes for you like a peak of a triangle or mountain with time spreading down its sides as in *Sphere* 47–48. The event of the moment is a "riding horseback between / the obscure beginning and the unformulated conclusion." The poet seems often, as Heidegger says, in this state of "betweenness."

A. R. AMMONS: An event can only occur in time. If you have certain subconscious or subterranean forces or energies, they, after their coalescence or occurrence as an event, become recognizable and knowable as forces. My poem, "Clarity," which begins, "After the event the rockslide / realized," is about this. So, though I don't have a theory of time, I would think about time as the procedural necessity of an event.

The most interesting thing about a poem is that the motion occurs through time to a still point, from the verbal to the nonverbal level. The most interesting motion to me is the coincidental, peripheral event, the simple, minute particular that leads to something inevitable; that is, you see some peripheral connection leading to something more central, becoming more binding until the poem completes itself in an inevitable place. This whole motion suggests something as demanding in its rigor as a traditional form. So, from my own point of view, I like to be between the local periphery where no fact is excluded and some point where certain timings can begin a train of necessity toward a realization of itself. This is the way that I have tried lately to alert the deeper symmetries of the self. I try to recognize certain events on the surface mind, or the periphery so to speak, of our perception. Then the process of making connections can begin that reveals what Coleridge calls an undercurrent of feeling which is not at all coincidental, but is staged within us permanently in its quality.

POETRY MISCELLANY: In "Hibernaculum," you describe a possible hell as "the meaninglessness of stringing out / events in unrelated, undirected sequences." I think you have been suggesting that when we move from random series to the orderly sequence of the poem a certain stillness emerges. In the context of this movement, and of the narrative nature of the poems, I think of Tzevtan Todorov's definition of narrative as something that "puts time into motion and suspends it."

A. R. AMMONS: Yes, I think we use the word "narrative" in too limited a way. That is, any qualitative progression is also a narrative. I like to have the narrative of the surface, the actions and events that are described, but in reading the poem one should realize that a deeper narrative has taken place. That narrative is made up of the shifts in one's feelings and sensibilities about things.

However, a poem doesn't exist only in motion, in time. It seems to me that when you know the poem intimately you know it radially and complete. You have a nonlinear perception of the whole thing. If you have a single dancer on the stage, she exists in one body and does one thing at a time as she dances across that stage. At the end you recognize that certain figures have been repeated, that there has been a certain narrative. Something has occurred that is more than any single event and which memory recalls. The same is true of the poem. Once you know the poem intimately, why then you come to a still contemplation of its component parts, and of its vacant center perhaps. At that point, it seems to me you can deepen your awareness of things yourself *without* the help of the poet. He has brought you to this still point, and now you have your own resources. It is here that words can become the cure of words, motion the cure of motion. That is to say, when the verbal construct creates a place that is nonverbal, then the very verbal construct has been criticized by itself. This is appropriate in that it heals the division in ourselves between thing and word.

POETRY MISCELLANY: This relation between language and things, the verbal and the nonverbal, is very complex. Language, you say in "Essay on Poetics," and other places, can reduce the world. I think of Wordsworth's "Note" to "The Thorn" where he talks about the proximity of words and things. In "I'm Unwilling," you say, "things / keep nudging me / to siddle with / them into / words."

A. R. AMMONS: At some point in our development words and things were indistinguishable, and words had power over things. That is no longer, I think, feasible, except as a primitive impulse or desire.

Perhaps it is not only a dichotomy between words and things, but also between us and ourselves. There are certain resources in ourselves that are nonverbal, and only at a certain level, as we said before, do they start to become represented as words: I think that some of this internal energy remains latent and we want to believe in a validity that the sound system of the poem might have.

Though words and things exist in different realms, the motion of the poem imitates the motion of reality, mirrors the motion of things. Perhaps that is as close as we can get to a correspondence between this system of language we have invented and use and the system of reality that is so profound.

POETRY MISCELLANY: You talked a few minutes ago about the function of the poet diminishing as one comes to know the poem. What, exactly, is the function of the poet? What are his responsibilities?

A. R. AMMONS: That is something that has troubled me all my life. My poems have not dealt directly with definable issues of my time. Only recently have I begun to realize how I operate. I feel myself to be so peripheral that I don't address groups but look for the single person in his room. He's the person I try to mean something to. I don't address an already defined stratum of society or a particular cause. Poetry has never seemed to me to be the best instrument for communication of a practical kind. In this respect, I think of the hermit lark, a shy bird with an unlocatable, indescribable sound. I identify with that in myself and in the poets I read, too. There is a one-to-one correspondence, a relationship between poet and reader whose undercurrent may radiate outward to affect the way other individuals perceive things.

POETRY MISCELLANY: One interesting aspect of this is the notion of the "Anthology." You say in section 16 of *Sphere* that "the anthology is the moving, changing definition of the / imaginative life of the people, the repository and source." What, specifically, makes a poem part of this anthology, of what Foucault calls the "archive"?

A. R. AMMONS: I think a poem must be entertaining, and it seems to me that the dialectic of one and many that we have been discussing in several ways is likely to produce this entertainment. That is, it is likely to produce the tissue, the weaving in a poem sufficiently complex so that the thinking mind can dwell upon it and find it enjoyable as an artifact that mirrors the mind and its world. I don't think a poem that is propaganda or speaks to a specific issue is capable of entertaining the many-sidedness of one's assent to and exception from realities. I think we want a poem sufficiently complex so that we are willing to invest in it a dwelling of our time because it corrects our narrowness, our smallness. I think that the people gradually approve of those poems that have this truth or openness toward things and will make these poems part of their imaginative reality.

POETRY MISCELLANY: I think you have struck the balance between the philosophical or unified statement and the multisided, unordered periphery very carefully in your poems. It is that balance between the repose and the whirl, stillness and motion, too. What has always struck me about your work is that there is always a potentially dichotomous vision that threatens to burst apart the world the poems operate in, but that the poems nevertheless achieve the "wholeness" you hold so valuable.

A. R. AMMONS: You erase all possibility of wholeness if you eliminate one side of the dichotomy. When you have an enlargement of vision, it is to provide a landscape in which to see the particular, the differences among things and not just their sameness, their unity.

POETRY MISCELLANY: This notion of difference is an important one for you. Your description of it in "The Account" as an almost imperceptible trace is close to how Derrida describes it: "something finer / than perception, a difference / so opposite to ground it will / have no mass, indifferent to mass." And in "The Flaw" it is a difference from sameness that defines a whole world. Of course, that is only half the problem—the other half is how differences are related, or as you say in "Essay on Poetics," a "preservation of / distinction in a seeming oneness." In *Sphere*, section 117, you say, "the poem insists on / differences, on every fragment of difference till the fragments / cease to be fragmentary and wash together in a high flotation / interpenetrating much like the possibility of the world." The fragments, together but distinct, are to form, to "declare a common reality past declaration." So the problem is that "something / thin & high / cuts through whatever is / and makes no difference of difference." Could you talk about the play between difference and indifference, about the "reality past declaration" that emerges from this play?

A. R. AMMONS: This has been a concern of mine since the 1950s when I used it in conjunction with a sense of risk and possibility. Possibility occupies the same world for me as event and coincidence. That is, it is because of chance that one doesn't have to conform to given structures—possibility is open. In this context, I think of difference as an enrichment. In the poem, "Possibility Along a Line of Difference," there is a flat, western terrain. A river goes through the terrain, but from your perspective you can't see it, can't see the difference ahead. The invisible difference creates a terrifying enrichment because there is no longer simply the flatness or evenness of the ground but a dramatic change. All these other actions have become possible, terrifying and beautiful, because of that gully washing through the terrain. The difference then would be to retreat from the high unities and amassings into the minute particular, the single event, the perceivable correction that criticizes the unifying tendency of sameness.

POETRY MISCELLANY: I think of this poem, like your others, as being in a conversational mood. A poet like Ignatow has an interrogative mood, Pack a suppositional mood. There is a sense of continual dialogue with readers, listeners, the self, even the world (whereas in some poems you have a conversation with things in the world—a feather, a mountain). It is a dialogue mode, I suppose, a mode of exchange, dialectic. Heidegger recounts a favorite phrase, from Rilke, I think: "Since we have been a conversation."

A. R. AMMONS: I think that this is a variation of the "one:many" notion. That is to say, the dialogue would be between the ambivalences of the one:many situation and represented by a dialectics of two voices. Voice, then, in its largest possibility, would tend toward the summary, and tone and variety of effect would tend toward the periphery, toward difference. Voice would then be the bridge between these two sets of possibilities. I am bothered by certain courses where students are taught to concentrate on voice and tone in a narrow sense: what happens is that the poet begins to identify in himself something he calls voice but which is really becoming only a mannerism. But voice philosophically, as we mean it here, is a re- solved action of many voices, a large sameness in the Coleridgean sense of a unifying sameness in difference.

As far as the actual conversations with things in the poems go, obviously I didn't believe that mountains talk. But I did believe that when you stand in front of a mountain you have a certain impression of majesty; what you have in the poems, then, is what majesty or height might say. In those poems, I'm often the little figure who comes up to ask what it is all about.

POETRY MISCELLANY: Isn't that dialogue mode related to your use of colons and more recently to the parallel columns in Snow Poems? I mean, these techniques certainly allow the poem to have motion in time, to be open-ended, to chart out certain directions, but they also provide the still- ness you described earlier, doubling back, a return, an exchange or dialogue, a reversibility.

A. R. AMMONS: Yes, I think they are related. The double columns in Snow Poems have unnerved some people, I suppose. They are intended to be playful; they can be read one at a time, but with an awareness of the other column, the other perspective. Once the center of a poem is found and established in the way we talked about earlier, then the poem is both closed and open, and it will have a dialectical form.

POETRY MISCELLANY: This notion of vacancy has become increasingly important recently, though its roots go far back. In "Hibernaculum," you talk about two kinds of "nothing"—one beyond, outside, and the other at the center, inside. In *Snow Poems* you talk about a state where all will be "an illustration of, allegory of, nothing." For you, it seems a state that enables continual beginning. It is related to the absence at the center of things in *Snow Poems*, "an empty-centered space." A basic absence is that of the self as in "The Hieroglyphic Gathered"—

> the central self unattended,
> unworn while the untouchable
> other, far and away, calls forth
> the bark, the slaver, the slobber,
> scenting: to pull up stakes!

Could you elaborate on this nothing, absence, the silent self as opposed to the verbal other?

A. R. Ammons: It seems to me that in both amassing and excluding you come to nothing. I wrote about this aspect in "The Arc Inside and Out." If you amass all your perceptions, the sum becomes undeliverable as a verbal construct. You have to break things down. But when you begin to break things down, you eventually come to an equally nonverbal inside, an equal nothingness. It seems to me, then, that language is an area of knowledge of contact with things; beyond that is the nonverbal, and within that is the nonverbal. That frightens some people, perhaps because silence is associated with death. But life can also be silent, and as we were saying earlier, it seems to me that the cure for words and the divisions of words resides in both that amassing of exteriors and that breaking down toward the unconscious interior. That seems to be a sort of healing, a place to begin anew. It is really the source of the erotic in poetry—some things move at a level without definition before they move into definition, are refreshing, inform our lives, and give us energy.

Carol Muske, 1981

Stepping into the Sky

POETRY MISCELLANY: One of the most compelling aspects of your poetry is its search for origins that seem always already lost, deferred, deflected. "Coincidence," for example, presents a groping back to define a love in terms of the self's origins, to find the self and the other coming from the same origin: "I remember you / like the first extension of myself / in sunlight." But the search goes even "further back. The beginning of the body / in other bodies, the hall of mirrors / from which we are borne." The origin here is an endless labyrinth. Even in an earlier poem, "Birth," the "cypress, unbridled, give birth / to something lost, / something tricked in the wind's clear pitch— / its bottomless circling." The speaker in "Coral Sea, 1945" tries to define her own origin by appropriating images from the outside world into her experience of existence in the womb. In "The Invention of Cuisine," too, the thrust is back toward an origin, this time toward an origin of the race, and toward an origin of imagination in our imagining back then. The origin is like the "presence" of gaps, absences, holes that "elude" the character in "Photographer." I suppose in this context that all poems become voices of desire.

CAROL MUSKE: I read somewhere that "birth canal" experiences, the whole process of birth, is a trauma from which we never fully recover...or remember. If you think about it, the notion of being thrust toward the unknown by contracting walls, pulled head or feet or God-knows-what first into an alien environment, beaten into a scream which is *breath*, that first entry of oxygen into the lungs—does present a convincing argument for our semipermanent disorientation on this earth. Perhaps poets have particularly traumatic birth experiences. I do believe that birth is the *end* of one story— and the beginning of another. Life in the womb fascinates me. Conception, then the months floating, the magnified sound of the mother's heart and breath, all the information passed along by the mother's body and mind to the fetus—all this as important as the formative years learning behavior, then language. The loss of the mother's body as world is the definitive loss. Birth is also a separation from another kind of language. Time in the mother's body is a time of talking, an extended dialogue of sounds, blood-touch, emotional messages. The thing about this language is, it is complete and sufficient. It is a language which manages to convey love completely, to articulate subtleties of emotion and stress. Though the mother may move through a world of anxiety or adversity and some of this blips through, it is essentially a language in which there is no loss. The tenant floats buoyant, reassured in his/her rent-free bubble. Loss, falling, emptiness, abandon-ment—none of that happens or is understood, until birth. Then it is under-stood catastrophically, indelibly, forever. Certain "languages" that hark back to this womb-language, this mother tongue, fascinate me: nonsense, com-fort murmurs, crooning songs, lullabies, sleep-talk—another level of artic-ulation and communication. Frost once referred to the sentence as a clothesline of auditory expectations, upon which we string words like clothes. He talks about "images of voices speaking."

My first most dramatic sense of language was at that level—auditory expectation and fulfillment. Going to Catholic school and stepping into the cathedral of Latin, I learned that language year by year by osmosis, by singing it, by hearing it daily echoing from the altar in the hoarse voice of the priest, in the antiphonal voices of the choir, the voices of the congrega-tion. When I finally studied it, formally, in high school, I found I had a map, finally, to a country whose terrain I already knew blind, by heart. *By heart*. That's how we learn language.

In the years before school, I remember that I often totally divorced the sense of words from their sounds, which were hypnotizing, thrilling, nearly tangible. Bits and scraps, rhymes, children's repetitive chants, impassioned speech—I would make up a magic ring of words to bless and protect. We all continue to need language on this level. I think that's why all these people are out "recovering their mantras."

All this by way of explanation about the "presence" of "absences" which you noted in my poems. I think a lot of the musing and circling in my poems is homage to this holy language, its loss. You're right about "Coral Sea," "Birth," "Coincidence," all of them are concerned with this. "Coinci-dence" goes a little further, in that it presumes another way of knowing, prebirth, which takes the form of "Fated Love" later in life. This is hard to talk about, that's why I tried to write a poem about it, instead. "The hall of mirrors from which we are borne" in "Coincidence" precedes the womb, it is the gene cathedral.

In Heidegger's "On the Origin of the Work of Art," there is the statement which clarifies "Coincidence" for me. The human being is both "thrown" and "projected" in Heidegger's terms. "Coincidence" is about the *second* existential being, projection, *entwurf*, the human being in possibility. Differing notions of will and fate, or determinism, would come to bear—but I see the line "I remember you / like the first extension of myself / in sunlight..." as an act of will, as extension which is conscious cooperation with the inevitable, like a tropism, an unfurling of a leaf toward light. Or an act of love as a conscious choice of what one *inevitably* will love.

If this sounds confused, call my mother—*she* knows everything.

POETRY MISCELLANY: In that essay Heidegger also talks, I think, about the essence of origins, how all poems retain a trace of their lost origins, how that trace is always unspeakable yet uncovered by the movement of the poem. Language always fails to contain the origin. I think of "The Fault" in this respect with its search for "roots" and the way it ends— "It's light again / and again I sign love, / my imaginary name." What language does is repeat again and again its losses, like the goddess in "Chasers," "making us paint the same landscape / again and again till we began to see it," to see the vision. In a way, poetry seems like the child in "Elocution: Touch" who "can't name the thing / he sees / or puts his hand on." The language of origins is always "a language we have yet to translate," as you say in "Her Story, Leaving Eden." I wonder, in this general context, whether there is a kind of suspicion, as Charles Simic calls it, about language, a sense of the "heresy of language" ("Idolatry"). At the same time there is also a sense of the way language supplements a lost origin, as in "Ransom," where the poem becomes a sort of ransom note for the lost life. In other words, language as always an insufficient supplement, the holder of imaginary names and myths, the thing we must keep repeating, using, in order to get at the unspeakable. Language, then, would become like the camouflages we use, the masks, the possibilities:

> What I am speaking of
> is possibility: trout
> moving through tea leaves
> white rabbits flying in snow.
> ["Camouflage"]

CAROL MUSKE: Language keeps calling attention to its own inadequacy, the way a literary conceit implies a habit of thought, an inclination of manners by its own insufficiency in bridging thought and manners. Language keeps saying what it cannot say. The poet's preoccupation becomes with how language fails us, at the same time as he/she glories in the attempt to overcome this failure. Gaston Bachelard writes about this in the *Poetics of Reverie*, the attempt to find words for the mother tongue, through dreams, reveries.

Marvin Bell has a new beautiful poem which *stammers* in the attempt to get it right, to say it, which talks about the language before language, cries, grunts, inarticulations. That's what I was trying to say in "Elocution" about the language "we are born speaking" having more "content" than "mouth," "darkness," "heart."

The goddess makes "us" paint the landscape again and again in "Chasers," because "we" have superimposed so many layers of thought on what is before our eyes that we do not see. This same process in reverse occurs in "The Painter's Daughter"—the child is imprisoned in the vision(s) of the father. He cannot see the fox without "painting" it in his mind, with his eyes. He cannot see the child without "painting" her. Painting is in one poem a means to "see," in the other it is a willed blindness, a total imposition of the intellectual on the landscape of sentient objects and beings, the equivalent of "false art."

It's true when I'm using the words "see" or "seeing," I'm often opposing the purely visual with opening, integration of the senses and thought. I do therefore have trouble with purely imagistic poetry. On the other hand, I also have trouble with hyperdeveloped symbologies, closed systems. I know I do love the fact that there's a character in an Ionesco play who murders another person with the word "knife." (I just remembered—it's *The Lesson*, and it's a teacher killing a student—must have been an MFA writing workshop.)

In poetry, language is palpable, thing-in-itself, and in that sense, *original*, retaining the origin. When it is poetic, it is also not anthropomorphic, unlike most of the sciences and some of the other arts. It's a mystery, it's much bigger than our minds, our selves.

POETRY MISCELLANY: One of the most interesting things you do with language is to suggest a sort of interpenetration of words and things, of fiction and reality, imagination and the world. I think of poems such as "The Painter's Daughter," where the images in the paintings are bits from the real world, and these paintings in turn make a context in which the daughter operates; or "Chapter One," where the novelistic and actual worlds define each other—"I can't go anywhere / unless someone writes it first"— as if we were all characters in a novel. At the end of that poem there is an opening toward the possibilities of language we were discussing, an opening toward "unwrit heavens" the character leads toward. There's a sense in your poems that anything that exists must exist in language, but also that what exists in the language is objectlike, tactile.

CAROL MUSKE: The "interpenetration of words and things"—that phrase brings two things to mind immediately. One, the first, is the biblical genesis-idea of the Word as flesh. I supposed I absorbed enough of that to last a lifetime. Then, I think of another climate (which perhaps proceeds from the first) I was steeped in—a sort of Midwest, prairie-America awe of the book, of print, of what was "writ." People would say: "But it says right here in this book..." or "It says right here in the paper...," as if in order to refute what was being said you'd have to argue with the words themselves, the print, as if the words were human objects.

"Chapter One" is meant to convey that aura of sleepy, summer afternoon, front-porch kind of dream of the power of words. It is the moment of belief that words can change one's life. It is also the moment of betrayal by words—the chafing under the supremacy of the author's consciousness, the wish to change the story, which I guess is the first recognition of one's own desire to write.

There is a level in both "Chapter One" and "The Painter's Daughter," however, that I want to reemphasize: the level at which books, print, words-on-the-page, the smell of binding, the spoken word, words as a kind of paint (what Gertrude Stein does so brilliantly in "Tender Buttons"), the exquisite, literal apprehension of language in its natural and private habitats is the whole point. Language moves from the purely ideographic into alternative responses which have nothing to do with context or logical meaning.

I think about Mallarmé in this regard. If you remember his quote, "Je dis: une fleur!...," "I say: a flower! and out of the oblivion into which my voice consigns every outline, apart from the known calyxes, there arises musically the delicate idea itself, the flower absent from all bouquets." But he was obsessed with the abstract, with making that flower bloom totally apart from its animating principle: the senses. The impasse he came to in his work was created by this desire to sever the two worlds completely. Then Valéry went in the opposite direction—trying to prove concretely, calculatedly, how poetic composition worked. Bergson's is, for me, the closest to the kind of thinking a poet can find useful—he comes close to illuminating how a poet needs to speak to what is *substantial* in things, in beings. A poetization of human experience.

POETRY MISCELLANY: Another interpenetration occurs with time, and in fact your handling of time throughout is quite sophisticated. There's the linking of times we already saw in "The Invention of Cuisine" and "Coral Sea, 1945," of course, but also the complex movement in "Short Histories of the Sea," where there is a parallel history to recorded history, a history of the genes that writes us, that determines us. Curiously, the second half of this poem turns to a mythic history in the context of the *Aeneid* where the sea becomes both a strange, mythic place and a source for history, for historians, for poets. There's also the way time itself operates the poems rather than just being a subject, such as in "Worry," with its associative memory structure, and the general way in which many of your poems open out by linking bits and pieces of images, metaphors, memories from various times. It's as if any given moment can't exist by itself, but is only a part of a spider's web of moments.

CAROL MUSKE: Time doesn't exist in poetry. Or conventional notions of time. I suppose, as Marvin Bell said, time doesn't exist at all. There's an essay by Russell Edson I like that *Field* published, about how time flows around the poem, not through it.

Whatever one thinks about time I find is irrelevant in writing the poem. It is truly a spider's web, the complexity of threads unwinds from the navel. The only history of any substance is the history of dreams, inventions, the imagination. I see sequential time and cause and effect as ideas that war with the human spirit. If you untie those knots, each event, each object, each person appears absolutely new, out of context, unjudgeable before us.

"Coral Sea" was a dream I had, but I felt it was a dream that belonged to my mother equally, a dream she had while she was carrying me that flowed from her sleeping brain into mine enclosed in the womb. There is no time in that poem, as there never is in dreams. The "1945" is ironic, as is the wartime landscape—these details are there to underscore the insignificance of recorded chronology.

My mother's mother died when my mother was sixteen, during the 1930s. My mother had a dream about the day before my grandmother died. The dream was actually a memory of seeing her mother coming toward her from the garden on a sunny day, wearing a picture hat with a veil, in Wyndmere, North Dakota, in the 1930s. Her mother, my grandmother, seemed to be *floating*—it was the day before her death, and my mother thought how beautiful she was, but how strange it was that she did not appear to be walking, but *moving* through the air. So North Dakota, the 1930s, my mother's age meant nothing—she transferred that diamond whole into my unconscious—and I've been dreaming the same dream since. It's all there, the roses in the garden, the dusty air, the sunlight, the picture hat, the veil, the movement of this woman toward her daughter who within hours she would never see or touch again: I have it. I feel as if I was present at that moment; through the dream, I was there. I am there. As Gertrude Stein demonstrated, the tenses themselves are a dictatorship of time.

POETRY MISCELLANY: We've been talking about a kind of doubleness. It takes on an uncanny force when it becomes represented by a sense of Otherness. We already implied a sense of the Other in "Coincidence," but it appears also in "The Visitor," where the dream lover appears, or in "Traveling" with its sense of separation. It's probably climaxed in *Skylight*, by the poem "Androgyny." Sometimes the poet becomes like the "Trance Artist," living other lives; perhaps this accounts for the way various voices seem to emerge from the poems. On a larger scale, as in the sequence "Siren Songs," different voices sound as if to call the dead child back. At any rate, this sense of an Otherness to the self seems to be a major force in the poems. In her essay, "Origins of a Poem," Denise Levertov talks about Heidegger's notion that being human is *being a conversation*. For her, the nature of our lives, and so poetry, is a dialogue. I think your incorporation of the Other is a stunning affirmation of this.

CAROL MUSKE: I like the Heidegger quote through Levertov. Karla Hammond asked me, in an interview, if I thought of my "voice" as actually many voices. I think of *Camouflage* as a kind of chorus. Now I'm a duet. You're right about the double, the other. That's what happens when you sit down to write—you stare the doppelganger right in the eyes. Then you see through what you fear the most, confronting the self, the other. You see clear through. "Androgyny" is about the gradual loss of all the self-defining aspects of gender, *past* that predisposition of flesh into pure human consciousness, like the child in the womb—floating, unaware of its sex, the limitations of the body.

POETRY MISCELLANY: This doubleness also suggests the movement of your poem, "Par," where the colloquial and the metaphoric flow, where words like "par," "course," and "good sport" are puns that generate the flow of the poem as it explores a sexual awakening. It seems that this sort of linguistic "production," as the semiotic essayists, such as Michael Riffaterre, call it, is one of the basic ways your poems are generated. There's always a double-edged movement, both toward and away from one term of an analogy—"the surprise backhand motion of thought / evading itself," as you call it in "Choreography." It allows the poem to concentrate and expand at once, and the effect is like "the steps leading up, / the ending in sky," or "an elevator / that never stops rising"—the play between the expanse seen through a skylight and the confinement of its shape ("Skylight"). In that particular poem, the aftereffects of the lost love get defined by the double sense of release and imprisonment. That seems to be a typical product and process with this technique and accounts, I think, for the complexity of feeling and thought in the poems. I think that double movement, in connection with the various kinds of interpenetration and the search for origins, the notion of the Other, makes your work unique.

CAROL MUSKE: I'm very interested in the "double movement" you describe. I love contradiction, I love the mind when it holds opposing notions, each perfect, in its spotlight. I think we've all felt the "backhand motion" of thought evading itself. The mind shies away from recognizing itself, its business, it does not want to identify itself. We pull away, in our consciousnesses, from unpleasant, painful, or confusing thought—even apperception, that mental sleight-of-hand. I swear I can sense the different hemispheres of the brain at war with each other, countermanding each other, *conversing* through the *corpus callosum*, the connecting circuit running down the brain's center. My former husband, the brain specialist, provides me with graphic portraits of cerebral architecture. I incorporate these into my imagination. Though his descriptions are technically brilliant and comprehensive, I still enjoy thinking of the brain as a tribe of tiny spirits who need blood to survive. Each spirit has a voice, an opinion. Because of the nature of associative thought, the brain is full of so-called "logical" contradictions. The child walking across the golf course in "Par" is thinking simultaneously, "I hate clover—I love clover." Jung was right about the simultaneous manifestation of ideas. And Keats was righter than anyone in his invention of "negative capability," the capacity of the poet to exist in doubt and dread, in contradiction. You're right about "Skylight." The architectural image is meant to be one of apprehension of total expanse (the sky) and confinement within shape. And you're right about the poem itself. The skylight here is the house itself, "a house built in the sky," that provides a daily overwhelming sense of limitlessness, coupled with the sense of imprisonment, the self held within another's imagination, let's just call it the "architect's" imagination, imprisoned within another's idea of the self. The self, the speaker, is full of anger and grief, trapped in the false, literal poetry of architecture—"a literature that dissolves into air." It is a poem about being held against one's will, it is a poem about hatred of the self and the weak in general for cooperating with the colonizers of the spirit, the high-rollers of illusion. But it is also a poem of release, liberation, a poem about, finally, stepping into the sky.

POETRY MISCELLANY: It's interesting, finally, how this process of emergence structures whole books. They grow by a sort of organic form. I'm thinking, really, of Denise Levertov's essay in which she talks about the necessity for gaps, rifts, that must be leaped over by the linguistic impulses of the poem. That's what your books do to the gap or absent origin. Do the poems emerge in the context of a larger pattern after a number of poems for a book get written? How would you see the pattern in *Camouflage* and *Skylight?* And how do you see the relationship between these two books? It's curious, by the way, that those two titles suggest the two poles that have been implicit in this interview—the opening up and the interpenetration (camouflaging) of elements in the poems.

CAROL MUSKE: I think *Camouflage* and *Skylight* are opposite poles, too. But I understood this fact and many others, in retrospect, *after* the poems were written. It would be pretentious and deceptive to say that I know what I'm doing when I write, that I have a pattern in mind. I work, like everybody else who writes poems, intuitively. I think that one is born with one's "themes," what you're here to talk about, so to speak. How these themes come alive in one's poems, how they interconnect and pattern—that's a mystery to one (me). I'm glad that it's a mystery. I think your delineation of the two "poles" in my writing is right on target—I have to say, though, that that's something I *feel*, or think/feel, rather than understand in a way I could develop into a theory of process. The two books couldn't be more different. *Camouflage* is a book of masks, conscious imitations, instructions, it is a limited book about limitations. *Skylight* is (if it works at all) a projection into the dream, the *real* dream, the open. Its language is meant to be the language of direct speech—by this I mean not just the colloquial, the speech patterns, but also the direct words of the dream, the consciousness-in-extremity, passion, the divided heart. It's a book that hurts me, but makes me happy, too. Ah, to place the word "light" on the table and have it begin, all by itself, to illuminate the room. Forget Ionesco, that's kind of the point, isn't it?

W. S. Merwin, 1981

Unnaming the Myths

POETRY MISCELLANY: In *The Nation* in 1962 you wrote: "Symbolism is never far from man's efforts inevitably, in acts of conscience—he is reduced to consoling himself with considerations of what his project might signify rather than what it might accomplish." The context for the statement was ironic, one of those political writings you did for that magazine. And yet this might be a good place to begin for us because your poems have, often, a mythic quality, and myth often seems to be a teasing out of narrative from symbol. I think "The Dwelling" does this. There's a way in which you see stories or myths behind everything. "Oh objects come and talk with us while you can," you say in *The Carrier of Ladders*. Perhaps, then, we can talk about myth, symbol, narrative.

W. S. MERWIN: When you say that myth is a teasing out, that suggests that symbol and myth operate on the same level and that symbolism is a static version or aspect of narrative. That may be so, but I am rather chary of these words; we would have to define our terms, which we may not be able to do to start with. I suspect symbol is more static than myth and probably closer to allegory, which sets up a one-to-one correspondence with what is represented. Myth is pretty hard to isolate. It's a dimension underlying sensual experience; if sensual experience is seen with sufficient intensity and identification, then you are already treading in the preludes of myth. That is, you're realizing your own dreams. You analyze them and begin to come out with symbols, but from beginning to end you know you're walking in the place where myth is happening. So I don't think of myth as a teasing out, but as a dimension where you and time are inseparable.

POETRY MISCELLANY: I wonder if all myths are inevitably, in some sense, creation myths.

W. S. MERWIN: I've wondered that, too. I think they probably are, not in the obvious way we were taught in school, that myths are a way of explaining how things came about, but that myths are touching the origin of everything. They are touching the original dimension of everything.

POETRY MISCELLANY: Perhaps that touching of origins explains the non-human voice that occurs in some of the poems, a mythic voice, prehistorical. In a book like *The Lice* that voice becomes bitter, political—"There is no season that requires us," you say in one poem. "Tonight once more / I find a single prayer and it is not for men," you say in another.

W. S. MERWIN: In *The Lice* in particular that overt misanthropy was more or less deliberate. *The Lice* was a book that was written for the most part when I felt the historic future was so bleak that there was no point in writing toward it. One element of the feeling in that book is still with me— the amazement at the terrible arrogance of our own species, which is certainly the most destructive on the planet. What we are prepared to do, to ensure our comfort or convenience, to the rest of the world—to the trees, to other cultures, with nuclear weapons or whatever!

POETRY MISCELLANY: Sometimes it seems that the nonhuman voice brings you to another consciousness, another perspective. Maybe, in the mythic sense, it allows a rebeginning. Do you think that's true?

W. S. MERWIN: Yes. If a perception is really intense enough or clear enough, it is everybody's perception, as well as an individual's perception at a given moment. Our awareness of the rain is everyone's awareness of it—we don't have to name them or us because they are part of the same perception. I think so-called primitive art is doing the same thing.

When you look at children's pictures, there's sometimes a little house with no human beings, only sun, trees, houses, and so forth. And the assumption is that humans *are* in it because humans are looking at it. They are there, and it's an important place for the humans to be.

POETRY MISCELLANY: And yet there is a sense in the poems of a distrust of the language, a sense of how it always fails us, and a sense of how this failure is what motivates, generates narratives, explanations. In *The Lice* you explain lives like "I who always believed too much in words" and in *The Carrier of Ladders*, "It has taken me this long / To know what I cannot say." But despite this distrust, things are always said— "I sing to drown the silence of far flowers," you say. There's an insistent vocabulary that defines each book and is developed from book to book, a vocabulary of things that can't be said yet are. I mean words like emptiness, distance, window, door,

silence, mirror, echo, and the like. This vocabulary provides a certain resonance, a feel to the language, a sense of the language's being able to *presence*
what it can't accurately name.

W. S. MERWIN: I think you're describing well the way I've come to feel
about language. There's a sense in which language is always inadequate. We
don't have to be metaphysical to see this—the cushion here, for instance,
can't be named. You can call it a cushion, but that finally is no name; it does
not call itself a cushion. There is that aspect of language which is always a
gross approximation to the uniqueness of any perception about any experience. Language is fairly general—the color red has to apply to every red in
the world when actually each red is different. The more you use language
imaginatively, the more you try to describe what's unique about something,
the more you realize the inadequacies of language. On the other hand,
language itself is unique; it has a life of its own which makes it a part of the
uniqueness of everything. Its life is the life of everything. It is, for example,
what makes conversation possible. So there is a simultaneous reverence and
distrust of language.

POETRY MISCELLANY: Some cultures don't have words to describe some
things we see or feel, and we don't have words for some things they see or
feel. I guess the classic case is all the Eskimo words for snow.

W. S. MERWIN: Sure. You don't see the cushion, you hear the word. And
it's important to be aware of that. That's part of the clarity and intonation of
your perceptions. The articulation of any word is at once absolute and
inadequate. In fact, if you are not aware of the inadequacy, then your
perception is going to be terribly eclipsed by the arrogance we were talking
about earlier. Human arrogance extends into language, as though we
thought the naming of things were actually a substitute for things
themselves.

POETRY MISCELLANY: Words, I guess, are ways of lifting veils and finding
more and more veils. We're always going toward something that's always
out of reach. The experience of language becomes the thing itself.

W. S. MERWIN: You say "toward," and yet perhaps it's there all the time,
unnamable. And of course a poem just doesn't name a cushion. A poem is a
huge leap—from the kind of basic, primitive use of language to a basic,
primitive use of poetry. Poetry is in a way the real use of language because,
though we can't name the cushion, there is a way of making a poem in
which the cushion and one's experience of it are not apart. Then you reach
the point where you can't name the experience, but where the poem is the
same as the experience. They become one.

POETRY MISCELLANY: In a way, your own language has become more
filled with objects, especially from *The Compass Flower* on. A poem like "St.
Vincent's," for example, or the new poem, "Strawberries," has this quality.
We are immediately in a more tactile, directly touchable world.

W. S. MERWIN: Yes, we can't move forever away from referents. If we do that, then we have nothing to refer to. It's so easy to get too abstract about these things, just as it is to get abstract about something like time. Our notion of time is of something we're outside of, for the most part, say, as when we watch a train go by. That sense of time simply isn't so. All that we know about time is what we are. That's all we'll ever know about it. Time is simply a way of living in the world that changes the world.

POETRY MISCELLANY: Well, I get that sense with all your words for doors and thresholds. Or take a poem like "Air" and that walk between two deserts. Time is always something we're in the middle of, a between, something always beginning and rebeginning in us.

W. S. MERWIN: I hadn't thought of that, but you're describing it very well. Parents are a myth that runs through the whole of one's existence, and I find myself writing about them. I keep trying to move away from the subject of parents, but the faster I try the more it keeps recurring. I guess they provide some sense of confluence, of returning and beginning.

POETRY MISCELLANY: The emphasis is always on process, not on ends. Everything is always in process in your poems. They deny, in a way, last things. There's always a new perspective to turn to, perhaps in the poem, perhaps in the next page, someplace just past the print of the last line that is where the poem is taking you. "The Helmsmen" with its two metaphoric perspectives, of the day pilot and the night pilot, one following charts, the other stars, suggests something of this.

W. S. MERWIN: Yes, I can't imagine writing the "final poem" or the "final Word," and it's impossible because of that double aspect of language we were discussing earlier. One of my heroes has been Thoreau, and there's a passage where he asks something like, "how can we find our ignorance if we have to use our knowledge all the time." Your life and your writing don't come, finally, from your knowledge.

In *The Maine Woods* there's an incredible passage where they're standing in the forest and they hear a thump far away; the Indian has to tell him "tree falls." When you look at *Walden* and *A Week on the Concord and Merrimack Rivers*, where he is talking about wildness and savagery, you have to realize he's just on the outskirts of Concord. And even at that time the rivers were tame. I find this aspect funny, and sad, and very revealing, and touching because it makes you aware of how very little he had to go on. Things in this book came out of immediate experience.

POETRY MISCELLANY: And on the other side, there's always a threat of nothingness, a word, too, that comes up more in your earlier poems. Still, there's "Tergvinder's Stone," that crazy stone in the middle of a living room, which is about as concrete as you can get, yet it becomes a kind of hole in the darkness, nothing. Nothingness seems to have become less a simple absence and more a container for everything.

W. S. MERWIN: It's the unnamable aspect of the cushion, say, out of which the cushion comes all the time. If one tries to live in a way that does not recognize this, then one slips into arrogance and exploitation. It's only if one is aware of the aspect of nothingness in everything that one begins to see things as having a real source, as distinct from just having a beginning. The beginning is measurable, but the origin is always a mystery. When was the origin of the cushion? In the idea of it? In some experience that led to someone's recognizing a need?

POETRY MISCELLANY: And along with the problem of origins is the problem of boundaries. How, for instance, do you conceive of the two books of prose and the prose that you're doing now? It's not what we would traditionally call short stories, and it's not the traditional prose poem.

W. S. MERWIN: One of the things I was trying to do at the beginning of *The Miner's Pale Children* was to call into question all of those generic boundaries, so that one can seem to be like a story, and the next one you say, "What is this?" I wanted it to be left open again and again in the book. The boundaries dissolve. I suppose I was feeling the limitations of traditional genres and decided to see what could be written in a short form. I was less bound in the second book, but I still had that aim in mind.

POETRY MISCELLANY: In the newer poems you've broken the line in a way that recalls, to some degree, Old English. But the rhythms have more flexibility for you.

W. S. MERWIN: That's true, and the rhythms of contemporary blank verse are different from the rhythms of Christopher Marlowe, too, but it's still blank verse. I think the Old English line and the blank verse line have changed in the same way. I believe that the parallelisms of Old English poetry and Middle English poetry are the underlying rhythms of poetry itself. Like any convention, the line I have been working with has its limits, but it seems to have many possibilities partly because it's been ignored for so long. In fact, I think there are real wells of energy there still in the language and the experience it has gathered and transmits. I think there is an untested youth in this ancient parallelism and tension, and I think it's related to the way language renews itself—and renews us. Language— new experience arising and being transmitted out of old—it may be our original myth.

Robert Penn Warren, 1980

On the Horizon of Time

POETRY MISCELLANY: Let's begin by talking about time. In a *Paris Review* interview a while back you talk about the distinction between William Faulkner's "still moments," the "frozen moments" that solidify meaning, fix it against the rush of time, and Ernest Hemingway's moments that "are key moments in themselves, moments of action." There's a richer sense of time and history in Faulkner—and in your own work. One of the more interesting things I find in your poems is the way you can counterpoint specific acts and larger contexts of history as in the lines "we think, Hear / The earth grind on its axis, or history / Drip in darkness like a leaking pipe in the cellar." Very often a character finds himself in a context in which the horizon itself is past and future, time, history—a large set of forces beyond him, like at the end of "Tale of Time," where the character stands at a threshold, the edge of the woods, and sees the heat lightning play like time over the horizon. But "time / Is only a mirror in the fun-house," you say in *Or Else*; "You must reevaluate the whole question" (of identity). I could continue to cite these marvelous images for obviously time and history are important questions for you. Could you begin by sketching out a little of how you conceive time and history? how you see it operating in the poems? in you?

ROBERT PENN WARREN: When I'm stuck with the question of time in some larger sense during the process of writing a poem, I'm following my nose, as it were, following an instinct about the material rather than following a theory. The general thinking, except in rare instances, has to be done far from your typewriter and far from your poems. The poem has to write itself rather than be planned out; a notion about time comes as a kind of flash when you've bumbled your way into the poem.

But let's look at time as an abstract question and see what happens. For one thing, there are two basic senses of time—or rather images of memory, to approach the question in another way. If I say, "your mother," an image pops into your mind. It is probably your mother in some characteristic attitude; it is a symbolic moment that comes to your mind. With the other kind of time, of memory, you may get a whole episode, or a whole life story piling into that moment. So one kind of memory is symbolic, the other is narrative, usually a fragmentary narrative; one is out of time, as it were, the other is a sequence of time. In poetry you're playing back and forth between these two kinds of reconstructed time.

Now, another and quite different aspect of time is the formal element. If you take a line from Pope—"and wretches hang that jurymen may dine"— and put that against a full-bodied Shakespearean pentameter line— "Unarmed Eros the long day's task is done"—one feels twice as long as the other though they are both ten syllable lines. The interplay of long and shorts, metrically, is an extremely important thing in poetry, and not just as mere variety but as expressive variety. For instance, I would go one step further and say that to read a poem you have to read with your whole body, not just for the sound. There is a muscular involvement, everything from your toes to your larynx. The Pope line spits from the front of the mouth. How does your whole body feel when you pronounce that line? The Shakespeare line has an openness and depth; there's a relaxing, a muscular relaxing all over. Now, these are questions of time, too, for they imply a short experience and a long experience, but they imply it muscularly. This relates to the other notion we were discussing in that you have to know what kind of experience you are talking about; you have to discover what rhythmic, oral, and muscular qualities may be involved. In Pope there is the tight, satiric, spitting, ejective "haste." Shakespeare's line, after the battle of Actium when Anthony relaxes, falls, "loosens" into despair. What I'm talking about is time as an experience. This idea comes into common speech. You can say, "I had a thin time of it," or "We had a big time last night"—there is a thinness and thickness of time.

POETRY MISCELLANY: For example, several of your poems, especially in the last three books, are structured by having someone confront a sense of the timeless and then having him move back into a consciousness of time, a world of time. I think, for instance, of "Snowshoeing Back to Camp in Gloaming," where in a "motionless landscape" the speaker "stood on that knife-edge frontier / Of Timelessness" and then moves out of that "Un-Time" through memory and anticipation to return to time and camp. Well, it seems that time is the thing that defines us in these poems—even that time and the self are one, or at least interdependent.

ROBERT PENN WARREN: I suppose the poem is built on the contrast of static time—time as a "being" and time as flow—here toward the life force of a loved one.

POETRY MISCELLANY: Is timelessness a void? a silence? an absence? a threat? Could you see the structure of some of the poems as attempting to establish a time, create a time, to supplement the void?

ROBERT PENN WARREN: Yes, the question of time as subject matter is another thing. *Being Here* is a kind of shadowy autobiography. It begins with my boyhood and my relationship to my grandfather. He is an old man who has passed through time, contrasted with the young boy for whom time waits, like a beast. The subject matter of the poems is the nature of that movement through time toward the events with my own son. Time is, narratively considered, your identity. You are your history. Symbolically considered, you can assume some existence, some essence which is outside an event; the soul, it corresponds to the theological soul and not auto-biographical history as a narrative. On a more secular level, the symbolic time sums up the character of a person; it is a way of abstracting out of biography to give an essence, a way of paraphrasing soul.

POETRY MISCELLANY: This business about time as identity reminds me of your poem, "Antinomy: Time and Identity." But the movement of that poem seems to go beyond autobiography toward something almost Emersonian.

ROBERT PENN WARREN: Yes, that poem, about getting into a canoe and going out into the black water alone, lit by stars here and there, is based upon an experience that happened when I was twenty-three or twenty-four years old. It became a poem only a year or so ago—about fifty years later. It has a more abstract treatment of the question of time and timelessness and identity. In one sense, identity ceases as time goes into timelessness, that is, as time becomes static. But against that is set time as movement—with past, present, future—and the reality of the crow's instantaneous call. "Antinomy" comes into the title because there are two opposing kinds of "identity" in the two orders of time. The poem winds up with a question about the future, with the simple image, the crow's call in the sky, which is a thing that can't be named, is just there, an essence of the universe. So identity can be more than with yourself, your history—also the instantaneous "ALL." Another example occurs in the poem "Night Walking," where I follow my son out and watch as he holds his bare arms to the moonlight in the mountains; he's seeking another thing, to identify himself with that ALL. Sometimes the identity could be with the land as in the poem about the Indian and the white man looking at the plain—for the white man, a shaven wheatfield.

POETRY MISCELLANY: The structure of the longer poems like *Or Else* or *Audubon* or even "Tale of Time," "American Portrait: Old Style," or "Synonyms" is essentially narrative, but different from prose fiction narrative. Discontinuous moments come together in the context, the thrust and rhythm of the poem, like touchstones arranged in a significant sequence. Perhaps this problem of discontinuity is addressed in "Tires on Wet Asphalt at Night," where the speaker, caught in the present, remembers something from long ago only to conclude, "I wish I could think what makes them come together now." Perhaps you could talk about the nature of narrative in your poems and something about the way the poetic narratives differ from prose narratives?

ROBERT PENN WARREN: For some years I tended to start poems from abstract ideas or from a specific line or two that evoked an idea. To some critics they seemed metaphysical. But almost all of my shorter poems from the last twenty-five years have had germs of narrative in them. They have usually begun with an actual episode. Take the poem about seeing the boy dance at sunset on an island in the Meriterranean; the origin was in an episode when we were coming down from the mountains and I saw my son go black against a sunset, like a figure on an antique coin. Now, the poem itself is always different from the original germ of the story. I know a thousand stories I could write poems or novels from; the question for me is why do I choose particular ones, or why do they choose me? The process of writing becomes a long meditation on this, one time as long as twenty years. I ask the question over and over again trying to follow the logic of the story. I never have the answer until at least halfway through, and the ending I originally have in mind turns out not to be the end at all. *Brother to Dragons* is a good example of this process—I heard the story first as a folk tale, then looked up court records; I didn't know what the story really meant until well into the writing.

POETRY MISCELLANY: A number of key images keep recurring in the poems. Some, like the horizon, we've already mentioned, and we could have mentioned "drowse" (*Being There*), "dream," "mountains," "darkness," "birds"—but more important, the particular image that seems to gather everything around it in a poem and becomes its nodal point—like the "leaf stem, at bough juncture" in "Acquaintance with Time in Early Autumn." Do you organize poems around images like this? Does the image come first? The image provides a point of contact with a physical reality that allows you then to take off on some of the implications of the situation, sometimes philosophically or theologically, and still keep the poem rooted. How crucial are these images for you?

ROBERT PENN WARREN: I see what you mean, and there are several answers. I can trace some of these images. When I was a boy I was in the woods a lot, and the birds always caught my attention. I didn't realize I was using so many bird images until critics pointed this out, and there is certainly a depth of meaning in that use that I was not aware of. As far as the mountain images are concerned, I have learned a lot in the far West, and now I spend my summers in Vermont, and the sun sets just beyond the mountains we stare at. The entire landscape begins to talk to you. The bird image, on the other hand, might be associated with a more distant memory. Let me say, too, that I try to avoid abstractions and that these images help the poem arise out of a dramatic setting.

POETRY MISCELLANY: Let's talk some about "voice" in the poems, that is, about the speaker and his relation to his audience, to his poem, to the author. For instance, we might focus on the nature of the "you" that is addressed in the poems, sometimes imploringly, sometimes in a directive, sometimes as intimate. How do you conceive of this "you" as generalized other? specific addressee? part of yourself (your speaker's self)?

ROBERT PENN WARREN: Sometimes the "you," as I use it, means "one," all of us, and is a way of suggesting identification. Sometimes it suggests a difference, even a tension between the speaker and the "you." But it can also work both ways in poems. This is a question I always deal with as I come to it; I have not thought abstractly about it at all. I don't want the use of the "you" to be a "mannerism." I don't want to use it to make the poem chummy. It sets up a little drama in the poem.

POETRY MISCELLANY: It is used often in contemporary poetry.

ROBERT PENN WARREN: Some modern poetry, free verse of a certain kind, gets so casual, so lacking in control, that it uses the "you" as a way of making the poem appeal to the reader. There is a long history of the direct address in poetry, obviously in epistles, but what we are talking about is not the epistolary "you." I really haven't thought about this, but perhaps the increase in the use of the "you" is because the modern poet no longer sets himself off as a seer. There's an effort to get more drama, an implicit dialogue, into the poem.

This is probably related to the "I." So much of Yeats's poetry, for example, is autobiographical. Thomas Hardy, too, has an air of autobiography about his poems; think of those poems about his dead wife, his first, horrible wife—when she died, he wrote the most beautiful poems about her. There a dramatic tension exists between the "I" in the poems and the original autobiographical "I."

POETRY MISCELLANY: There are often great shifts in diction—say, at the end of "Natural History, I," where you exclaim: "Beauty / Is the fume track of necessity. This thought / Is therapeutic." I mean that there seems to be a way, at least since *Incarnations*, in which you intentionally rough up the language. You talk about this idea, though, as early as "Pure and Impure Poetry," where you say that various "cacophanies," "technical" words, "jagged rhythms," and the like are "things which call us back to the world of prose and imperfection." I wonder if you could talk a little more about this notion. I wonder, too, if what I think is an increased use of techniques as your career has progressed is the result of a change in vision and principles or even helps effect any such change. To what extent must the poem avoid "poetic" language or use it?

ROBERT PENN WARREN: A lot of the poetry I was writing in the 1920s and 1930s was formalized poetry. "Monologue at Midnight" and "Bearded Oaks," for example, had a formal diction. Now, this strain disappeared in my poetry in the early 1940s—by "The Ballad of Billy Potts" it had vanished. When I began to write again in the 1950s—I had stopped writing poems and only wrote novels for a long time—I began to free the vocabulary, to mix formal and informal diction. I had no theory, only that I felt better doing it.

I always wrote some free verse but published very little of it. And I did start very early with a kind of balladry, much of it thrown away. The poem "Pondy Woods" is one that I kept, for example. Several of these had to do with country life. One poem, "Vinegar Hill," was about a Negro graveyard. That's a beautiful name for a graveyard, by the way, with its echo of Golgotha. That poem was no good, however. Some of these early poems used folk idioms.

Something else happened with this change in the 1950s that sometimes is still not understood. One recent reviewer talks about my not understanding meter. Well, I think I could teach a class in meter if I had to. But more and more I began to think in terms of rhythmical units and not in terms of meter even when I'm writing in a fixed meter. In any case, even with a reformer's regard for meter, the meter is always being played off against rhetorical considerations, word lengths, syllable weight, and so on. It is not a metronome. The pentameter or whatever I was writing in worked out all right, but the overriding rhythm began to be more important to me than the rhythm defined by the meter. I *think* and *feel* in that rhythm rather than in meter. Also, I can play back and forth between them, begin regularly and then move away from the regular meter. The rhythm becomes, not by plan but by process, free verse which is heavily marked by rhythmical units. At the same time, I write in fixed forms: I have a new book that will be out in 1981, and half the poems in that are in fixed forms, but fixed forms modified by rhythmical impulses. The meter's there, but not as apparently as it is in ordinary fixed forms.

POETRY MISCELLANY: On a more metaphysical level, language is very problematic in its relation to truth. I think of the notion that some sense of being and time is beyond words. I think of the end of *Audubon*, the end of "Sky" ("Its true name is what we never know"), and the opening of "Truth" ("Truth is what you cannot tell"). "Yes, how many names has truth?" you ask in "Ballad of Your Puzzlement." What, would you say, is the relation between language and truth? One of the ironies, of course, is that even while the speakers bemoan their inability to name truth, they are perhaps being most truthful in their use of language—close perhaps to the nature of being, time, and truth itself. Is there, for you, a "suspicion" about language, as some modern philosophers call it?

ROBERT PENN WARREN: You have raised many deep questions here. I'll simply stick to the simplest of answers. In *Audubon* the shift in time at the end is from the objective story of Audubon and its meaning for the boy (me) by the roadside at night caught up in the mysteries of nature. That last stanza says that a man like Audubon by his commitment to nature gives a story of delight—a rare type of human experience. The end of "Sky" is relatively simple. The body of the poem describes the coming of a summer storm. But there are other "storms" to fear. At the very end of the poem we ask what is the real enemy. Do we ever know it, really? About "Truth," take the Genesis story as the germ and carry it as far as you can.

But your whole drift here about language raises another kind of question. I know by experience that you sometimes write four or five lines and you know the language is wrong for the poem. Half the poems I throw away because they get bogged down somewhere. Perhaps a style has crept in that was never intended by God or me. "Tale of Time," for example, began as a blank verse poem. It was overformal and rigid in that form, though. I wrote twenty-five lines and it was awful, just awful. Several years later I came across some old fragments—I keep all my old fragments and keep them as a mine—and I read it out loud and saw that the blank verse was killing it. I took the first several lines, broke it into rhythmic units, and forgot the rest. The language changed immediately, and I felt like a new man. The poem had started out in the wrong language, as a formal elegy, in fact. The change in rhythm, then, caused the change in vocabulary.

A similar thing happened with *Audubon*. It started out in blank verse with a conventional, formal narrative line. When, twenty years later, I was again reading Audubon's works, the first line popped into my head and I saw the poem immediately as a series of angle shots, as aspects of Audubon's life rather than as a narrative in the conventional sense.

POETRY MISCELLANY: I was reading Eudora Welty's "The Still Moment" the other day. Audubon is one of the characters in there, and the whole story leads up to that one moment, which is structured, has a texture similar to the moments in *Audubon*.

ROBERT PENN WARREN: Well, I'll tell you, that was one of the things that started me reading Audubon again. That's a wonderful story. She's a great writer.

POETRY MISCELLANY: Perhaps this is the place to talk about the kinds of truth a poem brings us. "Where is the Truth—oh, unambiguous— / Thereof?" the speaker exclaims in "Safe in Shade." The questions, the techniques of roughing the poem up, the problematics of language all tend to defer the answers. The poems ask questions, put in motion thought/ feeling processes—and in some sense the truth seems to lie in the aptness of these processes. How do you conceive of it in poetry?

ROBERT PENN WARREN: I think a poem is a way of asking a question rather than answering one. You're trying to find out what's important to think about. You're trying to dramatize your human wants. You're trying to ask questions about yourself, about what your values really are. It is more important to ask the questions vitally than it is to give an overall answer. If you know the answers, you are a very lucky or a very stupid man. In any case, a poem is not a story or an essay. It ultimately deals with something not workable otherwise.

POETRY MISCELLANY: Perhaps we could finish by discussing ways in which you arrive at a book of poems, or how you conceive of a book as a unit.

ROBERT PENN WARREN: Each book except for the first which was simply a collection of the best I had at the time, completes a phase of my existence, a phase of my thinking, a phase of my own feeling. My new book, for instance, is a development of *Being Here* yet is different from *Being Here.* Months passed before I began this new book, and now I'm finished. I always know when I'm finished with a book. I've also got another book, about Chief Joseph, that won't be out for another year or so. It is not a narrative except in the sense that "Ballad of Billy Potts" was a narrative. It's a short book like *Audubon*—narrative plus other kinds of commentary.

Marvin Bell, 1980

Distilled from Thin Air

POETRY MISCELLANY: In one of his notebook entries, Theodore Roethke exclaims: "Make the language take really desperate leaps." I'd like to put some of your own lines next to that. In "Self-Made Man," you talk about "a mixture of alphabets, unrolling and unfolding / from all directions." In "To No One in Particular" you say, "I speak to you in one tongue, / but every moment that ever mattered to me / occurred in another language." More recently, in "The Canal at Rye," you say, "The natural end and extension / of language / is nonsense." These citations simply codify a tendency in your poetry toward leaps, ellipses, shifts, fragments of scenes and stories that make up the grammar and syntax of your poetics. Earlier, the language moved by more intense, local effects like puns, and lately the movement is more a stream of larger elements as in, say, "Birds Who Nest in the Garage." Though the irrational elements, the leaps, are still present, there is a greater self-assurance in the newer poems. In "The Hedgeapple," for instance, the fragmented narrative, the attitudes toward the woman, the discussion of the tree, the sense of self-realization come together in a more expansive way than you could have achieved earlier in the more close-fisted language of the first four volumes.

MARVIN BELL: That is a good question for me at this time because my language is undergoing a change, as you suggest. I did teach myself to write mostly by abandoning myself to the language, seeing what it wanted to say to me. That way, I could find out not only about language, but about myself, which was, and probably remains, a bundle of inherent contradictions and paradoxes. Now, what poetry can do, what it reveals, is always tied to language, but it also depends on transcending the language, going further than ordinary language. The lines you quoted reminded me of how often I've distrusted language, how much I have wanted my poetry to express what is inexpressible. How does one get at the inexpressible? I suppose by letting the poem respond to the implications of words and phrases, by shifting contexts so that words and phrases take on an irrational or a-rational sense.

Most of the early poems use a language that turns on itself to ask whether it can say what it has said or to question what it means. That listening to itself, responding to itself in the language of those poems is a way of making the poems whole and less and less paraphrasable. Now, *Residue of Song*, as the title suggests, is an almost antipoetic book, and from there I was able to write the poems of *Stars Which See, Stars Which Do Not See*, which is the best of those books, one where the poems are most opened up. Yet I still think of them as beginner's books. Ever since *Stars Which See*, though, I have been trying to redefine the poetic imagination and its language. Perhaps there's a self-assurance, as you suggest, a willingness to bring in bigger pieces of the world and not to have to try to tie every little bit together. I'm embarked on a risky experiment to see how much of poetry can be sensual and imaginative and not verbal first. That is, how much can the materials of poetry include the preverbal. There is a poem by James Wright that has the line, "I have heard weeping in secret." Without considering the special context of that line, we can say that it touches the essence of poetic imagination. We've all heard weeping and secrets behind doors. The problem for the poet, though, is how to use this elusive material, how to make it part of his sensibility at that moment in that poem. The whole history of poetry turns out to be a history of poets finding ways to incorporate what was thought to be nonliterary or secret material into their styles and content. There is always an undercurrent, the mystery. In "Stars Which See," the glassy surface of the mirrorlike water and its promise must break because things are not what they appear to be; there is always something more, different, an additional reflection, a secret. It involves the preverbal realm, and it is this realm the newer poems try to appropriate.

POETRY MISCELLANY: Your lines have also loosened up, become more spacious. In the light of what you just said about language, how do you conceive of the play between words, lines, phrases, and sentences?

MARVIN BELL: There has been a lot of talk about the line. One of the problems free verse has had is that many poets feel it should distinguish itself with special effects, particularly in its line breaks. In those cases the line has become too important. If you're just going for effects, for interruptions of the natural phrase to show off what can be done, then perhaps you are syncopating, jazzing, surprising the reader too much. Perhaps you should opt for a more seamless verse. The line length has to hold hands in some sense with the phrase. We should remember Pound's admonition: "As regarding rhythm: to compose in the sequence of the musical phrase, not in the sequence of the metronome." I think the musical analogy is crucial, for I do think there is a thing called an "ear" and that free verse depends on this ear. It is intuitive. It has to do with responding to different kinds of music and speech rhythms. I like speech rhythms myself, that is, a language which is opposed to what we can only imagine as written. Poems, in other words, are not written by word; they're written by phrase.

POETRY MISCELLANY: This seamless verse reminds me of the way William Carlos Williams's "Asphodel" strings out its sentences.

MARVIN BELL: Oh, yes, all kinds of sentences, all kinds! Sometimes he had to invent punctuation marks, like the comma followed by the dash. Williams was such a virtuoso with syntax; the line itself means nothing to him; only its relation to syntax has meaning.

POETRY MISCELLANY: Let's talk a little about the relation between language and meaning. There's still an undecidability in your poems—not the early, intense questioning, but a playful undercutting. I'm thinking, for example, of "Life," where the letter that is sent out like a poem contains "the spot in which it wasn't clear, perhaps, / how to take my words, which were suggestive, / the paragraph in which the names of flowers, / ostensibly to indicate travel, / make a bed for lovers." The problem is one of referentiality. "Yet what the symbol is to the flower / the flower is to something or other," you say in "What Lasts." And in "The Hole in the Sea," there is that "one word" that lies "in the hole of the sea," with a pun on whole, "where the solid truth lies."

MARVIN BELL: I suppose part of this problem goes back to my suspicion about language. You can't separate language and content. I've always secretly considered myself a poet of content, and still do, less and less secretly. It is curious that so much critical attention has been lavished in recent years upon poets whose poetry has *no* content. I think that sometimes teachers want their activity to be safe from philosophical and other concerns. The perfect tautology, the sweet song of nothing, has always been better received because it is safe. Several poets of my own generation, for instance, write beautiful, jewellike tautologies; these poets are practitioners of a limited aesthetic. But the rough piece can get at the impure world better. Picasso said, and then Stein picked it up, that "works of genius are always ugly." Part of the problem is that critics don't often see the buried metaphors, the richness, of colloquial language. They don't see the special precision of it, only a folksy translation of what they prefer to be elegantly said. But that colloquial language can hold a great deal of "meaning."

I have the feeling that American poetry can go on writing the same poem over and over again, that many of the vessels we're using just aren't going to save us anymore. It is going to take an enormous effort to break those vessels. For example, I've greatly admired Wright's *Two Citizens* and *To a Blossoming Pear Tree* and Galway Kinnell's latest work, but these poets have gotten progressively worse reviews. Wright was accused of being too sentimental; emotional, passionate—yes; but sentimental in the sense of emotion in excess of the event?—No, I don't think so.

POETRY MISCELLANY: In an interview in 1966 you said: "I write to make discoveries and inventions, as a necessary strategy to get things said.... I write to change my life." There's a sense of the self defining itself by speech, by passing beyond itself. I think of Stevens's "The Well Dressed Man with a Beard"—"a speech / Of the self that must sustain itself on speech." What seems important is not the statement but the saying. This leaves us with the strange relation of the poet to his material; as you say in "We Have Known" about poems, "If very little / can pass through them, know that I did, / and made them, and finally did not need them." More recently, in "Haleakala Crater, Maui," "I wanted something beyond me." So let's talk some about writing and the self.

MARVIN BELL: One can labor for years, say as Eliot says, to get a thing just right, and then discover that it's not the thing one wants to say anymore. Poetry is often talked about as a grapple with the mind for that very reason; the mind doesn't hold still for anyone. What we have in the end is an exhibit of "passage," as Eliot calls it in the *Quartets*, something that came out on the way to something else. One has to be careful here, careful about the voice, careful not to use this idea as an excuse for bad writing. Half the battle may be knowing who you are at a given time.

When I made the statement, "I write to change my life," I had just articulated many motives for writing, and that sort of encompassed the others. I think of Auden's line, "Poetry makes nothing happen"—I don't believe that. I believe poetry changes individual consciousnesses. When I read back over my poems I do see a person who has changed, though it would be hard to say how much the poems changed the person and how much the changes led to different poems. No one can know. I believe, at least, that there's a great benefit in doing anything seriously for a long time, and I'm not sure it matters what. Poetry can become a way of life. For me, writing poetry *is* a way of life, indeed down to my metabolic needs. I can't go very long without writing and not become crabby, hard to live with. I always feel better when I write, when I go to my study out back under the wild cherry tree. It only takes a few minutes before I say, "Why didn't I come out here sooner?" It feels wonderful! It's almost as if now I'd like to reserve the term "poetry" for a quality of imagination which is beyond technical analysis.

POETRY MISCELLANY: The self always seems at some threshold, always about to fade even as it begins to emerge. In "Trinket," in *Stars Which See,* you watch the water ooze through a crack in the pot and say it is this "that gives the self / the notion of the self // one is always losing / until these tiny embodiments."

MARVIN BELL: It is true that I think of the self as very small, and it is true that I think what can be known about the self is possible to know mostly by looking outside the self and not into mirrors. There's an essay by Rilke about Rodin in which he talks about Rodin becoming a great artist whose every moment was caught up in the greatness of his art. When he begins to describe the sculpture in terms of surfaces, he realizes what the implications of that are and says, "Okay, I've been talking about surfaces, but isn't everything we know about life a matter of surfaces?" Poetry looks at a surface until depth is achieved, that is, suggestiveness and implication. But we look at the surface, the threshold, nevertheless.

POETRY MISCELLANY: As if the surface were a transparency?

MARVIN BELL: Yes, as we were saying before, there's always something more. I believe that about the self, too. "Self" is a very iffy word for me, for in a funny way we are selfless. The word has become more problematic for me than "soul." American poetry has been limited in large extent, whatever its achievements are, and they are many and substantial, by two characteristics. First, I think that our technology is translated into a belief in technique in literature for its own sake. Second, there's a terrible burden, which the first characteristic often hides, that the self can expand, optimistically, to legislate what is right for other selves, whether they want it or not. America has always been a country with a vision, even if the vision may have been built on self-deception, manipulation, imperialism, commerce, self-interest, whatever. The vision is always translated into a myth, a moral imperative. It is this sense of vision which defines that American self and perhaps accounts for a blind faith in that technology/technique which is the means of achieving that vision.

POETRY MISCELLANY: In "The Self and the Mulberry," you say, "I kept losing parts of myself like a soft maple," then decide, "That was the end / of looking in nature to find a natural self." But one keeps hearing the children's ditty and realizes how they define themselves in the group game and in the saying of that song. That tension about the self seems to be the motivating force in the poem, perhaps throughout *Stars Which See.*

MARVIN BELL: That's terrific. I never thought of that. Well, I keep making a distinction between what we make of nature and what nature is in its indifference. Nature is not a phenomenon with a consciousness, though we often treat it that way—hence the title, *Stars Which See, Stars Which Do Not*

See. We look at the stars, and they seem to look back. What are they? They may even be long dead as their light reaches us. We seem compelled to speculate. In the Mulberry poem the distinction is between whether we see the mirror or nature itself when we look at it.

POETRY MISCELLANY: How does a poem like your recent "Late Naps" fit into this problematic sense of the self and its world? Specifically, it deals with the soul, though in a comic way.

MARVIN BELL: It's a poem about going to bed with a bad feeling; one takes a late afternoon nap with a sense of things still nagging, incomplete, done poorly. Anything can cause the bad dreams—"the dreamworks run on an oil so light, / it can be distilled from thin air." One thinks of the soul as laughable, as something that can hover in the air like a ghost, as insignificant but yet mysterious, as something that slips away in dream and yet haunts, nags like those bad feelings. We're weakest when the soul floats up and away, most vulnerable to discontent. The poem doesn't really engage so much the question of the soul as much as a certain kind of spiritual discontent—a spiritual pit in the stomach.

POETRY MISCELLANY: That sense of the soul going out suggests the notion of the Other. There is, for example, the play of self and Other in *The Escape into You*, of self and divorced self. And in "The Perfection of Dentistry," you see things, as it were, through the caretaker, and you "lead his concurrent lives." I think, too, of the recent poem, "Someone Is Probably Dead"—"It's stupid to pretend we can be someone else, / when someone else is dead."

MARVIN BELL: Well, "The Perfection of Dentistry" tries to find a way to see those lives concurring, one life taking place in another. We're all linked that way through imagination. I'm reminded of a poem in the forthcoming book called "A Motor," where the speaker identifies with someone who is up in a light plane and who is probably coming down to go to a hospital for cancer treatment. The poem ends, "Myself in the clinic for runaway cells, / Now and later." The Other here involves a possibility in the future as well as a certain sympathetic understanding now. But then there is the other side of the coin. There is Pindar's famous question, which I use in the title of a prose poem, "What Are We, What Are We Not." Rather than finding ourselves in others, there may be no others, no selves.

POETRY MISCELLANY: The way you use the "you" is perhaps as elusive as this Other. How do you conceive of the Other that is represented by "you"?

MARVIN BELL: I've tried not to use the "you" to mean "one," though I perhaps have sometimes done it ill-advisedly. I'm really addressing someone I know when I use it, though the reader may not be sure of whom. "The Canal at Rye," meaning Rye, England, where Henry James lived for a while, begins: "Don't let them tell you." Later in the poem you can figure out that "you" has to be a child of the speaker. Now, someone like David St.

John writes a poetry that is always fiercely intimate; it seems to depend heavily on addressing a someone as if that person were anxious to be addressed.

POETRY MISCELLANY: Let's extend this notion of otherness even farther, to other times. To what extent does a consciousness of the past or history enter your poems? In "To His Solitary Reader," you say, "Memory is what we are." In some poems, such as "Virtuoso of the X," history intrudes in images like "an aroma of gas remains in the showers." At the same time, this is not a cheap or nostalgic sense of the past, but a way of presencing it, as in "Father and Russia," where you repeat "you" as if to presence him: "Now I want you as you were before they hurt you, / irreparably as you were as in another country."

MARVIN BELL: It may be that memory *is* the sum total of our experiences, but it may also be that poetry includes memory and loss too easily. There's always the danger of nostalgia, a poetic attitude we ought to be a little more careful about—a certain tilt of the head, a certain longing look backward. Now, I did set out to write a book-length series of poems to my father who was already dead at the time. I thought of myself as completing a conversation that never took place because he was a father who didn't speak about many things. It became the sequence of only thirteen poems in *Residue of Song*. I was conscious of the danger of poetic nostalgia. Even the past tense has an aura about it. I like to write more in the present tense, or to write in what one might call the immediate past tense in which things haven't happened so long ago that one has to question "when"? In some ways, the poems are about possession, as in the poem where the three people pause for a moment at the edge of the road to look at some hedgeapples. When the lady appears at the screen, we suddenly feel as if we are spying, trying to take possession of something. Though we didn't take any hedgeapples, we felt as if we had.

POETRY MISCELLANY: Your sense of time, generally, is a dynamic one. Time becomes a futural thing, something we have to structure for ourselves. In some sense this is possible, I think, because you think of time as disguise; in "New Students" you talk about a "shapeless universe disguised as time." It's also a matter of point of view; in "Dew at the Edge of a Leaf," you have the lines: "Everything green is turning brown, / it's true, but then too, / everything turning brown is green!"

MARVIN BELL: I really do believe that time is an illusion. I can conceive of a gigantic scientific breakthrough that would see through time by seeing into materials. The idea of space travel today is senseless. You put up a few people in a capsule and they have children and their children do and so on until whoever arrives whenever doesn't know where they came from and are at a place they don't want to be. So, the only way to go from one place to another on that scale would be to defeat time, perhaps through cybernetics, by changing matter. It would be like turning on your TV and actually having the thing before you, not some representation that is always trapped by time. The poem "Viet Nam," from *Residue of Song*, opens by saying, "Viet Nam // is a place you will hear of / in the future, / which is not to say tomorrow merely." When you think of time in terms of a memento or two, a nostalgic memory from the past, something the clock has marked as ended, you reduce time. There is something larger—"Though we know better about time, / we know nothing about peace, / which is a function of time and war." Time is not a form, but a content; it has to do with material.

POETRY MISCELLANY: And it has to do with presencing that otherness. I was just thinking how often the word "elsewhere" or something like it occurs in your poems. It suggests something of the inexpressible, the secrecy, the otherness we've been discussing.

MARVIN BELL: Yes, elsewhere. In fact, I almost gave *Stars Which See* a different title—*Poems Which Came from Elsewhere*.

POETRY MISCELLANY: The elsewhere occurs in "The Hedgeapple" as the place you'd wish you'd gone back to. The refrain, "We should have gone back," keeps appearing at regular intervals. And yet, the poem itself is a going back, a fulfilling of the opening line, "I wish we'd gone back." The elsewhere is perhaps that preverbal space, but here made present, brought back into the time of the poem. The second half of the poem becomes more authoritative, at least relative to the questioning and subjunctive moods of the first half, almost as if you were going to say, "Okay, this is how it is," and then you end audaciously, "So: here." You've taken the elsewhere and presenced it, denied, undercut the refrain and opening line. It's like the old gossip who says, "I never should have repeated that story." Of course she has to, again and again.

MARVIN BELL: Yes, I agree with all you've said, but more compelling is your example. As soon as you say that, I'm interested in it; I want to use that line. That's terrific. What an opening line—"I never should have repeated that story." That to me is where poetry is. How could you not read the next line in a poem that began that way? That works like the opening of Wright's "The Old WPA Swimming Pool in Martins Ferry, Ohio"—"I am almost afraid to write down / This thing." You have to read on. There's so much urgency, so much private power, such a sense of secrecy. Once you've said that line, you've got to write it down.

John Ashbery, 1981

The Imminence of a Revelation

POETRY MISCELLANY: There is a certain kind of cryptology inherent in your poems. In *Three Poems* you write: "We have broken through to the meaning of the tomb. But the act is still postponed before us // it needs pronouncing. To formulate oneself around this hollow empty sphere." Later you write about "a word that everything hinged on and is buried there," yet "is doing the organizing." The text seems always a supplement for the lost word, for something always unspoken, unwritten. More recently, "The Hills and Shadows of a New Adventure" explores the problematic of naming; here one must deal with "certain illegible traces, like chalk dust on a blackboard after it has been erased" (*Three Poems*). How much does this notion of poetry as a putting into play of traces and lost names figure in your poetic? How much of poetry, I wonder, proceeds by an essential misnaming?

JOHN ASHBERY: As it so often turns out, something you've just read or are about to read turns out to be very useful. There is an essay by Borges called "The Wall and the Books," where the narrator reports that he read not long ago how the "man who ordered the building of the almost infinite Chinese Wall was the first Emperor, Shih Huang Ti, who also decreed the burning of all the books that had been written before his time." Borges goes on to make parallels between the two actions. He says that "perhaps he called himself Huang Ti in an endeavor to identify himself with that legendary Huang Ti, the emperor who invented writing and the compass and who, according to the Book of Rites, gave things their true names; for Shih Huang Ti boasted on inscriptions that still exist, that all things under his reign, had the names that befitted them." I think there's a parallel here to Harold Bloom's theory of the Anxiety of Influence in the desire to destroy or negate all previous writings in order to give things their true names and at the same time to build a wall around an impossibly large area. Further, at the end, Borges gives an almost Paterian definition of creativity: "Music, states of happiness, mythology, faces molded by time, certain twilights in certain places—all these are trying to tell us something, or have told us something we should not have missed or are about to tell us something. The imminence of the revelation that is not yet produced is, perhaps, the aesthetic reality." The imminence of a revelation not yet produced is very important and hard to define in poetry and probably is the source of some of the difficulty with my own poems. But I don't think it would serve any useful purpose to spare myself or the reader the difficulty of that imminence, of always being on the edge of things.

POETRY MISCELLANY: There's always a deferral of meaning, I guess. It's curious, too, that you have so many mentions of marginal places in the poems—bridges, paths, medians, porches, verandas, horizons, boundary lines, edges—places that situate the poem as an event as well as provide setting.

JOHN ASHBERY: I never thought of that before. In fact, I just wrote a poem this morning in which I used the word "borders" but changed it to "boarders." The original word literally had a marginal existence and isn't spoken, is perhaps what you might call a crypt word. I think this happens often, though, with other poets; Kenneth Koch told me once about a creative misprint he had made on the typewriter when "singing" came out "sinning."

One thing that I've noticed about my own poetry is the prevalence of indirect movements such as in the words "seep" or "leach," or, in other words, where things get from one place to another in an unorthodox way. This might be part of the impulse that also results in talking about marginal places.

POETRY MISCELLANY: Probably, this lack of closure, an insistence on deferring the revelation, defines the nonreferential, or self-referential, or even endlessly referential dynamic of your poetry. "All things seem mention of themselves / And the names which stem from them branch out to other referents," you write in "Grand Galop." There are also poems like "Worsening Situation," "Voyage in the Blue," and "No Way of Knowing" that begin with no strict antecedent and so suggest inexhaustible relationships. "All of our lives is a rebus," you say in *Houseboat Days*.

JOHN ASHBERY: I've noticed that the word "self-referential" is often used as a pejorative term in criticizing poetry today, and I'm glad you don't use it that way. It seems to me that poetry has to be self-referential in order to refer to something else. I think many people feel a poet should take a subject as an essayist would and then write about it in order to come up with some conclusions and the whole matter would then be solved to everyone's satisfaction. But poetry, as has often been said, is made out of words; it is an affair of language. The situation is parallel with painting, for a painting does not make a "meaningful statement." I think that this is why the Impressionists were harshly criticized at first, yet their work is actually a kind of realism superior to what had been done when they began to work. The interests of realism in poetry are actually enhanced in the long run by a close involvement with language; thought created by language and creating it are the nucleus of the poem. Self-referentiality is not a sign of narcissism, but actually is a further stage of objectivity.

POETRY MISCELLANY: What seems important is the process of generating possible revelations in language. Language, as some contemporary thinkers have begun to theorize, precedes existence in a certain way. There is no "bottom line" for there are always more words, the imminence of new words.

JOHN ASHBERY: In other words, we're never allowed to relax or rest. We're constantly coping with a situation that's in a state of flux. When I was writing *Three Poems* I became interested in the Tarot cards, and although I couldn't remember now what I learned then, I do remember that the images are not exactly what they seem to be, the most obvious one being "Death," which can imply a further life. There is not a one-to-one correspondence but a looking ahead to what the next situation is going to be, a process, a flux.

POETRY MISCELLANY: And there's just as much an undoing as a generation that goes into this process. In "And UT PICTURA POESIS Is Her Name" you deconstruct, as Derrida would say, traditional poetics "so that understanding / May begin, and in doing so be undone." And in "Flowering Death," you write, "We must first trick the idea / Into being, then dismantle it, / Scattering the pieces on the wind." I think also of "Five Pendantic Pieces," in which you write, "The poem of these things takes them apart." The poems tend to take apart or undo what they refer to in a way that reminds me of the writings of such contemporary thinkers as Derrida, Foucault, and Lacan.

JOHN ASHBERY: I think that it is probably not a coincidence that we've been addressing ourselves to similar problems and that these sorts of things tend to happen simultaneously in history from certain causes. I know, for example, that Raymond Roussel, who has been characterized as a kind of primitive Mallarmé, was asked in a letter about his opinion of Mallarmé, and he replied that he was unfortunately not familiar enough with the poet to give a serious estimation. So, while I am not very familiar with these authors, you may have a point in mentioning them.

As to the notion of undoing, let me say that it very often serves a purpose. Penelope's tapestry may have looked senseless to her entourage when she kept weaving and unraveling it, but it had a concrete purpose. In my case, the purpose would be to draw attention to the continuing nature of poetry, which has to come into being, pass from being, in order to return to a further state of being. This is really an affirmation of the way things are treated in a poem. I don't begin with the intention of writing a particular *thing*, though I can often look back and see things that must have been part of some unconscious intent. I actually try to begin writing with my mind a tabula rasa; I don't want to know, can't know what I'm going to write. So, too, interruptions are very important for they are part of the composition of life—a phone may ring as it did just then, and the interruption will provide the break, the space that allows me to go further on, perhaps in another direction. I have a line in one of my poems, "Syringa," about the way things happen, moving along, bumping into other things, which occurs in the context of a stream or river. That's not a very original metaphor, but in fact its triteness is one of the reasons I'm attracted to it. My mind wants to give clichés their chance, unravel them, and so in a way contribute to purifying the language of the tribe.

POETRY MISCELLANY: Many metaphoric situations are hidden in clichés, especially when you decide to take them a little more or a little less literally than they're usually taken.

JOHN ASHBERY: And I think they have a beauty because of being hallowed somehow by so much use, by people who are just trying to say what they had on their minds. Thought has taken this form again and again, and that should be respected.

POETRY MISCELLANY: You mentioned "Syringa" earlier, and in the context we have been discussing I'm reminded of the end of that poem with its insistence on the author as fiction, a kind of library of Borges, or an archive of Foucault. In "Self Portrait" you talk "until no part / Remains that is surely you." There is always an undecidable element for the "I" as single ego—a plurality of voices, voices lost in a labyrinth of textuality.

JOHN ASHBERY: Well, I'm notorious for my confusing use of pronouns which, again, is not something I consciously aim at. There are questions as to whether one character is actually the character he's supposed to be. I feel not too sure of who I am and that I might be somebody else, in a sense, at this very moment that I am saying "I." But doesn't this open up a book and make it more available? A book is going to be interpreted or misinterpreted in as many ways as there are readers, so why not give them the maximum number of options to misinterpret you, for these are all only interpretations. This seems part of the nature of any kind of interpretation.

POETRY MISCELLANY: There's a casual tone in your poems that allows you to confuse words and things, too, not just persons. Take the opening of

"Grand Galop"— "All things seem mention of themselves"—a low-keyed line that brings together world (things), resemblance (seems), language (mention), and the self-referentiality we talked about earlier.

JOHN ASHBERY: The tone is a humble one, and its casualness goes with the blank beginning that I talked about earlier. We always start from that point when we read. As to the bringing together of words and worlds, I don't think we can separate them in poetry. The physical and meaningful aspects of language always reverberate with one another in a way that leads to further language. As you know, I've been involved with contemporary art, and it just occurred to me that in Cubist still-life paintings there will be, say, a word on a wine label that extends off into space as an object in itself. Perhaps there's an affinity of tone, too. I'm certainly aware of trying to view things from different angles as the Cubists did, but I don't think it's a question of influence, only that general cultural concern we talked about.

Isn't it interesting, by the way, that this urge to depict an object from every possible angle is doomed to failure, yet the work resulting from the failure, is what makes it so fascinating to people? In a way you fail, yet in ways you also succeed.

POETRY MISCELLANY: And there's a sense of waiting, as in the lines near the beginning of "Grand Galop," where the "we" is always ahead or behind. "Nothing takes its fair share of time."

JOHN ASHBERY: Yes, I was thinking of that. The idea is probably the result of living in a large city where you always have to wait, whether it's at the bank or the doctor's. It's an agonizing problem, to know what you're supposed to be doing while you're waiting, because waiting doesn't seem enough, but it is possible to force oneself to realize that waiting is actually enough. Waiting is part of an endless series of stages of which the so-called objective is only another stage. I've been influenced by the music of John Cage in which there are long periods of silence and where the noises of the environment will be picked up and perhaps replayed at some point. I think he's trying to draw attention to the fact that every moment has a validity; it's a valuable unit of time, and the things that might be happening at any time have a value and even a beauty.

POETRY MISCELLANY: I think this relates to the sense of chance that informs your work, not only in the sense of the interrupted moment we were discussing earlier, but also in a more conceptual sense. There's the word play like the chance/dance rhyme at the end of "Fragment" or the "Indelible, Inedible" link in the poem by that title where letters can't be erased, can't be consumed. I suppose that, in a way, some of this originates in surrealism, if we can use that term with any accuracy today. Chance is important, isn't it?

JOHN ASHBERY: Yes, chance is very important in those ways we've already mentioned. On the other hand, I don't think it's the entire motivating force behind whatever you're writing. You shouldn't, for example, mistype every word in a poem. I think that promoters of surrealism have narrowed it to a function of the unconscious alone, yet we have to take account of the rational. I once interviewed Henri Michaux, and his opinion about surrealism was more or less mine, that it is *la grande permission,* with the French sense of permission as a leave, like a soldier's leave, but also the usual English sense of that word. Perhaps chance, then, is involved in this permission of language, the way words tend to try to have a life of their own, to take over at times, in fact.

POETRY MISCELLANY: In *Three Poems* there are two figures, the prism and the parallelogram, that suggest a double movement, a synchronic and a diachronic progress. This double motion has to wait until "Fantasia" and "Litany" to be enacted, though. The two columns or voices in "Litany" at times build progressively upon one another, at times reflect each other and so keep a parallel pace, and at other times seem independent of one another. This is related to the problematic of writing, of simultaneity. You say in "Litany" that "I want it all from you / In writing, so as to study your facial expressions / Simultaneously." This is a way of breaking down traditional relations of causality, of course, that is, a way of undoing, but it also demands a reconstructive effort on the part of the reader, who begins by overhearing a conversation of sorts, then must enter, make something of it, and so on. Roland Barthes talks about how such techniques force us to reread, a crucial procedure, for we tend only to read ourselves the first time around.

JOHN ASHBERY: The doubleness in "Fantasia" is fairly arbitrary because it would read the same if some of the he and she headings were left out. "Litany" is perhaps meant to be heard rather than read; at least that's the only way the experience of the whole poem could happen. I probably haven't gone beyond that because of the fact that we have only two ears and can only hear two things simultaneously. We're very often trying to hear two different conversations while we go about our business, or to read ahead or glance ahead a few pages. We lose a great deal this way, but that is realistic for we can't possibly absorb every aspect of any experience. A part may be momentarily lost, but then picked up to become unimportant later on.

I'm very interested in Carter's music, as you know. He is an extreme example of this presenting two or more trains of thought. He has a work for violin and piano, which I heard before I started writing "Litany." When it was first performed it was done with the violin on one side of the stage and the piano on the other side of a very large stage. It would seem as though they were talking about different things, but the one would become more intense and the other would somehow begin to fade at certain points, then the situation would change and the violin, which was already in an unequal struggle with the piano, would nevertheless overtake it and dominate it.

POETRY MISCELLANY: In "Soonest Mended," you talk about time as an emulsion, which I think fits in with what we've been discussing. Your sense of time seems to be something that "keeps percolating" possibilities, as you say in "Prophet Bird." The moment becomes evasive, always separating into parts, yet held in the emulsive suspension of the poem.

JOHN ASHBERY: When we experience a moment we feel perhaps a kind of emptiness, but when we look back at it there will be different aspects and the moment will separate itself into these aspects. We won't be sure what the dominant aspect was, and I guess that results in my sense of a permanent unraveling. This best describes how I experience life, as a unity constantly separating. It's difficult to get that into poetry, though. It takes time to write something when it is situated in a period of, say, half an hour. This form is really the base on which the poem is built; it's a conveyor belt and time gets arbitrarily snipped off at the end of the poem. Temporality is built into the poem.

POETRY MISCELLANY: And there's a desire to be at "the beginning, where / We must stay, in motion," as you say in "Houseboat Days." There seems to be an implicit desire to stop time from snipping at the end of the poem. In "The System," you describe coming to a fork in a road, taking one, and then ending up in the same place, the beginning, a parody of Frost.

JOHN ASHBERY: That was perhaps a half-conscious parody of Frost, but I was probably thinking of a radio program I used to listen to when I was young, "Jack Armstrong." Jack and his chums seemed constantly in a forest or jungle and constantly traveling in circles. This happens not only to explorers but to writers, to everybody. It's something I keep addressing myself to. I sort of see it as a series of overlapping circles and spirals. We're constantly taking two steps forward and one step backward.

POETRY MISCELLANY: We've been gradually working toward a consideration of form. How do you relate this spiral or circular motion to the parody of regular form in *Shadow Train*? There appears to be a form, but it is constantly unraveling because of the labyrinthian word play, the paradoxes, the irresolutions.

JOHN ASHBERY: To me, it's a kind of antiform, really, a lining up of four stanzas of four lines each. It looks sensible enough on the page but, in fact, it lacks the "meaningfulness" of the sonnet, a logical form. My intention was to give a sense of balance by having each section be of equal length and importance, therefore tipping it away from form. It's perhaps the sort of thing the minimalist artists of the 1960s such as Donald Judd were aiming at—four oblongs next to each other, rather than a hard, humanistic treatment of geometry such as you get in Piet Mondrian. It really is, then, an asymmetry, a coldness, an alteration. There was the sense of cutting things up, putting them in a kind of Procrustean Bed rather than letting them ooze out into a freedom of their own. I was aware, as I was writing, of the great irregularity of length of thought. One line would contain barely an idea while the next line would have six or seven slapped together. There's a relation between that and the almost brutal arbitrariness of the format of the poems. Format may be a better word than form for our purposes.

David St. John, 1980

Renaming the Present

POETRY MISCELLANY: *Hush* is particularly interesting for the conception of language that operates throughout the book. There is always something elusive. As Heidegger would have it, there is a presencing that does not presence, or arrive. The character in "Coming Home" is always in the process of doing just that, always being deferred. The elusiveness is manifested in your repeated use of words like "something," "or," and "perhaps"—there is a subjunctive or "undecidable" cast, to borrow from Paul De Man, to this language. And yet, this very language of absences can provide a Derridian "supplement," as in "Naming the Unborn," where the last son is named as if to presence him. And in the poem for Peter Evervine there is a similar presencing, here of a whole world, the son, the field that will be spoken in silence. There is an elaborate gathering of signs, of "traces," if we want to keep this terminology from linguistics and philosophy, that makes a presence of absence in "Hush." The poem becomes, as you say to your son, "The dark watermark of your absence, a hush." Words become not so much denotative signs but signifiers; a poem is made of "some few words that sound like music and the sea." Perhaps, in this context, you could begin by sketching your sense of your language and how it has changed.

DAVID ST. JOHN: These things that you mention have always been for me the most important aspects in poems. The episodic detail in all the poems is crucial to the way I want the poems to move, crucial to the texture of the language. I think of "Gin" as a kind of *Ars Poetica* with its fragmented newspaper account of murder at the beginning, the business of the friends complaining that "Even your stories / have no point, just lots of detail," and the other "disguises of omission" that occur. The false causalities, the positing of congruent alternatives through a poem are ways, for me, to describe through those "tracings" some area of concern. I'm not interested in trying to name something with one name because I don't believe whatever I'm discussing has one name. To name something in a fixed way involves a fallacy for me. In my poems there is that kind of "sliding of signifiers" that Jacques Lacan describes, the verbal texture that Barthes is describing in "The Eiffel Tower." What I mean is that there is a great deal of difference between the subject or sequence of subjects that a poem takes on and what I would call the "movement." I do believe in this context that poems are models of consciousness, and I think that's their value. Exploring or experiencing a poem has to do with exploring a progression of consciousness about an area of concern. This is why the episodic detail is so important; I try to allow the poems to propel themselves through narrative details that are distractingly specific yet have enough commitment to a beginning and an end so as not to prove merely frustrating.

Yeats's statement, "I seek an image of the modern mind's discovery of itself," seemed to define poetic activity in the early part of this century. For me, there's been an enormous revision of that; I seek the movement or progression of the mind's discovery of itself. That's an enormous distinction, because it takes the sense of the imagistic construct, which is necessarily and implicitly fixed, and suggests a more kinetic grammar of poetry.

POETRY MISCELLANY: There's a subversion of simple simile and metaphor. "A" is not simply like "B," but rather "A" suggests "B," which in turn conjures "C," and so on—Lacan's chain of signifiers.

DAVID ST. JOHN: Exactly. It's the movement that is important, not just A, B, and C themselves. I think that the experience throughout the twentieth century, after the lesson of *The Waste Land* and fragmentation had been learned, is that as experience grows more fragmentary and disjunctive, we need a model of consciousness that's more fluid and capable of absorbing those jagged experiences. A set, structured model of consciousness seems to me simply too vulnerable to suit contemporary experiences. Perhaps that is why the "deep image" seemed out of date so quickly, for however deep those images were, they were also fixed and static. On the other hand, James Wright's great value was not his reliance on that imagism, but his humanity and compassion, his enormous lyric gifts, his sense of the flow of things, of language.

POETRY MISCELLANY: This movement you have been describing tends to suggest a nonreferential poetry. At least, the poems are often self-referential.

A poem is always also about itself. And yet there is always a reference to an implicit "you"—Wright has this in a very different way—an "Other," as Lacan calls it, that provides a vague, even absent center. I've been reading an essay by Susan and Leslie Brisman that talks about the way all lyric poetry is implicitly an appeal to a supremely responsive auditor.

DAVID ST. JOHN: The poems in the latter half of *Hush* are enormously self-referential. That's also the reason that so many of the poems use the second-person address. It is a way to create tension, not only in the fact that the poems are to some extent also a self-address, but because with the second person I can evoke a kind of accusation to the reader as well. All the tension of the Lacanian Other is necessary for me. In most regards, in writing the poems I try not to be conscious of it in a pragmatic way, but the tension of the I/You address has always been crucial to the movement of the poems. In "Slow Dance" the conception of the "you" is probably the most difficult of any of the poems in *Hush*. It floats in and out of being more and less specific; there are times when it is very directed, times when it seems self-referential, times when it seems very general. Of the poems in the book it's probably my favorite because these kinds of maneuvers are done with as much grace as any of the other things I've done there. Now, I've tried to make the poems in *The Shore*, with the unavoidable exception of "Of the Remembered," less self-referential. But the others maintain the fiction of a specific Other, a specific "You" to which there's a specific relationship. That provides, I suppose, a more apparent and available surface. But what interests me is still the subterfuge, the maneuvers, the ways temporalities can be fragmented and superimposed, that tension between the namings and the misnamings, the verbal texture, the positionings of the "You."

POETRY MISCELLANY: What holds all these things together is *voice*. As this trace movement progresses, as the poems radiate out, often leaping dramatically, as does the opening poem in *Olive Grove*, for example, the voice provides a coherence, a believability. It allows the "stew," as you call it in "Gin," to disguise its origins without the loss of a base; it allows the poems coincidentally to "bloom / In such false directions."

DAVID ST. JOHN: Yes, to involve the kind of duplicities, the kinds of false presencing that goes on in the poems requires the necessary paradox of the strong presence of the voice. If the poems have any sense of authority at all, it's a sense of conviction that the voice presence enacting those poems is, if not to be trusted, at least to be heard. I feel that if I can maintain that and still accomplish the kinds of things I want to do beneath the surface, then that's as much as I can ask now. I like some of the poems in *Hush* to read as self-betrayals; the vulnerability is great in a poem like "Gin," where the details are given up, admitted by the voice. That's also true of poems in *The Shore*, though the narrative axis is more specific. The poems in *The Shore* were very single-mindedly thought out in terms of that voice presence. The riskiest poem is "Of the Remembered" because it generates multiple presences; the character of the voice changes from section to section as if the whole poem were a sort of autobiographical hologram that could create a sense of space in which I wanted to move. The presence in poems like "Blue Waves" and "Until the Sea Is Dead" is more consistent, a presence which is willing to posit an aura in a way the poems in *Hush* were unwilling, that were in fact resisting.

When I teach, the thing that concerns me most with young writers is that they recognize that poems are voice presences. It seems to take a very talented young writer about six years of trying on voices and masks to find the voice that most closely approximates the self or the idea of the self that occurs in the poems. It's this more intimate kind of persona poetry that interests me. I try to ask young poets to question themselves, to ask themselves: "Who's in that poem?" and "What presence, what self, is being portrayed in this language?"

POETRY MISCELLANY: On a nuts-and-bolts level, voice can be strongly given in the line. This has to do not just with the ways disparate items can be held in one line, but with the ways sentences and fragments interweave in the lines, play off against them. How has your sense of the line changed with your sense of voice?

DAVID ST. JOHN: In the last part of *Hush* especially in "Slow Dance," when I began working in longer lines, I was able to work a verbal suspension that the more specifically imagistic, short-line poems that I had once written simply couldn't hold. The longer line enabled me to create a more sophisticated verbal imperative. I could push a reader through a line and then drop the reader to the fragment or line following in a way that would, I hoped, accomplish that false causality, that suspension, and even more important, that sense of movement in which the poem continues to propel through the details and extensions of rhythm that mark a consciousness, a voice. In *The Shore*, particularly in "Until the Sea Is Dead," I began working with a shorter line again and found I was able to continue a kind of narrative movement, a kind of fragmenting of temporalities, but with a much more measured pace, with a less wild movement through the poems.

POETRY MISCELLANY: We've been edging toward a more direct discussion of the nature of narrative. A kind of Nietzschean genealogy seems to lurk behind what you've been saying. "The River" describes history as "taking every irrespective turn / Against the grain" and then "How / The sand is taken, only to be put down later." History becomes a matter of chance. Could you sketch out a little more fully your sense of narrative in relation to this sort of history? I'm thinking of section IX of "Of the Remembered"; there you talk about history, myth, and making up a story only to admit: "I've only taken pieces of several / To make one story I love, one chord / I hear most." These details give a sense of the poem emerging out of its own stuff.

DAVID ST. JOHN: Yes, that's what I want; I want the poem to arrive out of itself, to discover itself. The sense of chance is very important to me. I first tried to deal with it in the poem "Four O'Clock in Summer: Hope," which describes in the first section the painting by Yves Tanguy and the chance way the elements of the painting fall into place and out of place, could be one thing or another. There is a sense of randomness in the way the future passes back into the past. It was in a sense the falseness of drawing those distinctions that I wanted to talk about. The narratives of most of my poems are in fact dis-narratives; they exist by taking fragments and joining them as invisibly as possible so that the reader has the sense of a whole story controlled by the voice or voices that speak it. This seems to me a very realistic notion of how things work; just as in daily life our attention goes in and out of focus, we preserve a continuity in terms of our temporality. It parallels the way memory invades a present or the way dreams and desires, just other names for the future, invade the present. All of these invasions, these disruptions and eruptions, are very important to talk about. Unless we acknowledge them, they can be enormously threatening, even over-whelming. Unless you can maintain a narrative line in a poem that has as many scenes, sequences, and emotional temporalities as "Slow Dance" does, you'd get stopped at every point, swamped. The narrative has to create a movement strong enough—like the movement of the river itself, even accumulating not so important details—to keep the poem going.

POETRY MISCELLANY: "Until the Sea Is Dead" intermingles the Russian trader story, inserts a voice into it at the beginning, adds a sense of the real past in the story of the two, and in the last few pages produces that sense of the undecidable we were discussing earlier. The whole thing makes a complex web, a "supreme fiction," as Stevens would say.

DAVID ST. JOHN: There are two anecdotes that have to do with *The Shore* as a whole which deal specifically with what you're saying. The poems in the volume contain a lot of autobiographical detail, but they aren't in themselves autobiographical. They're fictions. After reading the manuscript, a very close friend of mine asked me how much was truly autobiographical, how much fiction, and she was shocked to find that only certain details were true. A great deal had been invented to duplicate the movement in types of situations, kinds of emotional concerns. The other anecdote is that when I received the proofs back from *The New Yorker* for "Until the Sea Is Dead" someone in their checking department had written in it that the story about the Russian trader was unknown to anyone who could be reached in Fort Ross. It seemed wonderful to me that someone just assumed the story was true.

I realized that part had been successful.

POETRY MISCELLANY: How did the poem originate?

DAVID ST. JOHN: I wanted to include a very defined story within a story. I knew when the poem began what the story was going to be in terms of the metaphor, the trader, the woman, and how I wanted it to return later on. Initially, the episode that now ends the poem was set earlier on, and then a friend who read that version said that the episode should end the poem. As soon as she said that, everything fell perfectly into place and I was able to end it in a few weeks. What I had tried to do was bring the poem to another climax before the end, but that violated the meditative movement of the last forty lines.

POETRY MISCELLANY: You've mentioned the notion of temporality several times here, especially in connection with the narrative movement of pieces. Your sense of time is one of the most sophisticated in contemporary poetry. Earlier, in *Hush*, say, in "Six / Nine / Forty-Four," there is a juxtapositioning of space and time. In "The Color of Salvation," the character's last friend lives in moments that are comprised of other times yet hold "all of life." But what I have in mind here is the more complex vision that informs *The Shore*. The past exists always as a fragment as in "Hotel Sierra"—at the beginning it is a "place without a past for us," but by the end the fragments have been so presenced by the voice that a past has been created. In fact, the two have all they can do to break away from it, to "travel in their own time," at the end. "The Shore" itself is an attempt to break away from the tyranny of the past which gets repeated in gestures like the watching of the scene below the people in the poem. "Elegy" attempts to create its own future. And even the past becomes futural in "Until the Sea Is Dead"—

> If you had been beside me, sleepless
> Or chilled by the sudden violence
> Of the winds, maybe you'd have walked
> Here with me, or come after
> To see what kept me standing in the night.

It's part of the structure of deferrals that motivates so much of your work.

DAVID ST. JOHN: I'm often amazed how rarely the problem of temporality gets talked about. It's true, I think, that the basis of my poems is elegiac exactly in the way you're saying. The poems exist in the subjunctive and conditional, the futural, and this seems to me to be the true state of experience. The passage that you refer to is where temporalizing occurs most dramatically. I wasn't sure whether I'd be able to get away with it or not, and it was the one passage I wanted most to get away with. There's a sense of being able to falsify a temporality and yet necessarily recognize the condition, the fact, of the present. There's an attempt to distort that present with the future and with whatever weight the personal past can bring.

POETRY MISCELLANY: And the distortions are owing to the traces, conscious and unconscious, the fragments in language. In "The Boathouse," you say, "I believed I'd take / What came, a life with no diary's / Hieroglyphics, / Only the crooked arc of the sun." But this pure presence soon evaporates into "habit," even when the past that informs it seems lost: "Every voice I hear / Within my own (*of the father,* / *the mother*) remains a saying so / Lost to its history."

DAVID ST. JOHN: And in that sense the temporality finds its way into the naming, the pattern of the naming. So in that way, to try to defy the temporality is to try to find other ways to name. It is to take the naming out of the frozen plane of a limited temporal orientation. In "Of the Remembered," the third section, with the epigraph from *The Wind in the Willows,* I wanted to talk about this sense of language, and in other sections of the poem the violations which that sensibility suffers.

POETRY MISCELLANY: Section VI of "Of the Remembered" begins with "now," a word it will repeat a couple more times and also subvert time in the way you've been discussing. The "now," the fragment, is seen as part of a web, layered as it were, like the whole poem. By definition, the whole thing has to be incomplete—"*blossoms in every last region of delay.*" It must continue on the way Derrida says in his essay on Shelley. But how did it come to be written?

DAVID ST. JOHN: I'd been wanting to write a section like VI, the italicized broken section, for a long time in order to talk about that "scripting" which occurs in language and which you've so accurately described. In fact, I had been wanting to write the whole poem for a long time, and it wasn't until I went to England, out of my daily literary routine, that I was able to make much headway. I had been carrying sections of it around for a couple of years. Originally the poem was in thirteen sections and had a very symmetrical design. Once I realized the fallacy of that type of unity, I could begin to see that it was necessarily partial, as you say. I settled for the present ten-part structure. The whole thing involves the play of forces, voices, against each other. I wanted the flatter, more prosaic sections to act as a kind of balance to the more heightened, lyrical sections—the italicized section, for example. I think the flatter sections are the more autobiographical ones.

When I was finished with it, finally thought I was done with it, I wasn't sure it had been worth it, though I feel much better about it now. I wanted it to be so good, my ideal of it had been made so present, that when I looked back on it, on the ways it had exhausted me, I doubted its value. I think finally that the poem is an interesting failure that doesn't cohere the way I hoped it would. But there are kinds of things I did in the poem that were, at that stage, crucial and necessary for the development of my work. At least I hope it proves to be.

Philip Booth, 1978

Lives We Keep Wanting to Know

POETRY MISCELLANY: Cézanne once remarked that his aim was to retrieve objects from behind the atmosphere impressionists drew over them. To do so, he said, he had to become part of the landscape: "The landscape thinks itself in me and I am its consciousness." One could begin to discuss your work by talking about its descriptive quality, that is, the nature of perception for you, the relation between the literal and the figural, the concrete object and the (subjective) image of the object. For example, in "How to See Deer," you seem on one level to prescribe a literal "See / What you see," and you take a similar stance in "Adding It Up." But the poems are obviously more than literal descriptions—as a poem like "Stove," where a whole narrative background is revealed as part of the meaning of the image of the stove. In all your poems, there is a way in which the world enters you as you enter it—perspectives blend. In "Let the Trees," you say, "let your two eyes / fill them, even as then / your own two eyes may / be filled," playing on the poem on "eye" and "I".

PHILIP BOOTH: In terms of the action of the poem, perception is very often visual. And also very often narrative in the sense that the "I" of the poem sees things in a certain sequence which then comes to some consequence—what the poem is about. I suppose I think with Stevens that description is revelation, but that the revelation from my point of view is the result of relationships, whether those relationships are as simple as between cataloged names or as complex as the ambivalence of objects and subjects as one perceives them. I think of myself basically as a namer; I continue to think of Adam as the first poet. I want to pare away excess detail toward a kind of essential specificity which may in itself, as the objects and subjects interrelate, come to a kind of revelation.

One way I might answer your question is to say that the poet doesn't choose his subjects or forms, that they, in effect, choose him. I think of myself as a participating observer; I don't think of the poem as a story coldly told, but I probably have a built-in New England reticence that I come by honestly. I like and admire Maine talk in its most laconic aspects. There's a great deal of selection that goes on when I write because I revise a lot. But I'm always after an illusion of spontaneity no matter how tight-lipped the poem may be.

POETRY MISCELLANY: Could you expand on your sense of the "narrative" element you have alluded to here? It seems refreshingly broad.

PHILIP BOOTH: Narrative depends on the sequence in which things are described—be they events, or images of objects, or states of being. I don't think of description for its own sake as being fundamental. I want to pare away anything that is merely ornamental—to get at an essence. That stark-ness is for me a way to let objects or emotions illuminate themselves. It is in the relationship between them that the event of the poem or the event of the metaphor occurs. They operate in time. I prefer a definition of narrative that includes Frost's "Neither Out Far Nor in Deep" as well as "Home Burial." Obviously, I do not write many straight narratives; probably "A Dream of Russia" is as straight a narrative as I have. But almost every poem implies a narrative to me in some way.

POETRY MISCELLANY: And in that poem, "A Dream of Russia," the plot unfolds in a "tight-lipped" manner, and it comes to a reticent close.

PHILIP BOOTH: I like the kind of stories I hear almost every day on the wharf here. They are almost always circular or egg-shaped, and they often come out to one word. Here is an almost literal transcription of what I heard last July fourth. A young fisherman and an older fisherman are talking on the wharf after the weekend of the fourth. The younger worker says: "What 'dya do ever the fourth—go out an' get drunk?" The older one takes a long time to answer, then he says, "Nope." Another long pause. The younger one says, "Didn't go out an' get drunk?" Another pause— "Nope." Then the younger one says, "Well, what didya do?" Another pause— "Stayed home." Then, after a while, "Suppose ya got drunk there." Then, finally, "Yup." And that's the whole story. I like its pace, its understatement.

POETRY MISCELLANY: The shortness, the tightness of your lines provides you with the basic technique to achieve this pace.

PHILIP BOOTH: I have sometimes wanted to write longer lined poems, but they generally come out in meters that don't interest me anymore. Merleau-

Ponty has an essay on the gestalt of film, the rate it reveals itself, which agrees with my concern with pace. The poem can't get started for me unless I feel it in motion. I think a poem begins with an image—I work from the simple image or the juxtaposed image—but unless I can get that moving, unless I can get some motion to it, it falters. For me, it's a matter of the rhythm of the phrase, the syncopation against that of how the line end works, and finally the pace of the whole poem.

POETRY MISCELLANY: Do you sense the rhythm before you begin?

PHILIP BOOTH: No, I don't hear it in the abstract, but unless I hear the rhythm in the words the poem is bound to go wrong. I remember when I first began to write I was subverted for months by the first line of Richard Wilbur's poem "He," which uses the title as part of the text: "He // was a brown old man with a green thumb." I feel very strongly that in the kinds of poems I write the line defines a great deal of what the rhythm comes to. I hear the caesura that comes with the break, the slash that's given when you quote, the hold you get in the double sense of both "wait" and "weight."

POETRY MISCELLANY: When you get going does the rhythm tend to steer the poem?

PHILIP BOOTH: No, I don't think it does, though I don't want the poem to lose that original impulse. When I say impulse I'm getting back to the possibility of a pulse, some undercurrent, some underbeat. But I want the poem to be able to shift gears rhythmically as, say, Charles Ives can change his measure in the process of a piece. I don't mean just a slowing down, but changing the time in which the poem operates. The poem is written in time to see what the poem outside time comes to.

POETRY MISCELLANY: This notion of catching, or to use your word from earlier, receiving the rhythm and then changing it, or receiving an image that then is juxtaposed to others rhythmically, perhaps altering its context, could be related to what we were saying earlier about perception—the relation of the perceiver to his world.

PHILIP BOOTH: Absolutely, and I think that as a poet you are necessarily changing the world. I think that we all want to modify our world so that we are not merely photographing it. The title *Available Light* plays on that possibility of photographic reproduction, which nevertheless involves selection, depth of focus, depth of field. I think that Auden is wrong, that poetry *does* make something happen. It makes the world more habitable. To make the world more habitable you build constructs in it, from it. The world is the more revealed, to go back to our original word, from the relationships that enter into the construct. So I do think of the poet as a maker as well as a namer. For me, the making function is superior to the naming function, not morally, but in the level of construction that's going on. Unless a poem does move, unless it has that motion we were talking about, it is not going to move the reader. I want the poem to move the reader off the page, not so much to extend the reader's perceptions as to "subtlize" them, as Melville says. One of the things I like about Maine speech, Maine laconics, is that you have to, living on the edge of things, between land and sea, treat things for what they are and sense the ambivalence in them without trying to build a program around it.

POETRY MISCELLANY: I wonder to what extent you think of the metaphoric "impulse" of poetry as essentially ambivalent. Metaphor involves a crossing over or transformation of the two juxtaposed terms, as you've described. It occurs as a blending in a more direct or extreme way in a poem like "The Owl," where you do exchange consciousness with the bird—and can thus proclaim at the end, "I begin to see," referring to sight in its various senses. In personal terms, any such exchange of consciousness is very difficult, if not impossible, as in "Lives," where one is always searching for "lives / we keep wanting to know." The aim seems to be to see things two ways at once.

PHILIP BOOTH: I think that the end of "Lives" that you quote comes very close to the ambivalence I'm looking for, a kind of perfectly balanced ambivalence. I don't want to say equipoise because that seems too static, but equal in tension. For instance, I understand those last lines to say both "lives we keep wanting to know us, in the sense of our situation," and "lives we keep wanting to know as we reach out to touch them." I want the space on the page, I want the line breaks, to invite the reader in that direction, to slow the reader down to that kind of ambivalence. A newer poem, which talks about people asleep in a village, ends, "people I cannot help love." Of course I mean it in the sense of the cliché, but also in the sense that I am helpless to help them love. Both these cases are fair instances of the kinds of ambivalence that I want the poems to make clear. We come back to "made" in the sense that the poem has to be "made" to make that happen. So one way to answer your question is to say that though I'm interested in the metaphoric in all its senses, probably my poems have become less metaphorical in the sense of conventional metaphor. I don't particularly aim for this, but I'm tired of, for instance, the kind of metaphor that is so programmatic and which is such a burden to the so-called deep image poets; I'm tired of what passes for surrealism and is so formulaic for the third and fourth generation "surrealist." My rule of thumb is "Honor thy subject in whatever complexity of perception is necessary." If I can make that perception clearly simple or simply clear so that both terms show equally, I'm happy, for it reflects my sense of the doubleness of vision we have. Always it's one thing in terms of another. If there is to be any revelation, it has to come from the relationship which by definition posits a doubleness.

POETRY MISCELLANY: Of course, you are distinguished from the "surrealists" by your overt consciousness and control, the distance your "I" often achieves from a scene. Still, more of your poems in *Available Light* are dream poems than in any previous book. Keeping in mind this doubleness, this controlled ambivalence you've been describing, could you talk about the role of the unconscious and the irrational in poetry? What, for example, makes a detail relevant? Freud describes the way the primary process is a wandering of meaning onto what might have been irrelevant details. Can there be an open-ended play between objects as determiners of meaning and objects as part of the world, between our inner drives to make something of the world and the world in which we find ourselves? The irrelevant detail takes on some meaning, for Freud, just by its context; could you see the poem as marking an emergence of form against the closure of the structure?

PHILIP BOOTH: This is exactly what happens in psychoanalysis; if the analysand can't free himself, if he has so much control he cannot let his Id go, not much is going to happen from the process. It seems to me that the wandering of meanings that goes on in psychoanalysis is something discernibly different from stream of consciousness. When you begin to deal with a single dream which may in itself undergo all sorts of condensation in the Freudian sense, but also may undergo editorializing, cutting in the sense of writing—when the dream undergoes these processes, it is because the writer has more of an inkling of how the latent content shows through the manifest content. I've kept some dream logs myself in difficult times, and I've found that only by waking myself up at night could I get the dream down; and then, only by getting down to the dream again in the morning could I begin to see the latent meanings coming through the manifest content. I think this process vastly extended happens in the poem. The poet is more in control because he is consciously revising; and that also means to envision the original vision. He isn't censoring the dream in the classic sense.

I used to be inclined to do what one of my students, Larry Levis, calls "tuck the poem under at the end." I'm now inclined to leave it more open-ended, more ambivalent. The horizon or edge or margin seems more terrifying now, but more wonderful. The margins themselves seem narrower, but within that narrowness I want to be able to look both ways, up and down, in and out.

POETRY MISCELLANY: Are there points in the process at which you say about an image or even a line, "I don't know why that's there but I know it should be there"?

PHILIP BOOTH: Sure, and a great deal of revision in the process of making the poem is for me to discover what those potential meanings are and to help the poem as a whole move toward some resolution of them. I don't mean a forcing of them to come to some consequence, but seeing in a sequence if they do come to some consequence. I don't want those phrases or code words to show finally in the poem, as such, but to have them integrated into the total meaning of the poem, the total flow of the poem.

POETRY MISCELLANY: Can this be seen as a tension between finished surface and original depth? I think this is playfully explored in "Strata." But take the poem "Photographer," where the poet goes to the depth of things in order to find "Shapes, pulsing" that can be captured. Perhaps the paradigmatic poem, though, is "Heart of Darkness," where the poet aims toward the "elusive" center, and the poem that would at that point "map the bottom" of things as "some sort of base / to start from"—which "might / enlarge our harlequin / mind." The perceived object is often like that—a center, a depth, a starting point from which an area of concerns can be mapped.

PHILIP BOOTH: It's a question of both where the poem starts from and where it comes to. Marlowe goes into the darkness following Kurtz. There is a part of any poet that takes him down into that part of himself where he would not otherwise go. I think that maybe the center, what you call the center, the depth, is inherently, implicitly what the poem starts from although it doesn't know it yet. Now, I want to go back to what you said about description. I do want an absolute clarity on the surface, and I want that surface of the poem not to mask the depths in any way, but to enable those depths to be revealed at a rate appropriate to the complexity of the seeing, of the looking in, of the looking down. I don't think a poem like "Photographer" satisfies me very much now, whereas "Snapshots from Kentucky" gives itself more opportunities through its screwy syntax and juxtapositions. The photographs in that poem are tied together in an imagined narrative, making a story as if the voice were telling about them as apocalyptic events.

POETRY MISCELLANY: Another way we could talk about this movement, the relation of the center to the unfolding poem, is in terms of time. In "Moment," time is a relentlessly linear progression, and moments must be perceived before they die, the focus being on the "now." And in "Graffito," "Time is nature's way / of preventing / everything / from happening all at once." But in other poems the moment is insufficient. I think the poem you referred to, "Snapshots from Kentucky," plays off what is captured on the photo against the narratives behind it, linking it to others in a very sophisticated manner. And in "Dark," the moment is defined by what is beyond it— "six months from now / to the moment," to be precise.

PHILIP BOOTH: In "Dark," various images provide for the speaker an access to the future, to the existence of a future, so that the moment in which the poem finds itself becomes part of a continuum which he can project. In "Moment," the process of the poem involves coming to an access of that moment itself. There is a more happy sense of the immediate moment than there is in "Dark," and I think that the distance between them accurately measures the movement of *Available Light*.

POETRY MISCELLANY: The structure of *Available Light* is fascinating. At the beginning, a speaker seems encased in literal or metaphoric winter scenes, looking out, and when he sometimes gets out, as in "The Winter of Separation," it is to be brought back in; at the end, the process is reversed, and the couple skating on the ice are looking at the world under the ice as if trying to get in. They are trying to get at a source, but a source that is found at the end of the book. The whole book is structured on these details or ambivalences, as you've called the relation of ins and outs. And it progresses from that enclosed world, to the freer world of the dream poems, to a continually expanding world.

PHILIP BOOTH: Would that all readers were as good as you. I don't presume to see all of those movements going on in the book, but I do intuit them to a certain degree. I put the book together in something like that direction. This does not mean that every poem bears on every other one. The epigraph from Karl Jaspers speaks to what the content is in large terms: "Being itself comes out of all origins to meet me. I myself am given to myself.... In losing the substance of my self I sense Nothingness. In being given to myself I sense the fullness...I can only maintain my integrity, can prepare, and can remember." This is the nature of the margin that the book iterates.

POETRY MISCELLANY: Jaspers talks somewhere about his aim as being a phenomenological description of the fringes of our experienced world. The margin, in terms of the ambivalence you talked about earlier, is a kind of threshold, isn't it?

PHILIP BOOTH: I think that about amounts to it—a threshold to what, one does not know except to say that it's always a threshold to death. My poems more and more sense life as a contingent process, the contingency enters into the poems not only in poems like "Panic," but also in the sense of the various contingencies we face through our consciousness of the possible ways of dying. There is the deepening watch on one's mortality in the poem called "Watch," and the valuing of that moment in the poem called "Moment," for what it is in its own rather than what it leads to. All these elements are more strong in my work now than they were.

POETRY MISCELLANY: Some of your poems have that sense that Jaspers describes of going beyond the boundary, but not in any transcendental way. In that space beyond is a strange, indescribable existence, not really free, not quite limited. "Voyages" describes it as an imaginative journey. Some of the mystery, and that's the best word I can think of, is brought out in "Islanders," where there is an island that exists beyond the boat's cruising "limits" and remains an enigma. More recently, "It Is Being" speaks in more philosophic terms about what it means to be—a going beyond the horizon to this mysterious world.

PHILIP BOOTH: There's an acceptance of being there, an acceptance of inhabiting that space—without much choice. That is, I suppose that in the process of such poems, the poem comes to discover that there is not much choice, that the movement of the poem is toward this end which is an end yet not a stasis, at least in the poem. I don't think of horizons themselves as limits because they move with us. Jaspers says that when one detaches himself from all determinant knowledge of being, one enters an indeterminate knowledge of being and can determine to be himself in that indeterminate knowledge of being. I think, if I got that said right, that this argues that poetry *does* make something happen, it makes it happen through the poet because of this ability to inhabit the realm of his imagination and being.

POETRY MISCELLANY: This making of the self, the poem, to share with the reader can be aligned with the double movement we discussed earlier, too. This is one of the curious things about "Strip," where you talk about the Mobius strip as a metaphor for this movement: "he // finds himself / turning // back into himself." Lacan and others have used the metaphor to describe the psychological action of the self, which loses itself among those wandering meanings we discussed earlier in order finally to find itself. The thing becomes both an impenetrable knot and a margin between consciousness/unconsciousness and meaning/image. How do all these things we've talked about today—margins, exchanges, crossings over, ambivalences, paces—contribute to a construction of the self?

PHILIP BOOTH: It's a fair question, but one I haven't thought through in exactly those terms before. I know that I'm not interested in constructing a mask for myself as Yeats did. What I admire rather is how Yeats in the end, and more particularly Stevens in the end, came back down to themselves from self-theorizing altitudes. I suppose that all the fictionalizing is an attempt to imagine himself into other lives so that he can work off some of his own anxieties, tensions. So I don't think of the Mobius strip as a knot, I think of it as the self and other, the two surfaces, reverse and obverse of the same life that does not add up to zero as long as one can see both sides of it. Isn't it Freud, or perhaps a commentator, who says that the ability to live with life's ambiguities is the mark of a mature spirit?

POETRY MISCELLANY: A kind of "Negative Capability"?

PHILIP BOOTH: I suppose it is, I don't know. I think of it more as an access, a way of returning to the world. Perhaps I've talked myself into a clarity about this today: the poet writes himself down into in order to write himself through, perhaps to some new realm of being which doesn't transcend the old, but gives him more access to what he has always inhabited and will inhabit. In that sense he is changed and so contributes to tipping the balance of the planet, however so slightly. Marianne Moore says in the poem "In Distrust of Merits," something like "Hate-hardened heart, how can I stop the war until I stop the war that is in myself." In that sense, I think the poet can bring himself through to be a survivor of margins, to inhabit the edges of his own existence. With his earned words he has performed a kind of act—to make the poem of the world more accessible to the reader, and so, change the day. Thoreau says somewhere that to affect the quality of the day is the highest of the arts. That seems to me to speak for any art and to be the implicit aim of any poem.

Heather McHugh, 1981

Doubling the Difference

POETRY MISCELLANY: The notion of difference seems crucial for you, at least in *A World of Difference*. It is curious, too, that "difference" has become a vogue word in contemporary thought to signify a philosophical idea that marks both self-division and self-definition—a separation from the self and from others opposed to, say, a naive transcendentalism or a desire for identity. I think, for example, of "The Impressionist," which plays off likeness and distinction, where a simple act "makes all / the difference." I think also of the emphasis on discrete moments in a poem like "When the Future Is Black," where, you say, "we make / a world of difference." Or we could refer to a poem like "Brightness," where specifics cannot be summed up. Could we begin by talking about this idea?

HEATHER MCHUGH: My first and Francophiliac instinct is to pose the question as a choice between opposites: *viva la différence*, or *plus ça change plus c'est la même chose*. But I mistrust binomial constructions; I suspect my two minds of making the world in their own image and my two hands of grasping only what can be weighed on one or on the other. So I generally find myself working to imagine opposites resolvable; and it's become an academic commonplace to suggest it—that mind is body, and vice versa. I remind myself, black and white have something in common (both are absolute). So, perhaps, yes and no are reconcilable. It's this maybeist in me that wants to vote *c'est la même chose*. This position has the ring of experience's

wisdom, profiting from improvements in perspective over time. It represents the concession stands in my nature, authorizes the "Like Me" mottoes,
tends to promote pacificist solutions (as does Ambrose Bierce's definition of
revolution: "an abrupt change in the form of misgovernment"), and fits my
relativistic bent: change your position and the object of perception changes.
Descriptions from the self are, to a notable extent, descriptions of the self.

But there are, *après tout*, men and women. This is not to be disregarded—
two wings, two gestures in the muscle of the heart; and I am not insensible
to two's beatitudes. One wants to argue *for* difference when resolution seems
too automatic an answer, metaphor a fashion, rather than a revelation; when
the lover wants to insist on his identity with the beloved; when not to
change becomes a refuge for the fearful; or when the instruments of comparison seem, as they often do, blunter than the instruments of contrast.
Sometimes doctrines of likeness appear to overlook the fine distinction,
doctrines of difference seem to confine truth to detail. We need senses of
both, or more, and doctrines of neither. I construe the writer's responsibility to be a practiced perspicacity—one, that is, not shaped by preconcep-
tion, but responsive to the patterns and surprises of terrain over a long and
moving present. I care, in my own habits of thought, not to sanctify the
habitual, not to dismiss the unfamiliar as peculiar, not to call disordered
those events and shapes in which I don't discern the rules of my own
backyard (the backyard being as big as a culture, or as small as a petri dish),
not to avoid the difficult, per se (in general, actually, to pursue it), not to
mistake comfort for love. I'd want to be mindful of at least four perhapses:
that I may be right; that the opposition may be right; that we're both right
(and there is no opposition); and that we're both wrong (there are *not* two
sides to every question, but three, or eight lying down). I take to the notion,
of some currency in the philosophy of science, that within likeness is difference and within difference another level of likeness, and so on. The
writer must keep his senses open, study without presumption, and love
both form and change (discovering each in each).

POETRY MISCELLANY: There are a number of techniques that convey the
ideas of difference. Puns, for example, make both a basic and an alternate
meaning—a word itself suggests a difference from itself. And there is your
play with everyday expressions as in the use of "good and..." in "Intensive
Care," the use of "making light" in "At a Loss," or in the use of "hold" in
"Language Lesson, 1976." Your use of these expressions allows a literal and
figurative meaning to coexist, even while we are aware of the differences.
Your use of parallelism is related to this. For example, you link "mind" and
"matter" in "Anniversary Song" by parallelisms. I think also of poems in
Dangers such as "Doing Time" or "Corps d'Esprit," where the climax in the
first and the whole texture in the second are based upon parallelisms. All
these techniques, and others, stop the notion of difference from simply

splitting your poetic apart, for they provide ways to link, to interpenetrate conflicting or supplementary ideas.

HEATHER McHUGH: It always seems remarkable to me how regularly the literal and the figurative levels of a phrase seem to oppose each other: making light of cold becomes serious when it's defiant of death ("At a Loss"); the title's "at," itself, suggests for loss a location; if "good and" means "very," then one can be "good and wicked," or "wicked good," in a manner of speaking, or Bangor, Maine.

I believe that remaining conscious of the physical senses of words, their etymological lives, we stand a better chance of remembering the world, not lapsing into automatic representations. The cliché is the word or phrase that comes to mind without its body; it's the easiest thing to say and forget to see, or say you see and forget actually to look at. I mean to study the cliché in order, working itself against itself, to remember: no insight and no justice come of ease. It is hard work to pay attention, but it is the writer's work.

And it's not just cute to note, even as I say so, that I'm using a language in which attention is treated as if it were cash, account payable. It is not incidental to find in such peculiarities the signature dispositions of a language and culture, to observe, for example, that ours finds its moral vocabulary in capital. A capital idea is a good one; merchandise is goods; credit is due the virtuous. It's no mean happenstance to find constraint in the language of banks—it's checks and stocks and bonds. At the ceremonies of naming, we unwittingly identify ourselves. It's to be witting one wants, not witty: this is not a matter merely of linguistic ornament, it's political. I mean to question the language I am given, and am given to.

POETRY MISCELLANY: There's an interesting way in which language and reality become metaphors for each other, or at least the play of language seems to be a metaphor for the play of differences in reality. In a poem like "Leaving" from *Dangers* the link between language and reality seems very close. "For My Fathers" and "Preferences" also come to mind in this context. Your poems, in many ways, remind me of how much the world we live in is a linguistic one, not just its materials, but our values and ideas about it.

HEATHER McHUGH: Writers have always referred to their work, but lately it's become fashionable to divest the piece of all other subjects. This amounts to a refusal of the old contract (what the reader used to love, forgetting he was reading at all; he entered a world, as if without a word).

Of course (the point's become a new platitude) language is itself metaphor. We cannot disregard, without injury to language, either its vehicle or tenor. They serve as mutual access. And I believe the world less rich to the extent that it denies language, just as I consider language less rich to the extent that it denies the world. That's why it seems so unwise to imagine that language is at best its own subject, to think the world at best its own object, unapprehensible by thought. Though we shine, reflecting on a Whorfian hypothesis (language is the shaper of our experience of the world, different languages make people see differently), still the world is not ours simply because we grasp it; and in a poem like "Field" I argue against the possessive intellect's staking out territory in order to call it known, or being more at home in the light of reference than in the light of day. Let us love the eye not because it makes the world (or makes the world small enough to fit it), but because it holds the world in regard. As a reader I am excited by that within a poem that cannot contain itself, much less anything else; that moment so greatened by experience that it breaks the bounds of propriety and discovers dictions no prediction would have authorized.

This is perhaps the time to admit how much I resist authorization itself. Isms, izations, ifications—what deaden a root with weight—I tend to mistrust, and the presumption that turns author to authority, potent to potentate. I mistrust the languages of rampant suffixing that crop up so inevitably in our government and commerce. In a culture so heavily invested in these domains, one is tempted to become preoccupied with the object of the coin itself, freeing it of representation, emptying it of its exhausted meaning, evoking its worn faces, its edge of fine lines, its physical feel (hot or cold, depending on the contiguous bodies of air or flesh), avoiding the corruption of its nature as a sign. But I prefer, I guess, not to be frozen in focus on the coldness of the cash. I mean, I miss too much the food and fire and wool it was meant to direct us toward. (I'm perhaps inordinately fond of the fact that the Bank of England heats its mint, in part, by burning currency.) If money is its own meaning, then you can believe all value to be symbolic, create value by making more signs of it, and wind up removing from the representative any direct relation to the represented. This is inflation, and it is so with language. I see our writers tempted to disinterest: the coin of language becomes divested of reference's standard, a curiosity; and the regard emptied of all sense of significance is, in the process of description, its own subject. Don't we want to remember how money was, once, the very wood we built a house with, or the leather and thread of shoes, the red pig, or the seed and spade? If we can't reach those things with our devalued language any more, if our fondest wisdom is that writing refers to writing, then we've lost our heart of power. And if this is true let's have a change of heart, rediscover language's power, not fix our affections (in surreal or thingian freezes) on its present and dispirited objects.

POETRY MISCELLANY: But there is a different aspect to language, too. Language always tries to capture the evasive, as in the poem "Syllables." Perhaps even more central in this respect is "Breath." Here words seem insufficient, only a reminder of "our history of longing." Language in this sense becomes fluid, a kind of metalanguage; "I want to call / you by a name that will not stay on the page," the speaker says in "A Nova Genesis." In fact, the whole notion of absence seems central to your work—I think of a poem like "It is 70° in Late November. Opening a window you nearly know."

HEATHER MCHUGH: Absence is an invention, like the self, of language. Numbers lead to zero, and a finity must be surrounded with infinitude. These concerns are no less powerful for being products of the imagination (popularly, the province of poetry)—perhaps more powerful because they can occupy immediately the stations of myth. The adolescent is almost fatally attracted to trains of thought having these destinations. I, myself, wanted the ultimate because the proximate was available to me. Perversely, I didn't study the wealth at hand because I thought it, in its profligacy, cheap. Now I hope to be, to say the least, humbler. I'm not *dying* to know more: I've just begun to study living. What is present seems inexhaustibly instructive to me now, and where once I wanted to make a big noise at once about nothing (and myself, my favorite subjects, perhaps the same subject), now I'd make (after long and peaceable study) a small noise about something.

The predication of absence, in such poetic vogue today, is a form of self-reference. But the self is greatened not by being lavished with attention, but by lavishing; not by focusing on itself, but by its own forgetting, in favor of the others it must not presume to be identical with it. Indeed, a love in which others (allowed by even the possessive imagination to be truly different from us) are held dear not tight, seems to me now our most difficult (which is to say our greatest) work.

POETRY MISCELLANY: The notions of difference and of the evasiveness of things also brings up what you call "doublings," a word that arises, in various of its forms, throughout your work. "The world / of doubles loves itself," you say in "Anniversary Song." And this also brings up the notion of the Other. In "Pupil" it is developed in relation to language; the speaker is like an "already translated" language, one whose "mouth doubletalks" in relation to the other person. The two minds in "His Lover Addresses So-crates," and the double in "Recip—" are also good examples. Perhaps, as "Blue Streak" seems to suggest, a consciousness of the Other is a ploy against the "I I I I I" of solopsism. In "Inside," the Other is an inner self, a further complication, a more psychological view. In "New Glasses," the relation between the you, the "second person," and the mother adds a kind of genealogical dimension. The whole notion is a very rich and complex one for you.

HEATHER MCHUGH: The double *is* the self and a function of language (itself a system of representations); the double is a favorite in contemporary poetry because the self still is (in disguise).

As soon as we learn to say "I" we represent ourselves, step out of our own presence. The self created the first person to keep it company. Adam is a form of self made by God; Eve is a form of self made *of* Adam, she's the second person. The mother holds the baby to the mirror saying, "That's you." So to the baby, you is I. This is a voice familiar in contemporary American poetry—using the you that really means I, the second person who is really a figure of the first, the mirror you see what you love in, a kind a complement, something fitting (perhaps as men and women fit, to recover the unity creation broke down into differences).

But it seems to me too easy, today, to stop at that wisdom. Self-love is our specialty: Freud and Einstein, locating the truth of an event in our positions relative to it, are the spokesmen of our age and sensibility, and like all heroes they are subject to diminishment by their admirers. The word "self" figures in a huge genre of best sellers. We are proprietors and mongers of the self, and the emphasis neglects what's so much harder for us: to value the Other without possessing it (since in possession we return to self-love). This is our work now, which writers perform partly through full consciousness of the errors language may have led us into, when it made property out of the self (something of nothing), and owe from own. And someday, maybe, we can come back to ourselves as if we had not bought them.

POETRY MISCELLANY: I'd like us to talk a little about time. In "Retired Schoolteacher," memory becomes a means of reimagining, a creative memory that allows the character to get at "the first touch of the starfish." What is the relation, for you, between memory and imagination?

HEATHER MCHUGH: As for time, it's hard for me to distinguish it from space. The answer to enumerators (in "When the Future Is Black") is the sky's answer (which once we were smart enough to make the map's answer): the space of minutes, seconds, what light moves in.

What can I remember of my life before time? Before I was taught that there were two of each, eleven and eleven, one and one, moments experienced as very different but clocked and named the same? Before I graduated to the time of lines, with past, present, and future for us to walk from, in, and to, respectively (our backs to history)? How great to learn there are other cultures which place the past ahead of us, metaphorically, because it's seen! And then there were the compositional distinctions: real vs. experiential time, with that latent bias—regular is real, variable imagined. (How this boggled me, who had thought imagination the source of everything permanent and eternal and unchanging, and who felt experience WAS real, leading us to what we couldn't, after all, imagine.)

We love our fortune tellers more passionately than our historians. And yet memory is imagined, and the record of presence itself (which is the work of attention I set for seers) is selective. So, yes, there's something of a return (to the medulla?) in the end of "Retired Schoolteacher," as I imagine relinquishing our special brightnesses, visual and cerebral, as I imagine what it is (was, will be) being born into another nature.

POETRY MISCELLANY: Your ultimate allegiance, especially in the light of the notion of difference, seems to be with the present. In "Refusal to Be Two-Timed," the doubleness of time refers to being beyond the now; as the speaker says at the end:

> there is nothing, past or future, left
> implicit here. I have unfolded
> its paper fist, I accept
> the present.

The contrast between a large pattern of time and the impulsive, intuitive moment is nicely drawn in "Reprise," which describes the singing of a bird who sounds "as if there were no knowledge / in design."

HEATHER McHUGH: As a matter of fact, I'd like to come to the world with no designs on it. At first (preposterously), my motives in writing were, I think, to confer upon the world the dignity of my own constructions, a kind of violence I did the world as if to forestall a violence being done to me. But the mark of the world is upon us, we were done the violence at birth, and if we remain open to the greater movements of nature (our nature, its nature, nature without pronoun) we may sense more about design than we could ever preconceive. The past and future seem to me to be records of present regrets and wishes, respectively (Bierce defines the future as "that period of time in which our affairs prosper, our friends are true, and our happiness assured"), and were I to believe in their contemporary architecture the past and future would converge on each other, leaving us no moment to be in, so I occupy a kind of undifferentiated time-space, a long moment, life of moment, in which what has been or is or will be are always extant, if not always manifest. If I live in the present, then it's one without ends.

POETRY MISCELLANY: Let's talk a little about perception and "truth." Poems like "Spectacles" and "Orbit" question the nature of perception, the first by drawing an analogy between a bike and a pair of glasses, for instance. "Letter" takes this questioning into the nature of "truth"— "The single truth is simply / false; the truth is never more / than an example." This is crucial for poetry, it seems, which has to remain open, exploratory. In "Futures," you talk about poetry as a dealing in the futures market, as a delight in the undecidable:

> Take a poem, for example. It will trade
> in hunger for a restless
> literate disease, stake out
>
> the fence around

what wasn't and what isn't, sink
your savings into fictions like tomorrow....

HEATHER MCHUGH: I suffer myopia's fascination with the lens. I love glass, it's such a slow liquid, gravity thickening our eye for the earth. I love that a line breaks it. I love that it focuses heat as if it were sight, until leaves ignite under its attentions. I love its reminder that we're attracted to the image of ourselves at the expense of the sight of others—that to make a seeing-glass into a looking-glass you have to black the other side. The cover photo for *A World of Difference* caught my concerns: in one lens of the poet's glasses is the reflection of the seen, in the other, the eye. Both natures work here in one moment, in one light: the seer and the seen are not, then, so different, but the difference is crucial. We may select our experiences of the world and frame them and then, even, call the world small, but we don't create the world itself. It is only with humility (the eye entirely taken with the world) that it can be caught—not as a man or animal is caught, but as a glimpse is: not (even beautifully) to be had and held, but (even plainly) to be seen.

Robert Pack, 1974, 1981

Questions of Will

POETRY MISCELLANY: A number of your poems contain references to the idea of beginning. In one poem, for example, you say that beginning "is a trick of gathering oneself / into what one believes / and stepping forth." Does the concept function for you as a metaphor for other sorts of beginnings?

ROBERT PACK: I think the value of considering any point in time as a beginning is that it adds a focused intensity to that moment. It is necessary not only to begin, but to be aware of the beginning as such. Whenever you begin a poem, you attempt a partial redefinition of yourself; there is something about yourself or about your sense of the world that you want to encircle in the act of making the poem. The idea of beginning, then, is very closely related to the idea of willing yourself into an intensified consciousness. The important concept is *will*—willing oneself to will, choosing oneself to choose. These are two aspects of the freedom that you win as you write a poem; you make a choice and will that choice into being. Here again the analogy with one's life is helpful; the feeling that you can control words within a poetic form strengthens the feeling, the belief, that you can choose to be the kind of person you want to be, given the history of your own life which imposes limits.

POETRY MISCELLANY: In "A Spin Around the House," you exclaim: "Everything spins / in its chosen space—I will it so." There's a way in which the suppositions that use words like *should, must, if, would*, become, by the end of a poem, propositions if not certainties. Questions become expressions of freedom; qualifications mark not doubt but a radiating out from a center. In short, the poems seem to will a certainty at the very threshold of doubt. The result is a world always beginning, always emerging. Yours is a poetics, I think, of thresholds and transformations.

ROBERT PACK: Yes, I like thinking of a beginning as a threshold. Standing in a doorway, one is aware of where one has been and where one is going. We are always arriving or departing, becoming ourselves and losing ourselves at the same time. The poet starts again to live and starts again to die in the intensified consciousness of poetic form. The poem's willed certainty, its fixedness, is a constant reminder that everything is being transformed and is passing away.

POETRY MISCELLANY: One of the ways you seem to sustain the movement from supposition to affirmation is by the repetition of certain key images— the sun, vistas or horizons, thresholds, trees—and certain key scenes, especially of the family. They give a sort of primal power to the poems.

ROBERT PACK: Yes, I feel the need to return to basic forms and images, and the primary image, as fact and as metaphor, is the sun. Also, if the will has to make choices by which it defines itself, it has to hold to some idea of what is good. I like to return to that simple word "good" as much as I like to return to the image of the sun.

I think the will to affirm is related to the need that the poet has to be convincing in his portrait of what is satisfying in life, and I think that satisfaction must be rooted in the most basic experiences: the experience of living in a world of light and dark, of natural forms, things that grow and move, the continuity between generations, the love between man and woman, parent and child. If the basic goodness of these things cannot be realized in a poem, then the poet lacks a complete vision and indulges himself in despair.

I like to pause in a very ordinary moment, one that is easy to miss because it doesn't seem at first significant, and then dwell upon it. It is necessary to shock oneself as well as the reader into discovering the importance of such moments. The difficulty of writing a celebratory poem is that it must challenge the reader into realizing his own capacity to affirm in the face of difficulty. It invites choice and responsibility.

The concept of the poem as a "cure" is a cherished one for me. I like to think of myself as part of the tradition of curative writing. Celebration is a cure because it demonstrates the ability still to enjoy. Celebration is the ritualizing and enacting of the inner capacity to enjoy, affirm; it is a social act simply because the poem is written to be read and shared. I believe the primary function of the lyric poet is to celebrate, to find a voice of sensuous praise.

POETRY MISCELLANY: One of the most powerful of those curative moments occurs in "The Kiss," where the simple context, your son's flying the kite, becomes suddenly transformed when you, in a way, replace the vampirelike kite, embrace, and kiss him. How are such moments, such dramatic transformations generated in your poems? For certainly they are plentiful, and they help account for the complex and ironic tone that so defines your work.

ROBERT PACK: I hope that the irony in my poem, "The Kiss," moves from the bitter recognition that destructiveness accompanies love to the playful acceptance of that recognition. Biting and kissing or strangling and hugging may be very close emotionally, and destructive desires may be just beneath the surface of affectionate behavior, but the awareness of human ambivalence need not be morbid or grim. Provided that you consider yourself capable and free to choose not to destroy, even though you feel destructive urges, awareness of your mixed motivation may be detached and comic. Likewise, to the extent that poetic form is an act of will, of chosen and controlled thought, it can be both playful and comic even when the poem appears to be most grave and serious. I wanted my poem to describe the most succulent kiss a father ever gave his son by means of sucking and slurping syllables, so I had to acknowledge the vampire aspect of myself. The serious scariness of a father's competitive and aggressive feelings for his young son should be seen by the reader as merging with and being transformed by the father's love and the father's need for the physical expression of that love. In sum, I'd want to say that the irony of my poem is comic irony or, to take the idea further, that all poetic form has either overt or hidden laughter in it.

POETRY MISCELLANY: In "Maxims in Limbo," you write: "For a poet, to name / an object carefully, is to submit to its power." You follow this with: "Wind ruffles and erases / the kingfisher's image of the lake. / Yet having said so, I see / it is still there." These two maxims "encircle," to use another favorite image of yours, the poetic territory you explore. On the one hand, the poet "names" the world around him, participates, like Adam, in its creation; but on the other hand, he submits to the power that the given world has always possessed: he marks absence and change and substitutes for that absence his own vision, his own presence. I think a poem like "October Prayer" with its interplay of world and imagination is a good example of this double process, of the doubleness in naming.

ROBERT PACK: All I can add to your lucid description of what you aptly call the "doubleness" of the process of naming is that even in submitting to the power of nature's necessities, the poet still is free to choose or create the attitude he takes toward those necessities of change and death. As an act of naming, the poem is the battleground of the will because in the making of the poem the poet exercises his essential freedom to choose how he will regard even his own inescapable anger or frustration or defeat. For every feeling that one has in love or combat that is determined by one's psychology and the immediacy of the event, there is also the aftermath of felt thought that regards the past event and may reconstruct it for the purposes of mythic or fictional truth within the chosen boundary of poetic form. You are right, in "October Prayer" the immediate physical moment of perceiving the fruit trees in an early autumn frost cannot remain separated from the memory of that moment and the further recreation of that moment, which is a fabrication from that memory. The moment, the memory, and the naming, the *recreation*—after all, that's what a poem is in both senses of the word: a playful act of creating again what already is there.

POETRY MISCELLANY: In "The Hearth," you worry at one point that "Something is changing" only to realize that in keeping watch, in naming and observing, you can hear the repetitions of a crow's call, and drawing from the idea that repetition suggests permanence, can then affirm a more hopeful vision where "Nothing has changed." The notion of repetition is an important one for the contexts we have been discussing, and it is also an essential element in form. In a way, all forms are ways of keeping watch, of ordering worlds, or at least of letting the music of words order worlds.

I think, for example, of "A Cord of Wood"—which I want to read as *a chord of would* to emphasize the musical way the repetitions and suppositions of the couple compose each other. Perhaps a more direct example would be "Looking at a Mountain Range While Listening to a Mozart Concerto." Here, vision, music, and the repetitions and modulations of form continually refresh the man's life. Form becomes, through the modulations of repetition, a way of creating what is to be celebrated.

ROBERT PACK: Here we return to the idea of will and choice. Once one has defined what is good beyond the poem, the goodness has been extended by virtue of there being another thing in the world, the past of the poem. A choice has come into being and is now a part of nature. What we are talking about, then, is the poet's energy creating and enjoying new energy. A poem without a felt form has greater difficulty in giving the reader a feeling of energy. To be experienced as such, energy needs something to contend against; energy is revealed in the palpable sense of options, of choices, such as when one chooses to repeat a sound or rhyme, or when to change or vary a rhythm. Energy is primarily rhythm, the feeling of rhythms generating new rhythms. In a poem with form, the reader feels what energy can overcome. The delight in poetic energy is the poet's way of reminding us that we are alive.

POETRY MISCELLANY: To what extent does music offer you a structural model?

ROBERT PACK: I think of every poem as a musical composition, a verbal arrangement of sounds and images. All forms of repetition and variation are inevitably part of the richness of the poem. There is no aspect of the art that interests me more than this. For me, it is in perfect harmony with the idea of celebration. The complete poem celebrates its own ability to celebrate. The poem may celebrate what is outside itself and celebrate its own ability to celebrate those things. An important model for many of my poems is Bach's fugal compositions, where the technique of return and variation produces a sense of having a given world to begin with, out of which many variant worlds are born. Musically speaking, to my mind, this produces a feeling of bounty, of plenitude.

POETRY MISCELLANY: Repetition, then, is associated also with the problem of ending, how to change the end into a beginning?

ROBERT PACK: The end that the poem modulates toward must be a new beginning, a new sense of discovery through the formal patterns established by the will. A new choice must then be made. There is nothing artificial about this. Each thing in nature has its own shape; a poem too must have a recognizable shape if it is to be itself. It is as much a musical shape as it is a statement which says what the poet needs to say to be what he wants to be. It is his way, within his limits, of being more freely alive.

POETRY MISCELLANY: Some of the monologues treat form ironically. In them, often repetition becomes a compulsion. A good example is "Coincidence," spoken by a potential killer or "Trillium," spoken by a father who may be having an incestuous relationship with his daughter. And some of the poems in *Waking to My Name* such as the sestina, "The Thrasher in the Willow by the Lake," spoken by another killer, are good examples. This ironic use of form has allowed you to vary the voices in the poems. I wonder what the relation is between form and voice, and what directions these new monologues might be taking you?

ROBERT PACK: Repetition in poetry may have a dramatic as well as a musical effect in that it suggests the powerful wish to return in memory to moments of intense happiness or the compulsion, as you say, to return to the fears and failures that never have been resolved. The killer may need to return to the scene of his crime or to repeat it, just as the lover returns to the home of the one he loves, or the poet returns to an image or a line in a refrain.

In the cycle of monologues I am now completing, all of my speakers are obsessed—some painfully, some happily. Many are obsessed with death and the need to accept death in a positive and life-affirming way, and many are obsessed with the need for greater intimacy in love. Intimacy, loss, and the need for celebration are the themes that obsessively reappear throughout the cycle of poems. All of the poems are written in blank verse because I, too—as so many before me—find that the obstacle of meter and of a given line length brings forth energetic verbal choices and still allows for a naturalness of diction.

All my characters speak out of apprehension, regret, or exultation, and the heightened rhythms of their language are, I hope, expressive of their passions. Not one of these characters speaks directly for me; all of them rationalize and at least partially deceive themselves, and yet when taken together, husbands and wives, sons and daughters, perhaps they form a composite image of my life and history. I don't mean my literal history, but the history of my imagination, the lives I might have lived being who I am. This emphasis is new for me, finding the expression for who I am in imagined characters other than myself.

Maxine Kumin, 1975

Settling in Another Field

POETRY MISCELLANY: The world portrayed by your new book seems more populated, its imagery more diverse, used more to counterpoint ironically some of the statements the poems make. Are you conscious of such a shift?

MAXINE KUMIN: Not really. I'm conscious that there is a continuing shift in voice, but it seems to me that it arises directly from the earlier book, that what had begun in *Up Country* simply gets continued in *House, Bridge, Fountain, Gate.* My intention is always the same, to be specific, clear about the naming quality of things. The focus, though, is continually narrowing. The more narrowed the focus becomes, then perhaps the more sharpened and ironic the language becomes. I think any shift is toward being more natural so that everything I write comes out of the world I am close to, out of the manure pile, out of the garden. That's the texture of the world I'm living in.

POETRY MISCELLANY: Your sequence, "The Kentucky Poems," presents a kind of self-definition, a focusing of yourself in a particular world.

MAXINE KUMIN: One reviewer, though she liked *House, Bridge, Fountain, Gate* overall, thought that this section was meretricious, that it focused on old themes, my sense of estrangement as a Jew. I was taken back by the comment because I thought she totally missed the point of the poems. She was saying that the subject was something I wrote less well about than the natural world, perhaps more so than the other sections. What I like about them is the way they deal with isolation by reason of place. The poet is placed in an alien place and confronts a whole new landscape. It's a way of testing the poet's own verities.

POETRY MISCELLANY: Is it a question, then, of relocating, say, the past in the present to prove and reprove a vision? In "The Knot," you have the lines, "in Danville, Kentucky, my ghosts / come along, they relocate as easily as livestock / settling in another field."

MAXINE KUMIN: Well, you have to come to terms with yourself if you're shut off that way. If an artist doesn't separate himself or herself from the mainstream no work will get done. That's why it was good to be plunked down in a totally different place. You know, that was exotic for me as if I had gone to—you know Thoreau's poem, "One need not go half way around the world to count the cats in Zanzibar, extra-vagrant, it depends on how one is yarded—" Well, I was yarded in Kentucky, and that was just as extra-vagrant for me as Zanzibar would have been. It was really exotic to be in the Baptist Bible belt; I loved it.

I think my poetry has always been rooted wherever I've been in time, in attitude, or in physical location. The new poems are very much a part of what is going on with me at this time in my life—living very intimately with the land and with the animals. I can continually be surprised and write about what surprises me. Like the chanterelles I showed you earlier. When we go riding, as I did earlier, I'm always delighted to find them, to stop and pick them.

POETRY MISCELLANY: Most of your books are built around sequences of poems that revolve around, explore, a location or a time.

MAXINE KUMIN: As you know, poems don't occur in the order in which the reader meets them. But as you acquire a sufficient body of poems and begin to think in terms of a book, then you're faced with the problem of how to structure it. As I was writing "The Kentucky Poems" I began to see that I was going to have a group. "The Knot," which I consider an important poem, was the poem that I wrote first.

POETRY MISCELLANY: That poem places two locations in contrast to each other.

MAXINE KUMIN: It's very autobiographical, very direct, very honest. Having to let go, having to undo these knots that tie us to family, location, or even a mental state is a very serious problem. I had just come back from Europe, from seeing my daughter. I felt very isolated and alien at first in this little town in Kentucky, just as I felt some alienation in the country of Belgium. I could understand what they were saying in both places, but the nuances of the language are so evasive.

POETRY MISCELLANY: There's also a process of taking hold. In "The Deaths of Uncles" is the description of a home movie where "the reel stutters and balks before it takes hold." I think this book confronts that process of stuttering and then consolidating more than earlier books.

MAXINE KUMIN: This book takes a lot more risks. For one thing, I seem to be willing to deal with more material, much of it heavily fictionalized. I'm playing around an awful lot more with narrative, which I love doing. I know that narrative is supposed to be dead in poetry. We are all supposed to be writing little transcendental lyrics about emotional states, but I so much enjoy the whole storytelling process. I like to read other stories. Bill Meredith's *Hazard, The Painter* is written with deft, ironic control. It is a voice very different from mine, but one that I find quite enchanting. I like the idea of the story coming back into poetry, and I wish I had a lot more stories to tell.

POETRY MISCELLANY: You often use the narrative and lyric modes to qualify each other, in the way you use locations, as in "For My Son on the Highways of His Mind," or patches of narrative to tie a lyric together, as in "Bedtime Story."

MAXINE KUMIN: The line in "Bedtime Story" is one that I like very much, tetrameters and trimeters basically. When I was writing the poem for my son I wanted to write it in that tight lyric line, which I consider Audenesque. But I couldn't do it. The best I could do was to produce a lyric refrain and then fit the narrative roughly into iambic pentameter.

POETRY MISCELLANY: There's quite a lot of interweaving of rhymed and unrhymed sections in your poems. Rhyme is very important to you, isn't it?

MAXINE KUMIN: Especially coming down to the end before the door is closed, I like to do that. I've been working on a poem for weeks which is just a sort of narrative country diary. I want to call it "A Mortal Day of No Surprises." It begins, "This morning a frog in the bathtub." The bathtub is one in a pasture. That's an almost daily occurrence around here, one small miracle in the mortal day of no surprises. I find that as I'm coming down to the end of the poem where I face, as I seem to face more frequently in my poems, the prospect of my own death, the lines are getting shorter, the rhymes are getting tighter, and there is much more tension in the poem.

POETRY MISCELLANY: There are a couple of ways of facing death, at least in the poems, aren't there? "That a man may be free of his ghosts / he must return to them like a garden."

MAXINE KUMIN: You know, you tend to get more deathy as you get older. You really can't help it, it's there. Not that I mean to become obsessional, but there's a sense of my own mortality that I'm more aware of. For example, in "Pairing the Geese"—that "slippage of my days" sort of thing. And yet it would be dreadful if we were immortal—nothing would have any meaning. There would be no poetry because poetry is so intensely elegiac in its nature. Without a foreboding sense of loss the poet would have nothing to celebrate, would not be moved to song.

POETRY MISCELLANY: I suppose that attitude is reflected in the phrase, "grand comedy of anguish"?

MAXINE KUMIN: Yes, Amanda's eyes are described as "rage red with toy worlds inside." I think of the twin masks of comedy and tragedy, the shape of the mouth in the tragic mask being so grotesque as to be comic. If you look at the face of a child about to burst into tears, it is comic at the same time it is anguished.

POETRY MISCELLANY: We were talking about rhyme. Does it provide a way of holding these two aspects together? Do certain kinds of poems demand it?

MAXINE KUMIN: If I had to give up rhyme, I'd have to give up being a poet. I have many students who say to me that rhyme is insincere, but for me it is not a question of sincerity. The rhymes are all there, all packed inside my head. It's a question of letting them all out a little at a time. Rhyme provides so much of an underbeat to the language of the poem, so much a measurement to the tension of the poem that I would be very hard put to write a deeply felt poem without it. I think that the tougher the subject matter, the more likely I am to use all sorts of metrical devices.

POETRY MISCELLANY: How important are tricks and games in composition? Do you play many games?

MAXINE KUMIN: Not as much as I used to. Probably the toughest poem I ever wrote was the elegy for my father "The Pawnbroker." When I wrote that I not only picked out an impossible to fulfill stanzaic pattern, but I began by writing it in syllabics, because I could hardly dare approach the subject otherwise. Then when it was done I went back and loosened it up, roughed up the syllabics so they don't show anymore.

POETRY MISCELLANY: The pattern, then, came first?

MAXINE KUMIN: Yes, you know, putting down the forms so you can pour the concrete and then taking away the forms when it hardens.

POETRY MISCELLANY: In "Living Alone with Jesus," you have the lines, "form can be seen as / an extension of content."

MAXINE KUMIN: I'm glad you picked up on that. I love that poem. It's a humorous poem which is, however, deeply felt. That whole business about having Jesus in a funny little backroom apartment is quite sincere because Jesus is the comforter of the lonely, the lost, the isolated. The line about form has an amusing origin. Diane Wakoski and I had met at Bread Loaf the summer before and I had just finished reading an essay of hers on how form can be seen as an extension of content. The phrase, which Creeley actually originated, rolled so deliciously over my tongue—with the business of the butcher shop and churches, all form and no content—the essay came at a very fortuitous moment.

POETRY MISCELLANY: Do you find yourself often saving scraps and inserting fragments like that?

MAXINE KUMIN: Yes, I write on scraps. I pull off the road to write things down. I do a lot of commuting back and forth to Boston, an hour and a half without a stop light along the highway. It's a good place to get some serious thinking done, and I generally have my manuscript on the front seat. I'll often stop to write things down. That's a nice thing about a poem, it's portable. If you're tinkering, trying to move lines around and get them right, a good place to do that is on a long distance drive.

POETRY MISCELLANY: You do a lot of revising?

MAXINE KUMIN: A poem is not a watercolor, you don't just get one shot at it. We all know that a watercolor either works or not in the first twenty minutes or you tear it up and start another one. But a poem does not, unless you're in the habit of tearing up your worksheets, and poets are too egotistical for that. You don't lose anything by trying again and again. I am an earnest adherent to the whole notion of revising, of tightening. I also believe in turning a poem face down and not looking at it for a week. I often have to do that to get any perspective at all for I still habitually fall in love with bad, rhetorical passages and it's hard to give them up.

POETRY MISCELLANY: These techniques, like using rhyme in tougher poems, or the whole notion of the effort in revising, the sense of difficulty define the world you live in and which the poems are a part of, don't they? I mean, even this area, Joppa Road, poetry is inherent in the "location" itself.

MAXINE KUMIN: Yes, this area is called the Joppa district because the early settlers who came here were from the land around Amesbury and Newburyport along the coast. They had named a flat there Joppa in recognition of the biblical Joppa, and when they moved inland they brought the name as a tribute to their origins. The land along the river bottom, which in those days I presume was much more open, was called the Joppa district, and so later when the road went through it was called Joppa Road. Now, of course, the land is very much forested because it's been grazed and whenever land is grazed, and then not used, it comes back up as trees. So what was once lovely meadow is the heavy growth that you see.

POETRY MISCELLANY: One of the "Joppa Diary" poems, "July 5," deals with that sense of decay inherent in the pastoral world, that elegiac sense of the struggle of living, as you describe the graveyard.

MAXINE KUMIN: In every one of those graveyard inscriptions there is a marvelous sense of faith, the sense that Christ is standing waiting to help the infant or the mother who died in childbirth or the man the tree fell on. These people worked so damned hard—fourteen, sixteen, eighteen hours out of twenty-four. It fascinates me to contemplate that, even with just the little brush I've had with it here, the physical labor involved in this kind of life. I have an increasing respect for the human body, its capabilities as well as its limitations, and an increasing respect for the poor dumb beast who dragged the wagon and pulled the plow. The patience of animals and the enduring humility of the human are things that we today are growing too far from. I think one of the great tragedies of our society is that so many people grow up on asphalt and never get their hands into manure piles and into gardens. My whole life is predicated on shit. I put close to a ton of horse manure on my garden in October, had plowed it in in April, and planted in May. I'm still enough of a city person, though, to be startled by the fact that you plant a squash seed and squash comes, you plant a beet seed and beets come. Now, it's a miracle to me that out of these little packets come incredible vegetables. It's like the unpacking of new leaves in "May 10th." I feel a sense of wonder and I only hope it lasts. That was the wonderment about the chanterelles I mentioned earlier. This is the season for them, and how lucky we are to have them. And it's more rewarding to gather where you didn't sow—wild mushrooms, vegetables, and berries are a great pleasure.

POETRY MISCELLANY: It seems that part of the way you come closer to this world around you is by being able gracefully to let go of parts of yourself, what you have taken to be parts of yourself. What I mean can be seen in "To Swim, To Believe," where Peter sinks because he thinks too much, whereas the secret, you say in that poem, is in "relenting the partnership." And the last poem in the book is a prayer to Amanda, "small thinker," hoping that the letting go will be natural.

MAXINE KUMIN: Yes, of course, there has to be some suspension of thought and belief to be able to walk on water. That would be my own prayer for death—I am without faith, but I often find myself praying. Mostly it is a supplication that things might persist. As now, we are forced with having to put away a dog. I hope we could do it in some graceful way. He's deaf and doesn't hear the horses, and I'm in terror that he'll be stepped on, have his backbone crushed. Then I'd have to put him away myself with a shotgun. It's pitiful. It's not a very dignified ending for a dog that had great dignity.

Stanley Kunitz, 1978

Living the Layers of Time

POETRY MISCELLANY: In her book, *Wordsworth: Language as Counter-Spirit*, Margaret Ferguson talks about the inherent link between discourse and themes in Wordsworth's arrangement of his poems. She calls the progress of his classification a "metaphoric journey through life." Could you comment on the relation of theme and language in the light of your own development from more traditional to more functional or intuitive ones?

STANLEY KUNITZ: My method of working is such that I don't predetermine the form. The form is what emerges in the actual writing, or—more accurately—"saying," since my writing develops out of a process of incantation. I am very fond of a dramatic structure, which isn't always evident on the surface, an image or episode that carries the action of the poem and gives it momentum. Once I launch into that action it more or less moves by itself because it has an end in view, an end that I can't see but which the poem does. There is another kind of poem to which I was particularly devoted in my younger days. It is a dialectical poem, in which I explore the contradictions of the self, the argument within. The poem unfolds in terms of that argument, which then proceeds to some sort of truce at the end. My meditative poems are an outgrowth of that dialectical approach.

POETRY MISCELLANY: The poems often have aphoristic endings, whether it's an aphoristic line like "The souls of numbers kiss the perfect stars" or an aphoristic event like the end of "Journal for My Daughter." The aphoristic ending sends the reader off into richly connotative regions, and the endings seem to be even more open in the late poems.

STANLEY KUNITZ: Perhaps I'm less positive about the meanings of things than when I was younger. I like the enigma of an ending that is both a door and a window. It's a release of tension to arrive at a point of clearing where one is able to affirm something, even if that affirmation contains a principle of negation within it.

POETRY MISCELLANY: That moment is sometimes like a meeting place of eternity and time, permanence and change, being and becoming. This concept seems very crucial for you. In "Change," for example, you talk about the mind's powers to move; man can adapt to change "Because the mind moves everywhere." Later in the poem you say how man progresses in order to define himself—"Becoming, never being, till / Becoming is a being still." Another example would be "The Mound Builders," where several different periods lend their perspectives against the speaker at the end.

STANLEY KUNITZ: I read Plato in my youth and never stopped meditating on the relationship between the worlds of being and becoming. In "Change," one of my earliest poems, the words "being still" can be read two ways—as suggesting endurance in time and as indicating a certain "stillness" beyond time. One of the things that has always fascinated me is the persistence of the psyche through all the changes of the body, all the phases of one's history. There is that self which is indestructible, at the kernel of everything one is and does. In my own case, I've been following its traces all this year, as I've been putting together the poems of a lifetime for publication—my first such comprehensive collection. I've been writing poems for half a century now—a staggering thought—and I've been through many transformations. Of course, my style has changed quite radically, maybe even become its antiself, but from first to last I can detect the presence of that same old vulnerable blob of protoplasm that has my name attached to it.

You mentioned "The Mound Builders." I'm glad you did, for it's a poem that doesn't seem to have attracted much critical attention. I wrote it in 1962, following a reading tour down South, in the course of which I had paid a visit to the Ocmulgee National Monument in Georgia. There I read the inscription, "Macon is the seventh layer of civilization on this spot," which somehow struck me as a rather depressing bit of information. Back in my motel room I heard, on the TV news broadcast, that President Kennedy had announced the resumption of nuclear testing—which made me wonder about the imminence of an eighth layer. In my poem I attempted to cut through time layers, expose them to view as aspects of the eternal present. History isn't a series of dots in a moving line, but a manifold tissue of events, connected with different epochs. In certain of my poems, particularly the longer ones, I seem to want to fold back these layers, to give a spatial extension to time. One lives in the present, but also in other times, past and future. I feel that I am not only living now, but also in other times, past and future. Now is one of the locations of my life, but so is my childhood and, beyond that, the childhood of the race. Even my own death is part of my occupation. That density of feeling, when it saturates a poem, is what I describe as psychic texture.

POETRY MISCELLANY: That sense of spatial extension is related to Coleridge's organic form and to that sense you described of the gradual emergence of the poem, isn't it? His poems spatialize time, too.

STANLEY KUNITZ: Particularly in his free-flowing odes. Coleridge describes two kinds of form, mechanistic and organic. Mechanistic form is predetermined, filled in by language. Organic form develops from the materials inherent in the poem. He uses the working of clay as his metaphor. The most appropriate image for the process may be that of a living thing growing, coming alive and sending out its antennae one way and another, as it searches out new areas of feeling or meaning. The concept of organic form leads one to try to arrive at some sort of satisfaction of an impulse by engaging it in an action which ultimately leads to its exhaustion. In that sense Valéry was right when he said that poems were not so much finished as abandoned.

POETRY MISCELLANY: Another way of presenting things is through the apostrophe or invocation, devices you use more than many other poets. Apostrophe resists narrative, sequential time, and yet it allows the poem to send out its antennae, as you say.

STANLEY KUNITZ: True, but one has to guard against letting the apostrophe become a merely rhetorical trick, a mechanistic shifting of gears. I'm not sure that I'm more addicted to it than other poets. If I am, it may be because I'm so aware of the divided self. Sometimes the person you address in a poem is your other self, that Other who is also you. At other times you have to call on an outside agent, human or divine, to spring you from your self-made trap. Another consideration is the monotony of simple declarative sentences in flat succession. Few contemporary poets, I'm grieved to say, seem to understand the importance of syntax as a means of modifying the vibrations of a line, or of propelling it forward. You need to change the pitch of your voice to keep your poem from going dead on you. You want it to open up, to rove free. This is something that Hopkins, above all, understood. He was a supreme master of invocation. And, of course, a great prosodist.

POETRY MISCELLANY: As a poem of yours opens up, it seems to confront a threshold. There is a whole section in *Selected Poems* called "The Terrible

Threshold." In "The Flight of Apollo," it is a threshold between our world and infinity. In "Robin Redbreast," the speaker looks through the bird's skull to a blue, eternal sky. There is always this sense of being caught at, but looking beyond, the threshold. For example, in "Open the Gates," the end becomes a new beginning— "I stand on the terrible threshold, and I see / The end and the beginning in each other's arms."

STANLEY KUNITZ: Yeats wrote, in a late quatrain, "It is myself that I remake." He was referring to revisions, but his observation is true in a larger context. The poet is forever making and remaking himself in an effort to surpass himself. I think of poetry as, above all, an art of transformation and transcendence. At every important stage in his journey the poet has to "cross over."

POETRY MISCELLANY: A number of your poems involve a kind of Jungian movement into and out of a mire, a mortality. In "Green Ways," you talk about the "self's prehistory." In "King of the River," you describe an evolution going from a salmonlike self to "the threshold / of the last mystery, at the brute absolute hour." You have the sense of inheriting a higher life and being always banished from it—an ambivalent endurance.

STANLEY KUNITZ: A lot of reasoning goes into the making of a poem, but the great leap is from memory and awareness to the rapture of the unknown. That can't be a wholly logical procedure. Reason can play all sorts of clever and even beautiful word games—that's what Coleridge meant by Fancy—but the imagination is a deep-sea diver that rakes the bottom of the poet's mind and dredges up sleeping images. The visionaries teach us that we have to become ignorant before we can become wise. Jung's special insight was that we need to go back and confront our past before we can become strong enough to move forward. The athlete who wants to jump over a high crossbar first retreats several yards, so that he can gain momentum for his leap. Poetry is our most sophisticated use of language, but it is also our most primitive. It has its source, deep under the layers of a life, in the primordial self. If we go deep enough, we may discover the secret place where our key images have been stored since childhood. There are chains of other images attached to them, the accretions of the years. A single touch activates the whole cluster.

POETRY MISCELLANY: Freud visualized a knot, an impenetrable tangle of images, leading in a number of directions.

STANLEY KUNITZ: His theory of neurosis led him to see these images as traumatic and repressed. No doubt many of them are, but an artist's key images can include some that relate to experiences of joy or ecstasy, images that give him his first glimpse of Eden. If you could plot all these images, as you do the stars in a constellation, you would have a reasonably accurate representation of the creative identity.

POETRY MISCELLANY: One of these image clusters, at least in the poems from your middle years, includes words like stain, defilement, contagion, corruption, vileness, waste, infection—the list could go on. In "Single Vision," you talk about the "stain of life," for example. The notion often seems to carry moral or theological overtones, too, like Blake's vocabulary in *Songs of Experience.*

STANLEY KUNITZ: To set the record straight, "Single Vision" appeared in my first book, *Intellectual Things*, published in 1930, so that I was in my early twenties when I wrote it. Of course I owed a lot to Blake, including the title of this particular poem and of the book as a whole. Even then I had a perception of evil, which wasn't based on much experience of it. It's true, as you point out, that in my middle years my vision really darkened. I went through a bad time. "My bones are angry with me," I wrote in a poem I called "The Guilty Man." In the catastrophic period that culminated in World War II and my four years of military service, I felt politically helpless and personally defeated. My "guilt" took on existential dimensions. I did not know how to live anymore with myself or the world around me. The original flaw, I perceived, was to be born mortal and fallible. We have all been expelled from the Garden, but the ones who suffer most in exile are those who are still permitted to dream of perfection.

POETRY MISCELLANY: The poet in your work often speaks "the serpent's word." As in "Science of the Night," he fails to make contact with others. The self dredged up out of the unconscious in "The Approach to Thebes" turns out to be a monster. Do these images have a general application?

STANLEY KUNITZ: They derive from the predicament of the artist in Western society. In the dominion of the arts nobody is more insecure than the poet, who has neither a community to address nor a commodity to sell. If he has a political function, it must be in an adversary role. With few exceptions, poets live separate existences, outside the mainstream, less a part of our culture than of our counterculture, of which they are an unorganized segment. So it is that, in a defensive reaction, their temptation is to become completely self-preoccupied, to lose the human touch, to devote all their energies to the cultivation of ego and sensibility. Paranoia is the vocational disease of artists. That's what I mean by the transformation into monster.

POETRY MISCELLANY: This tendency seems more pronounced from the Romantics on.

STANLEY KUNITZ: It isn't an accident that the beginnings of Romanticism coincide with the advent of the Industrial Revolution. We all know that the Romantics defended nature against the incursions of the "Satanic mills." What isn't so clear is that they were defending the craftsman and artist, the whole man making the whole thing, against the theory of the division of labor and the new technology of mass production. It's a rare artist today in whose work we perceive, above all, the emanations of humanity rather than the pride of the specialized ego.

POETRY MISCELLANY: In your later poems, the threshold, the self, seems less "terrible." The perspective seems to have become more ironic, perhaps more stoical, certainly less "angry."

STANLEY KUNITZ: That rage of my middle years almost consumed me. I suppose that I have made my peace with at least some portions of myself. This has modified my voice. Age hasn't made me more conservative—I still think of myself as a radical intelligence—but I have learned how to be less impatient with failure, including my own. I have chucked a lot of baggage and am stripping down, however reluctantly, for the last few miles of my journey. The immediately important things are to keep on living, to keep on working, to keep on building a world of affections.

POETRY MISCELLANY: The sense of being a father, say, in "Journal for My Daughter," deals with this, doesn't it? The image of the father is widespread in your poems, referring to your own father and to yourself.

STANLEY KUNITZ: In the constellation of my images I suppose that the quest for the lost father, the one I never knew, is pivotal. To find the father is to find oneself. And to become a father is to reenact an archetypal mystery. That's to become part of a majestic drama. At the same time, in another perspective, it's a curious and humbling phenomenon to step into one's place as an insignificant link in the infinite chain of being.

POETRY MISCELLANY: That finding of the self is often put in Wordsworthian or Blakean terms. "Poem" describes an experience that is "a dream...or not a dream" in which the speaker moves in a cyclic way between dream and reality, the outer world and the inner self, until they seem to coalesce. And "Geometry of Moods" talks about the coincidence of circles of self and world that never quite coincide, as in Wordsworth.

STANLEY KUNITZ: These early poems often announced themes that continue to haunt me to this day. I read Wordsworth during my school years, as I read Blake, and shared his excitement about the reciprocity between nature and self. I think, too, of Coleridge's exclamation: "O Wordsworth! we receive but what we give / And in our life alone does Nature live." Let me add that the natural world has been the most sustaining of all the forces in my life through the worst, the darkest, periods. The fact that I have an abiding sense of joy and participation in the natural world is fortifying; it compensates for much human failure.

POETRY MISCELLANY: There's a sense of intensity not only about your feelings for the natural world but for the world at large. Talking about the flowers, but also the whole world and his own ability to love and imagine, Coleridge confesses his dejection that "I see, not feel, how beautiful they are." Feeling is crucial, not knowledge.

STANLEY KUNITZ: Agreed. I keep on accumulating information, because I was born curious and don't know how to stop. But I realize that my knowledge is worth little to me, or to anybody else, unless I can incorporate it into a world of feeling. I suppose that's one of the reasons why I continue to write poems.

Daniel Mark Epstein, 1980

Double Vision

POETRY MISCELLANY: I'd like to talk first about what seems to me to be a cluster of tensions in your work, the basis for its very ironic character. Your work is characterized by a gesture of inclusiveness: "Like Noah I want to bring everything into the house," you say in "Summer House." But this inclusiveness is achieved in a startling way. At the end of the poem you refer to "the horizon / no man can see without turning his back on it." And you talk about being "a better neighbor to the unknown." Inherent here seems to be a necessity to see things indirectly or askew, to include things by turning from them, which perhaps explains why so many of your characters are excluded from society—misfits, assassins, people missing limbs, various hermetic types. An undercutting occurs here, then—a complex double vision that attempts to include the world, but from odd perspectives. There's an odd way, to refer to one other poem, in which the characters in "The Follies" all touch each other, include each other, radiating out from Mr. Cantini's baritone, yet in which they also remain separate, their perspectives detailed.

DANIEL EPSTEIN: It's amazing to me that you use the phrase "double vision." I have a new poem with me that I wanted to show you called "The Sentry of Portoferrario," and it focuses on a "broken boy" whose eyes "blindly fix upon each other" and who has been "Born lame as an old joke." He's the "sentry" and "keeps his watch high on the falcon fortress" with a "lonely insistence on heaven." The poem asks some questions about guilt and vision and ends with the lines: "But somebody has to pay for the hobbling climb, / somebody has to pay for his double vision."

What's the burden of any vision? Isn't it instructive that the Greek seers were so often blind? Perhaps the answers have to do with the relation between what we see or remember and what we imagine. There's always the Cartesian problem to be solved—"Is there really anything outside my own consciousness?" The world that seems most real lies in the imagination. That's frightening to me. It was frightening to Descartes. And yet I'm driven always to imagine the world as I've never seen it. The more vivid that vision becomes, the more inclusive, then also the more lonely it becomes. There's no company there. I made it alone.

POETRY MISCELLANY: Your poem "Rip Van Winkle" faces that problem, too.

DANIEL EPSTEIN: Yes, he wakes, and the last thing he can remember is this woman that left him. She had made him so angry he wanted to burn down a forest. Instead, he falls asleep and dreams the fire. In a sense it's a parable about double vision, about the real and the imaginary.

POETRY MISCELLANY: Perhaps "Nocturne" is the central poem here. In a typically inclusive yet paradoxical manner you exclaim: "By night and the powers of darkness / I am making a day to live in." As it turns out, in the course of "building a song to live in," you discover that it excludes you. The poem becomes a "white elephant" that you ask bids on only to undercut yourself: "Who am I kidding? / I'm the luckiest man in the world / if I can give it away." And then there's that moving resolution when you ask "for one who would hold me / through this single night."

DANIEL EPSTEIN: The first part, as you suggest, goes back to the idea of inclusiveness. I like to think of myself as an adventurer into the physical world and into the world of perception. I admire Allen Ginsberg and those poets of the 1950s who were influenced by Zen Buddhism and the whole business of "watching." It's very important for me to be watching, bringing as much of the physical world as possible into me, to predicate my vision of the future. The world of imagination is not *sui generis*; it comes from our experience of a real world. I met a wandering philosopher last summer who has been in and out of mental institutions, and when he's out he works very hard investigating his own life, his own perceptions, and he talks with others about them. He told a story that is a good parable for my problem in the world as a poet, and that has a good solution. He said that he was having this Cartesian problem of wondering whether there was anybody out there or not. He invented an imaginary lover who came to him nightly and made love to him. The figure of the lover was actually an instrument of masturbation. But one day when he was in the middle of making love to this visionary lover, the figure rose all of a sudden to announce who it was. At one point the philosopher realized that there really was someone else, that this was a real person. That is the solution to the problem of solopsism that is sought in "Nocturne." You need another person who is independent of you and yet whom you can love and make a part of your dreams and visions.

POETRY MISCELLANY: I suppose the very nature of the dramatic monologue, any dramatic poem, helps provide this solution.

DANIEL EPSTEIN: Yes, I think that's probably a reason I write as many of them as I do. I'm not content with living in one body, doing one life in one body. It's that passion for inclusiveness. Whitman is instructive here, the attention he pays to different types of psychology, ways of seeing, ways of living. But the impulse to create other characters comes from this discontent that you're only one person. When you really know other characters, historical figures or imagined voices, then in a sense you *are* them. You are freed from your own body and mind. That's erotic—and exhilarating—and expansive. Most of the poets I admire have been able to create a theater of other personalities.

POETRY MISCELLANY: I wonder in what sense you might see the reader as an Other, who must be appropriated and who appropriates, like the lover who saves you from solopsism or the historical figure you can become. Jacques Lacan talks a good deal about the Other, which he sees in language and the unconscious, but it's not unrelated to George Herbert Mead's "generalized other"—your reader, in effect. How does writing implicate the reader? I've always liked the way Wordsworth in "The Thorn" allows his narrator to con the reader into thinking the worst about the legendary girl, then pulls the rug out, and the reader realizes he's made a mistake by taking the narrator at his unreliable word.

DANIEL EPSTEIN: Certainly your reader becomes part of you; if you make a judgment and he accepts it, then, yes, it becomes part of him. He has to consider it or he's in moral trouble. The writer of "Rodempkin" and the reader of "Rodempkin" put that character through Hell. There are places in "Rodempkin in Hell" where the reader is upbraided, where the narrator says: You're collaborating, it's in your power to see it differently.

POETRY MISCELLANY: History and the past are also important as ways out of the self, particularly in *Young Men's Gold*. The lovers and then the groom's mother are haunted by pasts—"What spirits plot / love's ruin"—in "After the Wedding Party." The speaker in "Woman at a Prophet's Grave" exclaims about her son—"forgetfulness, / be still above my son," even while the poem itself is obsessed with her memories of him. And the "Old Man at the Wood's Edge" says, "The woods are full of skeletons," as he tries to prepare for his own death. The past is something that must be negotiated—that's what the poem "Young Men's Gold" is doing, isn't it (looking at past to understand future)? What is interesting in this context is the strong narrative base that most of your poems have—stories or fragments of stories. I wonder if you could sketch out your sense of what makes a narrative and how stories might be related to how you see the importance of the past and of history.

DANIEL EPSTEIN: History is narrative, of course, and I wonder to what degree fictive. It is selective. History decides what's important about the past, tries to figure out what would cause a war or a marriage. You have to do the same thing in telling any story. The whole process lets me understand what I'm doing now, where I'll be tomorrow. I'm haunted by certain kinds of stories. "Young Men's Gold," for instance, emerged out of my reading about the Civil War, my sense of some American fabric, a kind of mythic character and action that is the true meaning of events. I assume there is something like Jung's "Collective Unconscious," a collective memory that supplies such tales. It's important, too, that there is some element of mystery, something that points beyond my understanding. The gestalt of events, the contents of that collective unconscious, point to something outside the visible picture rendered by story and myth. And that leads me to something else—the story does not stop when I stop telling it; it goes on even years after I've meditated on it, made the selections, put it in the poem. It goes on as I try later to figure out what it means, what else could have happened that I haven't said.

POETRY MISCELLANY: That's like Barthes's notion of a "text" as a demonic plurality of meanings, as an engendering of new signifiers, new interpretations, as, really, the life of language. He opposes it to the traditional, static, monistic "work."

DANIEL EPSTEIN: Oh, yes, that's true. It is a Nietzschean idea. My idea of education in general comes out of Henry Adams, that sense of ongoing process. The process of learning is a historical process, a narrative one where you write your own life. But where do you start? George Eliot says at the beginning of *Daniel Deronda* that you don't start at the beginning, you arbitrarily dive in and make selections of events.

POETRY MISCELLANY: And the sense of time and history is paradoxical— you have both to immerse yourself in them and transcend them. That double sense occurs in "Old Man by the River," which is both rooted in the physical world of events—the boy who brings him the news, the blossoms, and moments of nature—and in the mythic sense that the poem as a whole seems to achieve.

DANIEL EPSTEIN: Well, it's the poet's duty, and especially when you use history like I've done, to get out of time. You do this by familiarizing yourself with history so much that you can consider everyone you read as your contemporary. In that way you get a broader view of things than if you saw them in a confined historical setting. That broader view is what a poem like "Letter Concerning the Yellow Fever" tries to do with a particular set of events around Baltimore in 1818. Richard Howard talks about the dichotomy of the poetry of experience and the poetry of imagination. I consider myself a poet of experience, finally, because I believe you can't cut yourself off from history, but have to make your place in it and continue this ongoing act of structuring it and yourself.

POETRY MISCELLANY: You have a new poem, don't you, where you talk directly to Vergil? That strikes me as putting into practice that idea of dealing with past figures as if they were contemporaries.

DANIEL EPSTEIN: Yes, the "Ode to Vergil." When I was living in Rome there were some violent things happening—like the kidnapping of Moro. I really thought I ought to write to Vergil in a sort of transhistorical dialogue. Not only is he a poet, but there is a medieval tradition of Vergil as necromancer. He turns out not only to be the correspondent, but also the participant in some hair-raising developments by virtue of his acts of augury. Well, the poem catalogs all these things and achieves, I suppose, a double vision about Vergil himself and the state of modern Rome.

POETRY MISCELLANY: Your language there is making the sort of leap we discussed earlier. You use a basically urban, cosmopolitan, technical diction. But several levels of diction are operating. The middle section is much more intense and incantatory than the first, and the poem relaxes just a bit in the last section. It allows for those various perspectives, and I think it's a link to the dramatic work—I mean to plays—that you've done. What special difficulties does drama pose for you, as opposed to dramatic monologues?

DANIEL EPSTEIN: First, let me agree that language itself is very important in that historical process; we inherit our language, and we complete the process of inheritance by passing it on revitalized in writing poems. And altering levels of diction lets you see the same thing in different ways. I think of Paul Blackburn, Frank O'Hara. I think of Whitman. I think of Hart Crane, who saw his city plainly along with a Platonic ideal of a higher city.

The writing of plays poses several problems. There's a technical problem first. When you have been writing lyrics for years, you have to learn to get the images out of the language and into the three-dimensional space of the theater. The transition is made in "Young Men's Gold," which has four voices in it. It is more dramatic than my earlier poems because the characters have physical presences suggested by their different speech rhythms. That's the beginning of theater. My next long poem was actually a six-character play where individuality is suggested not just by differences in diction but by the patterns of movement on the stage.

Eliot says the lyric poet who is going to turn to theater has to go through a spell of putting his muse on a very lean diet. He's talking about lyric imagery. You don't require much of that in the theater because there's already so much for the eye to be preoccupied with.

POETRY MISCELLANY: You've been working on a translation of Euripides. How has this affected your thinking about these things?

DANIEL EPSTEIN: Well, it has come after a six-month period of writing a long play of my own, which presented a number of problems of versification. Now I'm busy translating *The Trojan Women*, and it has confirmed a number of ideas I had about handling lines, suspensions in speech, how concentrated you can be, how to create suspense rhythmically. Euripides has been encouraging.

POETRY MISCELLANY: Your sense of rhythm is probably one of your most pronounced characteristics as a poet. In a number of your poems you use longer, often looser lines than do many contemporary poets, lines that may vary from three or four to seven or eight or more beats. Your lines seem to become more variable and more complex through the first three books. I don't mean this analysis to sound as if your writing is random or uncontrolled, because the sense of timing and pace—and these are also dramatic terms—is superb and finely controlled. You seem always able to achieve the rhythm of the plot, the movement of the speaker's voice that underlies any believable narrative.

DANIEL EPSTEIN: I don't know if I can add anything to what Pound has already said. Rhythm has to suit the emotion in each line. That can be more or less subtle; if it's too subtle you forfeit the drama and the force of rhythm. Most of what I've learned is from Latin and Greek, especially the Greek dramatists, which is not to say I write in those meters, or that I plan regular lines with formal and esoteric patterns of substitution. But in those dramatists you find lyrical passages that are nothing like the pieces of short dialogue, which are in turn nothing like more rhetorical passages of argumentation or lamentation. They're not totally regular, but the passages build through repetition. Say you have a line that you want to soar after a period, say of pondering, where you want the character who has a problem to break through, start singing. Well, you use fewer accented words. After a while, all this becomes instinctive. Rhythm is the way you perceive the world, and the varieties of rhythm that are at our disposal also allow us to see a greater variety of things. This takes us back, quickly, to the notion of inclusiveness that we began with.

William Stafford, 1979

Emergencies of the Moment

POETRY MISCELLANY: In your essay "Some Arguments against Good Diction," you talk about the way language both distorts and enhances experience. You talk about how "the successive distortions of language have their own kind of cumulative potential, and how under certain conditions the distortions of language can reverberate into new experiences more various, more powerful, and more revealing than the experiences that set off language in the first place." Words, in a sense, create their own world—or, as you say in an early poem, "open the world again and again." Sometimes, as in "Poet to a Novelist," syllables create "echoes realer / than originals." And in "Report to Crazy Horse," the Indians "are learning / to take aim when we talk," and their enemies "shift when words do"—the world and its words interpenetrate. So in "Report from a Far Place," you say, "Making these word things to / step on across the world, I / could call them snowshoes." Yet there is an irony—what you call a "hazard" in the essay—that appears at the end of the poem. The words "burn, or don't burn, in their own / strange way, when you say them." The hazard is that you enter the labyrinths of language: "inside / each word, too, that anyone says, / another world lurks, and inside that…" Could we talk about the way a poet tries to make his world, how it sometimes makes him, makes something else—how everything, any word almost, becomes part of a story that could be true—about the sense of being that is carried by language.

WILLIAM STAFFORD: Well, a writer is both a beneficiary of language and a victim of language. Language is bigger than any individual. For example, there are certain "places" that words reach where their syllables happen to be related to each other, the connections between these words being made by associations of sound, not conscious logic. There's a kind of tide of language, an undercurrent. I feel like a surf rider in the language; the luck involved is at least equal to any skill. I find myself being taken for a ride, and the ride always goes further than I thought I could go. Even when you think you're in control that wave is whipping you toward a part of the beach you've never seen before.

It excites me to think of the possibilities there are in language. If you enter into language hopefully, trustfully, your faith will be rewarded. Language is always helping you, suggesting resources for the emergencies you meet. But you have to be ready to welcome the distortions of your original plan that language presents along the way. In that sense I'm a happy venturer into the distortions, if you like, of what language gives us.

POETRY MISCELLANY: Could you relate this sense of possibility, of venturing, to your conception of form, which seems more open than that of many poets? You seem to emphasize pattern, an evolving pattern, perhaps what Coleridge called an organic form.

WILLIAM STAFFORD: Yes, the whole idea of pattern is a congenial one to me. I don't feel less concerned with patterns than are some more "formal" poets, but I feel that there are more patterns to be discovered than have been recorded so far in traditional forms. You have to find your own form; it's like a dog circling and getting ready to lie down in high grass—you sort of make your pattern according to how stiff the grass is, what the temperature is, lots of things. Now, that doesn't mean you don't get a feel for what the grass is doing—what your words and feelings are doing—only that you have to find more patterns than do people who are devoted to form. They are forced into a limited number of mechanical relations to the emerging poem. Our surfer/poet, on the other hand, constantly has to meet emergencies with new directions at the very crest of the wave. Saying of this poet that he has no pattern or sense of form is like chiding the surfer for not hitting the beach at the same point each time.

One of the problems with traditional formalists is that they often neglect the syllables that aren't in rhyme positions. But all those other syllables are like plankton, and you have to be able to scoop them all up, relate their sounds, find new relations. So suddenly I have a new program for poetry— "save the plankton." Save those little signals in language that are making so much difference and which are neglected in standard forms.

POETRY MISCELLANY: This sense of the depth of language also seems to inform your vision of things. For example, a number of your poems deal, as "Bi-Focal" does, with a doubleness in the world. In that poem, you talk about love on the surface and a legend underneath: "So, the world happens twice— / once what we see it as; / second it legends itself / deep, the way it is." And in "Ask Me," you talk about the moving current of a river under the seemingly still surface. This sort of Platonic metaphor occurs in the poem "Whispered into the Ground," where, dreaming of old places left behind, the speaker can exclaim, "Even far things are real." There it is not just surface and depth, but near and far. At other times there is a relation between here and now, or inner and outer— "Inside: the universe that happens / deep and steadily." But there is always one side of the dichotomy that remains distant; there's a sense of absence, loss, of what the psychological critic Jacques Lacan calls "otherness."

WILLIAM STAFFORD: These various images you've been talking about suggest to me my sense of the limitations of all human beings. We are only intermittently conscious enough to know the important things happening around us or even within us. Even a compass needle on this table would tell us something about the present that we don't know. There are vast forces that we rarely, if ever, perceive that control us. There is an awful lot that is getting by us. We already know that because we've invented instruments that tell us there are other things out there. My poems again and again are based upon the difference between our proud assumptions about self-control and our serious limitations.

Now, the ultimate significant Other is God, or something like that. The speaker of many of the poems, then, or whatever the intelligence is that inhabits these poems, is a person who is in league with powers greater than human powers. These greater powers can't really be known. The Other is also the location of another perspective, as in that poem where the speaker seems to walk alongside a Cree warrior. We have to listen, give ourselves over. We have to settle for things, for our limited understanding of things. I think "Traveling Through the Dark" is that kind of poem.

POETRY MISCELLANY: I think one of the healthiest things about the Romantic tradition, and it's a tradition I know you are part of, is its insistence on just such a sense of limitation. *The Prelude*, for instance, is structured as a sequence of failures that lead to higher successes. Wordsworth fails to get to the island in the rowboat episode but discovers the immense power of nature; he fails to reach the peak of the Alps or to see the sun rise on Snowdon but learns more "sublime" lessons. His original intentions are always thwarted, and a larger power leads him to other discoveries. The same thing happens in "Resolution and Independence" and his other poems. It happens to Shelley in "Mont Blanc," to Byron in *Don Juan*.

WILLIAM STAFFORD: Oh, yes, and it's a delight to find someone reading these things in the same way as I do. You can make wonderful poems out of failures. Those who feel they have to make the poem come out in a determined way are only depriving themselves. I feel that art is the acceptance of glorious failures. I think that Hardy is another we could add to our list. Many people think of his as sad poems, but they provide me with a great lift. I was on a panel a little while back and the question arose as to what a student should read to be a good poet—the answer was Wordsworth's "Preface" to the *Lyrical Ballads*, and I think that's good advice.

I guess I've said something related in "Writing the Australian Crawl"— you have to play your hunches, take chances. Everything helps, even those failures which may, finally, be incorporated. We have to learn to write more naturally, more openly. We have to be able to put ourselves wholly into our sentences. When we have done that, when we have given ourselves over to language, then there is a power that we can feel knowing just where we are in our sentences. That power enables us to absorb our failures, to transform them.

POETRY MISCELLANY: Related to this sense of transformation is a metamorphic impulse that runs through your poems. It has to do with finding a home or an origin. If we can get back to first things, or at least invent them in myths, a whole new world or a new idea about the old one seems to fall into place. Something like this is suggested in "For the Grave of Daniel Boone" and "Sophocles Says." Certainly it receives a full mythic treatment in "The Animal That Drank Up Sound," where the desire for origins and the sense of language we described before are blended. In "Our Story," ends and beginnings blur. Is that the basis of myth, to find beginnings in ends? to have a sense of things going beyond? Could you talk about the metaphors of home, origin, and beginning and about myth?

WILLIAM STAFFORD: Myth gets into poems because it is impossible to keep myth out. By the way, there's something about the idea of a "home" that occurs to me and can serve to link myth and language as I think you are suggesting. In readings, I've stumbled across the heavy occurrence of sounds that rhyme with "home" in my poem "The Farm on the Great Plains." And this is true of other poems, too. I think that the sound somehow suggests something about a number of linked ideas and feelings. This is something that goes far beyond dictionary meanings—the sound itself seems to have some significance we are not quite conscious of yet.

In other words, I'm not so self-conscious about inserting myths into poems as someone like Yeats would be. You don't have to try to put myths into poems. You'll be overwhelmed with them. You become overwhelmed by the strange images and associations that are generated as you write, especially if you begin to think of them as "mythic." Maybe running from a myth, then, is the best kind of myth. I think that all myths begin, originate, with the simple "what if...." That is, there's a kind of leap away from the present. Those two words, "what if," are probably the source of all myths. And they are the source of poetry, too. In that sense all poems and myths are about origins.

The strange thing about myths is the way they are so basic they can suggest several things. My best example of this is that poem, "The Animal That Drank Up Sound." I didn't know until I went abroad and was speaking in a dictatorship that it was a political poem. A translator who was going to assist me at a reading was afraid to translate it. At first I didn't understand, and then I realized that, yes, the animal would be the censor. It was an Indian legend to me, but for the Iranian it was a political poem. In a sense, these myths are all around us and suggest, like we said language does, things we were never aware of.

POETRY MISCELLANY: Yes, our very beliefs, our truths, are myths, too.

WILLIAM STAFFORD: Sure, there are myths that scientists live by; even though they believe them for a while, the most learned ones realize that one myth or model will be replaced by another. What we were talking about before in terms of failure, language, the Other, is called in science the uncertainty principle.

POETRY MISCELLANY: One of the ways you seem to be able to draw the mythic dimensions of your poems together is by the sense of time you create in your poems. "Time's Exile" is in a sense related to the question of origins. There you talk about being "alongside old happenings when they flare." But there is more than a sense of nostalgia—there's a sense you can control time through language. In "Spectator," you say, "Make the moment go rich in your stammering // ...the words though are old before they are said—/ you can have time surrounded." And in "It Is the Time You Think," you talk about the little "pause" or "trap" in which you might "manage Events"—something to provide "some kind of edge against the expected act." I guess what often happens is that, as in "The Whole Story," you arrive at a point where you can say, "I am time."

WILLIAM STAFFORD: It is uncanny the way it keeps appearing in the poems, this abstraction from sequence called time. It happens often, I suppose, because it is a myth. For the artist, the now provides all the signals. He has to reinvent the now again and again. If you have the feeling for continual process, continual transformation that we were discussing before, you can't be tied to prescriptions, but instead be ready to begin anew. You can't be tied to a simple linear sequence, but have to be able to interrupt yourself, create a new now. I guess I'm trying to say that for the poet, time only exists in this relationship between him and his material, at least any really meaningful time. It is a process. Just now, the best example I can think of is in Keats's letters; he continually shifts in mid-sentence to another context.

POETRY MISCELLANY: Some sense of this reactive movement occurs in the chapbook you did with your son where his and your poems alternate. There's a braiding of the two perspectives. There's a sense of the separation not only of time but of consciousness. The braiding is an attempt to try to achieve a unity that can't, after all, be fully achieved. The important thing is the process.

WILLIAM STAFFORD: Yes, I'm glad you got all those things togther. I get a vision, when you explain it, the way your hands go, of one of those cords that is braided in two colors. There certainly was that sense that both my son and I felt when we were putting the book together, but it's hard to explain. I guess that one of the things poetry does is to make an equivalent for those things we often do with our expressions and gestures as we talk to one another. The chapbook is trying to express that sense of braiding you do with your hands. And yet it can never quite do it. That's an ambitious idea. It's the ambition of poetry, an ambition always interrupted by the impulses of language.

Dara Wier, 1981

The Languages of Illusion

POETRY MISCELLANY: The last poem in *Blood, Hook & Eye* ends: "You look at the mountain / miss the mountainless space, / the mountain holding mountain in place." Something is always absent in your very concrete language that gives that language its sense of mystery; the invisible or the absent seems to order space, to hold things in place. There seems to be an invisible marginal script that links the intimacy of the moment with an immensity which is all that lies behind or beyond it, to steal a concept from Bachelard's *Poetics of Space*. In a more recent poem, "In Obedience to Absence," you talk about mirrors that "revise space"— "These mirrors will show you where / you would have been." Always, more or less is shown— "You've turned toward seeing / what you never intended." Perhaps we could begin by talking about this mystery that so characterizes your language.

DARA WIER: A mystery is something I wish to contemplate and to ask a reader to contemplate; it's not a puzzle to be solved. If you solve a mystery you're done with it, and I want the mystery to be one that resists a solution, that allows you to take off in other directions.

I think this may originate in the Catholic theology I learned in a very unsophisticated way when I was young. I was always told that you were supposed to contemplate a mystery, and I always wanted something to happen to me when I was sitting, waiting. The thing I missed was that I was supposed to make something happen. One day I realized that the body that embodied the mystery that I was to contemplate was more important to me than it should have been. I stuck to the subject too much and only saw what I intended to see.

Now that is connected to my sense of metaphor. There are two ways of thinking about what metaphor can do. One is that it is a nice, static way to present two things in an interesting juxtaposition. On the other hand, *metaphor* might suggest the kind of movement that a verb produces, a change— once you've changed something into something else, it's then ready to be changed into something else again. The first way of thinking about metaphor suggests a Protestant sense of communion in which the bread represents something; it's ceremonial and historical, a reenactment; there is no mystery involved. The second way of thinking about metaphor reminds me of a Catholic sense of communion—transubstantiation, something is changed; it's sacramental and timeless; I believe in the transformation that takes place when I make the metaphors I use. I want change to occur in metaphor—not just comparison or decoration. I'm not trying to show more clearly the first half of a metaphor; I'm trying to take it and change it into something else. I think "To Become a Field" is a good poem to talk about here because that's the one in which I discovered that what mattered to me was the way things can be changed, do change, are turned, transformed. Before that, what mattered was the pure possibility of what images can evoke, how they can resonate.

POETRY MISCELLANY: I'm reminded, as you talk, of "Colorless Green Ideas," where the dark is described as being like a horse in a stall looking down over some sleeping friends. Then the poem takes off and describes the horse. The night, the original image, gets left behind as a simple perception, though it remains as a trace, in a modifying or adjective function— "how difficult it is for nothing / to remain nothing." As the poem moves from one image to another in a rippling-out movement, some traces remain but the movement is more important. The traces are like the markings on those magic slates we used as kids, an analogy used by Freud and some contemporary critics, and they remind us of the dynamics, the movement, how far and fast the poem moves.

DARA WIER: That's good, I can see that. What you want is to imitate in the language the way your mind moves through perceptions and understanding. That's the way I think about catalogs, too. If you use a catalog and list five things in it, I think that implies there is an endless number of possibilities you might have used—the catalog is not closed. The movement is on the surface, and it involves some uncertainty. It involves an interfacing of different images, something I've always been fascinated with. I learned to be able to live in this world through something like Keats's "Negative Capability," or F. Scott Fitzgerald's notion that you have to be able to hold two opposed ideas in the mind at once and still maintain the ability to function. I disagree with Ernest H. Gombrich's notion in *Art as Illusion* that you can't see both sides of the double image at once. If you can't see the illusion, if the illusion is not clear to you, you can't create it, can't even draw the picture. I suppose that's like your idea of the trace, and its presence is necessary in order to have a poem move in the way we've been discussing.

In terms of language, I am very conscious of the different ways in which a particular word matters at a given moment, whether to name something or to recall a word's history. This consciousness can provide the poem with movement. For instance, "She Has This Phantom Limb" near the opening of *Blood, Hook & Eye* originated with a story a man told me about his aunt who lost a leg and felt phantom pains. I couldn't write anything interesting about someone not having a leg, but was able to write about someone missing an arm. There are so many things we do with hands, and so the arm's absence in space becomes more interesting. But I got stuck when the poem moved to the palm reader. I looked up *palm* in the *OED*, and there I found *palm* is related to the word *antler*, and that suggested *deerskin*, the gloves, and the poem took off. You're given something like that as a gift because of language.

POETRY MISCELLANY: I wonder to what extent language, vocabulary, determine the subject of a poem. I mean, I wonder how much this process we've been describing serves as author, authority.

DARA WIER: I think language determines the subject a lot. It's what we use to think, so it must. As I become more interested in particular words, they give me things I didn't know before. They give me an understanding of whatever it is I'm writing about and how I'm thinking about it. One of the things that made *The 8-Step Grapevine*, besides my interest in the characters, was thinking about all these words we laugh at when we use them—like *lollygag* or *dojigger*. I spent days making lists of these words, though I ended up using only fifteen or so. But the words determine the way the poems sound because there's a kind of foolishness in those rhythms. After I finished that book I had to put those words and rhythms out of my head, and I had to revise many of the newer poems in order to remove from them *The 8-Step's* quirky music.

I pretty much have faith in a unifying and generous force, maybe sometimes your subconscious, that provides you with those connections you can't rationally figure out. Language is part of that unifying force. I think I began to understand this when I wrote that new poem, "The Batture." The batture was where I began to write poems, romantically, as a child, putting them in little jars, throwing them into the river hoping they'd float to South America. I began, when I was writing "The Batture," to think of what the imagination offered—that gift bearer that gives you unifying powers, lets you write over the horizon, makes living endurable. What makes it interesting is to see which side of the coin you're going to be moved by, the

7:15 AM
Breakfast

8:25 AM
Morning prayers

...AM
...res

8:30 AM
School

11:30 AM
Lunch at St. Joseph's
Dining Hall, then recess

...0 PM
...School

9:00 PM
Bedtime for
younger students

9:30 PM
Lights out
for everyone

St. Joseph's student
daily itinerary

HELP US GO B

NAME: Jimmy Backpack

NAME: Jenna Highlighters

NAME: Glitte

NAME: Brady Calculator

NAME: Aiden Notebooks

NAME: 3 ri

Go to stjo.org/dreams
Lakota students

K TO SCHOOL

NAME: David
CRAYONS

NAME: Amy
Art Supplies

acy
ens

avannah
Binder

NAME: Nicholas
Pencils

NAME: Missy
Pencil Pouch

to help provide the
school supplies.

St. Joseph's Indian School
We serve and teach, we receive and learn.
PO Box 326
Chamberlain, SD 57326
1-800-341-2235 • www.stjo.org/dreams

6:30 AM
Rise and shine,
wash up, dress,
and make your bed

7:4
Househol

3:30-6 PM
Homework/extra-
curricular activities

6:30 PM
Clean up
from supper

6:00 PM
Supper

12-3

8:00 PM
Shower and gather
clothes for laundry

7-8:00 PM
Free time

8:30 PM
Bedtime snack and
night prayers

mountain or the mountainless space, and the imagination's part in that. It becomes a question of how far you'll let your imagination travel. And it has to do with creating those illusions.

POETRY MISCELLANY: One side of the coin we haven't talked about is the physical texture of your language. Even the movements in your poems are, to borrow a phrase from Bachelard, "movements that are engraved in our own muscles." There are images of meat, animals, flesh, earth, sexuality—a poetry crammed with tactile, visual, auditory images.

DARA WIER: Part of that is purely my own sentimental and nostalgic connection to a place and people whose own vocabularies and lives include and are reflected in my own language. But by sentimental I mean something like what Pamela Stewart means in her essay in *Intro 12*; one part of the word has to do with feeling and emotion, the other half with the intellect. I think the physical aspect of language is sentimental in this larger sense. Also, words really are physical not only because of the way we speak them but because we really do think of words as things. Each has its history which is a horizontal measure of its origin, whatever transformations it's gone through, wherever it's lived most frequently; and each has its own particular connotative qualities, its own several puns—and these are vertically suggestive. At the crossroads of these vertical and horizontal aspects comes the word, the word as we see and hear it most strongly. We understand something about a word, and a poem can begin to happen in several directions. That Bachelard quotation is wonderful in this respect.

POETRY MISCELLANY: In a way you don't know the object itself, though, because language is always there. If I rub my hand over the glass like this, I can't separate the physical feeling from what I know to be a glass, its history, purposes, associations, which are all given in language. I might associate the act with something I saw in a film or a commercial or read in a story or a poem.

DARA WIER: That's why I want all those things in detail, that's why I want the world in the poem so much. The objects we name recall sensations, other words and images. One thing I love about language is that it makes us think we know things that we can't know, because we have names for them, can talk and write about them. Actually, it's our only way to keep reminding ourselves there are things we don't know. So language keeps us humble.

When I was very young, there was something I feared, terrribly, that wasn't named. When Allen and I lived in Virginia we would drive to Richmond a lot, and it often was in cold weather. My lips would chap and I'd lick them; a fear would come exactly as when I was young. Finally, I began to understand that the thing I feared had something to do with a time when I was little and my uncle burned my lips with a battery—the acid—from a hearing aid. That's part of it, but not all. The point is, the discovery, though incomplete, began with the single sensation, and the object that was recalled may itself lead to other discoveries. I'd love to be able to put that back together.

POETRY MISCELLANY: I remember a comment you made once during a reading. You were describing those yards you pass which are strewn with reflecting bottles, statues, animals. If you think modern poetry is weird, you said, look at those yards. And what's so curious is the sensibility of these people; like the poet, they have one hand on reality.

DARA WIER: That's what's important. They are imagining worlds to live in, and they make worlds on their lawns that are unusual and strange. I love thinking of somebody putting two thousand little rocks together to build a little grotto in the front yard. And everything is always out of proportion, the color is never realistic—I like the juxtapositions of those things. And I like the fact that what is uncommonly combined gives pleasure.

POETRY MISCELLANY: The function of the narrator is crucial in all this. The narrator of the poem is, after all, putting the poem together, imagining a world to live in, and sometimes intrudes as in "Sherwood Street Talent Show," where she exclaims, "Wait / a minute...." I think that one of the strengths of *The 8-Step Grapevine* is the way the narrator moves in and out of the poems, but this occurs in all your poems to some degree. In "Lucille Examines the Family Album," we perhaps have a self-portrait of the narrator in Ernie, for we must be aware of "His style behind / or before the camera." He is "the fixed center / of all these turning pages."

DARA WIER: That last poem is certainly a description of the narrator's function. Yes, the "accomplice of *likeness*" is what I say Ernie is, and the writer is certainly that accomplice, too. I know that when you're writing it is very easy to imagine yourself as the reader. By becoming part of the poem, by putting yourself in the poem, sometimes you're letting the reader know how you're reading the poem as you go through it yourself. You become the reader's companion, and you take on one another's characteristics. When you intrude directly, you're in communion with a reader as you move through the poem. I think that is closely related to the first poem in *Blood, Hook & Eye*—the audience speaks the poem instead of the poet.

POETRY MISCELLANY: As in "If for a Night My Tongue Could Speak," where you are literally, if comically, putting words in someone's mouth.

DARA WIER: Exactly, and one thing I learned from writing some of the new poems is that the narrator not only wants to slip into the poem but also to slip into someone else's body, like putting on a glove, becoming that person. A while back I went to the Toledo Museum to see a show of Richard Estes's work. He's always called a photo-realist, but the interesting thing is that while he's completely true to some kind of photographic realism in terms of detail, there is always an overlay of abstraction in terms of color, design, and form. When I went to see that show I desperately wanted to put my arms into his arms and feel what the painter must. He has that double-ness that we were talking about in terms of language and so I suppose there is a kinship; he calls things out of the ordinary world and we see them in a special way. He has a lovely picture of an escalator that does that, for instance.

POETRY MISCELLANY: What sort of relationship does the narrator establish with the characters in poems? In *The 8-Step Grapevine* it seems more ambiguous but more engaging than the "One Woman" poems of the first book. What stake does the narrator have in the action?

DARA WIER: My intention from the first in *The 8-Step Grapevine* is to give the characters what they want. Each of them lets you know in the first poem, and the narrator gives it to them by the end, but I don't think it's given very graciously. As a matter of fact, it was Allen and Richard Dillard who pointed out to me that Ernie seems to have died when Lucille visits the mortician's wife. I didn't want that. Lucille does want to be a star at Ernie's funeral and is waiting for it, so I wrote another poem to keep him alive to keep alive her desire. The characters in that book mean more to me than the ones in the second section of *Blood, Hook & Eye*, the one-woman characters. Those women are vehicles more than anything else (but the characters in *Grapevine* delight me). Once they begin to take shape, once Ernie becomes hapless and begins moving toward the conclusion of the book, I follow his steps in the dance and am happy to go on through with him. When I enter that world, I'm able to look around and see where I stand.

When you're writing these poems, you think, "I've got to give them life," and you are always aware that they're invented so you can make them live any way you want them to. You choose all the time. What I found was that I wanted to give them what they wanted. But do I give them their wishes, then pull the rug right out from under them—which is so easy to do in language? I love those characters; I'm not disdainful of them in any way. I don't think their desires are mundane just because of the simplicity of the objects and events they decide to use to try to understand their lives. I think of Eudora Welty's story, "Petrified Man," which takes place in a beauty shop. What I love about it is that it shows you you can take any object, any setting, situation, and make it resonate in an important way.

POETRY MISCELLANY: The narrator in "All You Have in Common" starts off as an observer; then intensifies the use of "you," which is different, I think, than just a second-person address and seems to speak to an Otherness in the narrator; then can address himself later—"the narrator keeps calling your name." At the same time, the identity of the "you" and the events of the story begin to shift dramatically, establishing false connections and leads.

DARA WIER: Let's start with "you." When you're learning to write, you don't use the first person because you don't think you have earned the right;

you invent somebody to speak for you. In colloquial speech we use "you" reflexively as "I." In a lot of these new poems there's a "you" who is also an "I," and the two of these together get to be "we." I let the poems go ahead and do that. They often start with a singular "you" or "I" and then move to a "we." I suppose it's the way of linking the narrator and reader we were talking about before.

As for "All You Have in Common," that poem is partly wallowing in an enjoyment and understanding of how much you can manipulate a story, how many possibilities there are in any narrative. What is important is not the story, but how we get there; it doesn't make sense logically. The poem plays with and against absolute, rational causality, but the only causality comes from the language.

POETRY MISCELLANY: The problem of causality is really part of a larger problem, which is the way you perceive time. Let me outline a few aspects of this in your work as I see it. In "Complaints," in *Blood, Hook & Eye*, the past exists as a "trace," as "the empty tomb which bears my family name." There's an attempt simultaneously to retrieve that lost past, fill the empty tombs, and escape it by moving toward the future. More recently, in "Memory," you can "spend the last few minutes / chasing what can't by fever-weakened / hands be caught." The paradox of time is that it is there, but always beyond our grasp. This has one effect that seems central to your work; though you glance backward, you aren't trapped like Eurydice— everything is seen freshly, opening up. As you say in "Another and Another," "I run the clocks down. // Everything I touch for the first time. / No new beginnings only beginning." You're always beginning, always at the threshold; as in Nietzsche's Eternal Return, everything speaks of "Another identical matter." Finally, the threshold itself seems layered with time—time becomes a question of intensity. There's the 2.8-billion-year-old rock your brother brings back in another new poem, or the presence of layered time in those Indian mounds we visited south of here.

DARA WIER: The first aspect has most to do with emotions about things, a sense of preservation. In this sense, we participate in creating the past. Memory may provide a sensation, an emotion, say, fear or anticipation, but not until the memory can be understood by means of words does it truly step into the future. Memory keeps something with you that's no longer with you—exactly that sense of the mountain holding mountain in place. There's a sense of wonder, a sense that there are an infinite number of possibilities possessed by any one moment you remember. As you keep breaking it apart, you keep thinking that you'll find the core. But you never find it because that center opens up again, and you are able to keep filling in all around it, packing it with more things to shape it.

I've always disliked the expression, "a new beginning." It seems stupid, but we can say it, can pretend we know what it means. What I like about that rock that came eleven thousand miles is that it embodies the union of time and space. Now, this seems to me to have as much to do with language as with any sense of time. Language gives us and preserves for us a sense of time. If you write a story in the past or even the future tense, it is always in the present tense as the reader is reading the words. No matter how hard we try to place something in another time, in language it is always here, right with us. The narrator is always present, giving you the story, giving you a particular syntax that you follow. And it is always for the first time.

What's wonderful about writing is that you're multiplying time. You're giving it more room than you ever have when you move through a day. I guess we write partly because of that and can be satisfied because we can keep saving ourselves and saving time. Even though we can't be immortal, we can pretend that there is an infinite amount of time. The poem defers. That goes back, again, to creating an illusion. We can create the illusion that we can live forever. We can create the illusion of objectivity, which is really omniscience, omnipresence, infinity.

POETRY MISCELLANY: Perhaps one of your newer poems, "The Innate Deception of Unspoiled Beauty," best summarizes the sort of motion in time and language that your poems enact. Your "wish," which is erased, left as a trace, is "that those moments which the brain contrives / first to link, then to pull apart will find each // its place to settle, sink, sufficient while it turns / the scale toward no particular point." Several competing movements are described here, as well as the movement of the lives behind them. Everything is at the threshold, not looking for a solution, opening up mysteries.

DARA WIER: That's certainly an accurate description of why I like to read, why I like to write, what makes me think, keeps me thinking. I'm fascinated by that. "The Consequence of Weather" talks about a glass of water, a hanging basket, and a photograph, which all have different associations, worlds that spin off from them. But they're held together by the woman's crooked finger; that little physical thing draws them all together. That's one of the things poems can do for you, provide you with details or moments, worlds, unendingly.

Richard Wilbur, 1979

The Mystery of Things That Are

POETRY MISCELLANY: In your poem "A Summer Morning," you have two characters, a gardener and a cook, who view a great house and by their relation to it end up "Possessing what the owners can but own." In "The Undead," the vampires can "prey on life forever" but "not possess it." And your Aspen in "The Aspen and the Stream" desires to "drink creation whole." These and other poems seem to set up a metaphor system that distinguishes ownership as a passive and possession as an active, more imaginative mode of relation to the world. I was wondering how extensive this metaphor is and if it relates to a general conception of poetry.

RICHARD WILBUR: I think you are seeing something that I have not really noticed before. I guess that I do think in my poems about possessing the world or being possessed by it. My poor mind reader, in the poem by that title, is being possessed by the world. His mind, as the original of the poem said, is like a common latrine, and his real dream is an escape from consciousness. I have one other speaker in my poems who dreams of an escape from consciousness, and that is the Stream in my poem "The Aspen and the Stream" to which you referred. He achieves a true self when he blocks awareness out. The Aspen that you mentioned has a contrary way of being itself, and that involves an embrace of as much of the world as he can embrace in his own way. Now, I think one job poetry has to do today is to combat the neutrality of so much of our environment. Poetry can let us know more, specifically, about the world that surrounds us. The poet can be like the Aspen, and the poem can be his exercise in taking possession, by observation and feeling and form, of some part of the world. The poem can help us embrace the world more intensely than we would do normally.

POETRY MISCELLANY: The psychoanalyst Jacques Lacan says that language is connected to desire. If our language, as you say, can create "the dreamt land / Toward which all hungers leap, all pleasures pass," it seems always to do so inadequately, so that we must also exclaim, "O sweet frustrations, I shall be back for more."

RICHARD WILBUR: I think that Lacan is right. Language for the poet is surely always a language of desire. It is language, in other words, of Eros, of the Platonic Eros embodied somehow in the words of the poem. We create art because of what we can't have and because of our insatiable desire to have it. This reminds me of one of the early Yeats observations to the effect that it is the business of the poet to remember Eden.

POETRY MISCELLANY: In "A Hole in the Floor," you have the phrase, "the buried strangeness / Which nourishes the known," which seems to me to be an accurate description of your work. There seems to be an interplay between your sense of the actual world in descriptive poems like "March" and "Children of Darkness" and "A Late Aubade." But there's always a drive present to discover what is beyond the physical: "My eye will never know the dry disease / Of thinking things no more than what one sees." The poem "In a Churchyard" talks about "Pooling the mystery of things that are." Could you discuss the relationship between description and metaphor?

RICHARD WILBUR: I am very attracted to accurate description. There is a strong motivation for many poets to take some neglected phenomenon of the world, find exactly the right words for it, and write it down for humanity's sake. "Thyme Flowering among Rocks" is a poem where I simply look at the thyme in flower as long as I can and as closely as I can, seeing whatever botanical things make it be what it is. There is not much more to be noticed in that poem, once I'm through. I think one effect of that kind of exhaustive description is to take you beyond the object you usually perceive. You go away from the object as you do in a metaphor, but you do so by going into it. You reveal a world that ordinarily lies beyond human perception and you imply a further beyond. Now, in metaphor it is usually the force, the boldness of the comparison that carries you away from the object. Yet even the most modest metaphor carries with it the implication that all things are mutable, that all things are comparable. If there is no other idea in the metaphoric poem, there is that.

POETRY MISCELLANY: One of the things that characterizes your metaphors is their sense of surprise. I think of the stunning end of "A Glance from the Bridge" or the opening of "Walking to Sleep."

RICHARD WILBUR: "A Glance from the Bridge" is a description of the breaking up of the ice on the Charles River and a description of the large buildings just beyond the bank and the gulls pausing for a moment on the sullied ice. The last two lines describe, suddenly, the water's movement against this setting—"As if an ancient whore undid her gown / And showed a body almost like a girl's." Nothing in the early language of the poem anticipates the idea of prostitution. Of course, the poem does begin with a kind of romantic feeling in favor of natural freshness and against urban grime, so one can rather quickly associate part of the final image with that grime and part of it with youthfulness, with a surprising freshness. I think that quite a lot of surprise is what is needed for poetry; ordinary comparisons simply don't convey enough of the linkage, the interpenetration of things that we can discover of a sudden. If I say that life is like a mountain railway, from the cradle to the grave, the language doesn't electrify us— we've heard it already. Both terms of the comparison are not being taken with equal seriousness. So the surprise, then, must be appropriate to the subject.

POETRY MISCELLANY: There's a marvelous tension in that image, too. Isn't this kind of tension one of the effects not only of surprise but of metaphor in general? I mean, the language often strains against the subject by its suddenness until we see the appropriateness.

RICHARD WILBUR: Yes, that's very true. All kinds of strain can give delay, surprise, and emphasis in poetry. I have been translating a play by Racine in which the action is continual violence. That is what it is about. Yet there is an elegant surface, a courtly surface of elegant turns of phrase. I can think of some modern poets who have similar effects—Yvor Winters and J. V. Cunningham come first to mind. They both have great technical control while at the same time they have quite raging feelings underneath.

POETRY MISCELLANY: Paul Ricoeur writes in *The Rule of Metaphor,* "ordinary language now appears to me...to be a kind of conservatory for expressions which have preserved the highest descriptive power as regards human experience, particularly in the realm of actions and feelings." Often, though, the richness of language is forgotten by some of our poets.

RICHARD WILBUR: Whatever one may say against the poets of my generation, they did at least have dictionaries and know what words meant. Given the fact that today so much talk is moving toward the grunt, I am not surprised to find how many poems are now written in which words are shallowly used, as if they had no background. For me, it is particularly exciting when I can employ not only the present meaning of a word but its history.

POETRY MISCELLANY: There's that wonderful sense of play on the word "regard" at the end of "The Eye" in the ordinary phrase, "giver of due regard."

RICHARD WILBUR: I didn't have the foggiest idea that the poem was going to end with that phrase. I was quite surprised to find that it took on such a special flavor. The delight is in seeing it come alive.

POETRY MISCELLANY: In an interview a few years ago, you said, "I feel that the universe is full of glorious energy, that the energy tends to take pattern and shape, and that the ultimate character of things is comely and good." Could we talk a little about the relation between energy and pattern and the sense of a "truth" of things that "comes alive," that emerges from these in poetry? Frost said in a *Paris Review* interview: "The whole thing is performance and prowess and feats of association." For him, and for you, that "truth" is a dynamic thing, isn't it? It is the truth, say, of the processes of mind, the processes of transformation that occur in a poem like "Piazza di Spagna, Early Morning," as the poet observes the girl, wonders about her.

RICHARD WILBUR: It always vexes me when students demand, or critics explain, that a poem means this or that. As you have been saying, a poem is not a static thing but rather always a dramatic striving after some conclusion—not necessarily, I suppose, *the* truth, not necessarily a yes or no, but some kind of conclusion, some kind of concrete sounding of a subject. The striving is part of the truth itself. I can't separate Milton's assertions in *Paradise Lost*, for example, from the style of the struggle in which they are arrived at. That is why summaries of Milton's theological beliefs are so dull to read. The truth in Milton's poem is Milton bringing himself to say or perceive this or that.

I think it is very hard for people to get rid of the illusion that after a certain number of years they are going to know something, that their minds are going to jell. All this reminds me of those ads for pearl necklaces that used to be placed in magazines. You'd give some little girl on her twelfth birthday a necklace with twelve pearls, and then each year you'd give her another pearl. I suppose by the time she was really old the necklace would be dragging on the ground. Well, it is very hard to get rid of the add-a-pearl theory of Milton—or of poetry. I find myself coming back to what those critics or students, those pearl stringers, would say is an added truth, just another pearl added to my necklace. But I feel that I am not returning to the same truths and that the earlier pearls are being forgotten, are slipping away. Because the emotions and energy are different each time, it is never exactly the same truth that is tried for in the poem. Each time there is a different concrete inflection, a different dynamic situation. The whole process is more dynamic than the pearl theory of knowledge suggests.

POETRY MISCELLANY: What differences in this process are there between a brief lyric the size of "October Maples" and a long, complex poem like "Walking to Sleep"?

RICHARD WILBUR: I think that a lyric of the length of "October Maples" is written with much greater foresight of the conclusion than a long poem should be. A long poem written with that degree of foresight would be boring. There would be no struggle, no effort to get from here to there. I think there has to be, in the form in which you are working and in the argument you are developing, a certain amount of resistance. Even in a short poem you cannot anticipate everything. There has to be a sense of discovery. The long poem, though, can surprise in a wonderful way and amount to a revelation for the writer. "Walking to Sleep" really breaks down into two parts. It starts out by advising someone to get to sleep by means of carefully selected images which would flow through his mind. At a certain point in the poem that ceases to work. I didn't know, when I started writing the poem, that it had to go wrong. The poem was counseling a hopeless mode of facing the blank of sleep, and what had to be recommended was an openness rather than a safe selectivity.

POETRY MISCELLANY: Several of your poems deal with a dialectic between seeing and creating, reality and vision. For example, "The Eye" begins with the compassing point of view of someone looking through field glasses, but the vision itself is severely questioned. The second part of the poem seems to be a prayer to Lucy to "correct" the perspective. "In Limbo" is perhaps an even more severe questioning of sight and vision.

RICHARD WILBUR: There is an early poem of mine called "The Beacon," which is a poem about seeing and creating. The eye looking at the ocean seems to impose its own vision as it searches the dark for some truth. It suggests something of the limits of human perception. The poem "The Eye" is a very special inquiry. I think I have always been interested in the five senses and in the ranking of those senses, for example, in medieval theology. There the eye is supreme, the most spiritual. And I have always been interested in the way certain poets rebel against the eye. Walter Jackson Bate has shown that Keats is less visual than the other Romantics and that he was more interested in the "lower" senses. Among modern poets, I have always linked Williams and D. H. Lawrence as advocates of the lower senses. Charles Baudelaire is more visual, and this emphasis suggests a certain distance or detachment. He says somewhere that in smell one must actually take into one's body particles of what one is smelling—there is, for him, a sense of violation there. Now, many of these considerations lie behind my poem about seeing and creating, "The Eye." It began as a reaction to an actual experience in St. Thomas. The field glasses provided me with an extraordinarily powerful vision. I was fascinated by the consequences for the sensibility of being able to see more than the naked senses were meant to see. There was, I suppose, a sense of trespass there. At the same time, the validity of vision itself is questioned. That is why I chose the show-off couplet form—to achieve an air of self-mockery.

POETRY MISCELLANY: The form in the second half is more lyrical and resolved, isn't it?

RICHARD WILBUR: The second part was begun several times before I worked out the right balance for it. I think the second part is more blunt and more sincere; it was certainly intended to provide a positive correction. The difficulty then became how to pass from the heroic couplet to an unrhymed verse. I had to find a structure that would be muted, that would carry over some of the cleverness of the first section and some of its rigor, but also make possible a certain tone of sincerity. The whole poem had to seem like two phases of the voice, two moods of the same person.

POETRY MISCELLANY: And yet the questioning tone persists, too. There always seems to be something left over—perhaps that sense of mystery we were talking about before. This occurs even in poems that seem tightly closed.

RICHARD WILBUR: I think of those paintings by Degas which are like uncropped photographs, where there are parts of people, parts of horses running off the canvas. And I think of that poem by Robert Graves that ends on a comma. I think that sometimes the poet who doesn't think that there is a comma at the end of the poem may be closing the poem too hard. There is a certain relish in acknowledging, in the very moment which you are tying up the poem's argument, that all the possibilities have not been exhausted.

POETRY MISCELLANY: The poet, then, seems like your mind reader who discovers things that are missing from our consciousness, our perceptions. He uses tricks, techniques, to determine what we need to hear.

RICHARD WILBUR: As far as "The Mind-Reader" is a poem about the mind and its dealings with the world, it is also about the poet. Perhaps the ending, with its half-intentional evocation of the *Tempest* idea of the drowning of Prospero's book, often associated with the poetic imagination, helps to suggest that. I think of it as being, more importantly, a poem about the mind of God. When one considers the agony of the mind reader, one thinks of the unimaginable tolerance with which the deity is willing to listen to us all, be aware of us all. There is an utter incapacity of the human mind to tolerate what God would tolerate.

Donald Finkel, 1978

Before the Beginning

POETRY MISCELLANY: Many of your poems deal with the problem of beginning. Edward Said, in his book *Beginnings*, identifies two types—really two sides of the same coin. He calls a transitive beginning one that foresees a continuity that flows from it and is the product of the mind's desire to think everything through from the start. He calls an intransitive beginning one that challenges continuities, that may be disruptive, and that seems arbitrary and whimsical. I think this is a useful distinction for beginning to talk about your poems. In "Angels and Fools," you write about beginning as the choosing of a direction, a transitive beginning— "Before the beginning, / there was no direction." And in *Answer Back*, you ask the question—well into the book— "How to begin what cannot be ended"? It seems to me, though, that more poems begin intransitively. In "The Drunken Subway," you say, "How many ways into / the poem tracks / left tracks right." And "A Few Pointers" begins, "Above All, the road must not be too carefully chosen." In what sense is a poem the carrying out of an intention, and in what sense is it a playful beginning, a plunge to see what happens? How are these two beginnings related for you?

DONALD FINKEL: I seem to remember a very early poem that begins, "Let me find my way...." Yes, I'm very conscious of the problem of beginnings. Obviously, there's no simple answer. In a way, you can begin to talk about any subject, any area of experience, at any point, and find your way through it. Sometimes it reminds me of unraveling a sweater—you could take a snip at any point and end up unraveling it all. If you tried to cover an unexplored area, you might enter it at any point and then move through it in a random way till the whole landscape had been covered. In the longer poems, beginning with *Answer Back*, I developed what was for me a new way of writing— a method you might call collage. I discovered that if I worked in a totally linear manner, as I always had in the past, then the poem would quickly wind down to an end. With the collage, I could have several beginnings.

I think what I discovered was that my own insights emerged in flashes rather than in logically developed patterns. Over a period of time, I would recognize that the experiences I was having and the book I was reading would be interrelated, though I wouldn't see that until later. For *Answer Back* I allowed myself to move in several directions at once over a period of five or six months and then assembled it all.

POETRY MISCELLANY: It's a question of rebeginning, then? A poem like "Target Practice" playfully denies its own ability to report an absolute origin, to report what happened, or maybe never happened, in the past. "Neither is right," you say, "the fiction or the fact."

DONALD FINKEL: Yes, and it may be that poems like that made me see that I could take elements of what had looked like an inevitable progression and rearrange them in such a way as to establish new juxtapositions and new relations that were just as interesting and just as "true."

I spend a great deal of time gathering material for the longer poems, much of it unusable in the end. Then I spread it out before me and begin to assemble it into various possible sequences. Gradually, the bits and pieces coalesce into significant order. Afterward I might go back and write new sections, following out vectors suggested by some of these developing sequences. Sometimes I don't discover the best way into the poem until quite late in the process.

POETRY MISCELLANY: You become like Penelope-Earth in "Adequate Earth," who is "unweaving by night the mischief we spin / by day."

DONALD FINKEL: Well, I think there are two views of literature. One is that it is an aspect of our culture that we preserve in libraries or even remember on computers. More appealing to me is thinking of literature as a process of constant reconstruction of what we are given. If I were to turn at this point to a philosophical assessment of the activity of poetry, I'd probably turn to Lévi-Strauss. What he says the mythologist does, I think the poet does—he calls it *bricolage*. The *bricoleur* constructs functional objects from the fragments he finds about him—as Lévi-Strauss puts it, from "whatever is at hand." Some of the fragments the poet turns to account are mythological, some are historical or literary, and some of course are scraps of his own experience. From them he attempts to construct a complex image of his life and the life of his age, as he apprehends it.

POETRY MISCELLANY: As in "Finders Keepers," the priests in an oral tradition who each morning "construct anew" the "language of the tribe"?

DONALD FINKEL: Exactly. Or in the poem "Keeping Time," about the Gahuku-Gama of New Guinea who have a game that is over only when, after a long time, a tie is reached. Of course, that means they have to begin again and again. It's a cyclic view of time, in a way, but not so neat—it's more random, less defined.

POETRY MISCELLANY: In some ways there's a very spatial view of time and history in your poems. You have in the title poem for *Adequate Earth* an epigraph from Byrd's *Alone:* "Time was no longer like a river running, but a deep still pool."

DONALD FINKEL: I was very excited when I stumbled across that. Byrd was part of what I was reading when I started *Answer Back,* but I wasn't at all interested in the Antarctic then. I was mainly interested in the kind of meditation that develops in solitude—an interrupted meditation that is not linear.

It's certainly true that *Adequate Earth* spatializes time. That book gave me a problem to solve that was appropriate to the technique I was developing. It occurred to me after having spent a month in the Antarctic, moving around in that huge area, leaping from place to place, and never remaining longer than a day or two at one spot, that the only approach truly appropriate to the material was vagrant and discursive. In order to assemble the history and the geography of the Antarctic into one composition, I could discover no better way to begin than by piecing together passages from my notebooks and my journal with the fragments I had collected from sledging journals, personal memoirs, and contemporary scientific research.

POETRY MISCELLANY: The traces of history, even the landscapes, are so quickly erased, and the enduring images—the ice, the mountains—seems so eternal that it must have been a difficult task. For *Answer Back* there were more historical images to use.

DONALD FINKEL: In another sense, it was very easy. The Antarctic has a limited history—just enough for us to focus on, just enough to be barely manageable for such an enterprise—though it still involved for me a tremendous amount of preliminary reading. I like working in areas where there isn't too much material, too much commentary, too many earlier chronicles. Otherwise the danger is that I'll end up traveling over beaten trails, where the scent is so confused subsequent travelers can't distinguish the various essences.

POETRY MISCELLANY: It's a question, then, of finding a rebeginning that is always different, that stimulates a new outlook.

DONALD FINKEL: Yes. I'm working now on a new sequence that I've been gathering notes for—on interspecies communication. I'm fascinated by one of the more outlandish approaches to the problem, the Lana Project. It involves communicating with a chimpanzee by using a computer. Lana was set in what was called a "language training situation," a plexiglass room containing a keyboard to a computer, a monitor, which would display whatever she produced on the keyboard in linear fashion, and a bank or dispenser, containing her food, which served as a motivation for learning to communicate. In order to gain access to her food she had to punch into the machine the appropriate sentence—"Please Machine Give Lana Cookie." She could get the machine to give her food, play music, run a film, open a window to the outside—a variety of tasks. She would also communicate her needs to the technicians (that's what they call themselves): "Please Tim Tickle Lana." At a certain point, they decided to initiate what they called conversations rather than simple statements or requests. Here's what one of the "technicians" says: "The initiator of a conversation presumably starts the conversation with some goal in mind, and, likewise, the recipient of that information is also presumed to have a goal when in turn responding to the initiator." (That reminds me of what you referred to at the outset as a "transitive beginning.") It's totally alien to my notion of conversation. Consider how so many conversations begin. "Hot enough for you?" So often we're not at all interested in answers to our initial questions. If we have any goal in mind, it's probably the conversation itself. There's a kind of poetry that's similarly "goal-oriented"—its aim is to make some sort of statement, to assess or to explain some aspect of experience. For me, however, the most interesting kind of poetry is more tentative, more exploratory.

Even in the field of exploration one runs into the question of goals. The emphasis on the attainment of the North and South poles is a perfect example. Actually, the very idea of reaching either pole is wonderfully pointless. The ice keeps drifting, and you have to keep moving the flag that marks the place. I'm constantly fascinated by that sort of narrow motivation. Still, the approach that really appeals to me is that of Scott's companion and fellow explorer, Edward Wilson, the scientific director of both his expeditions. Wilson's tendency, like mine, was to gather odds and ends wherever he found them. His diaries are absolute treasure troves. He ended up dying with Scott on the way back from the pole because, among other things, he insisted on dragging along on the sledge about thirty pounds of geological specimens.

To return to the subject of conversations, I think that in some sense the way I write is developing more and more into a kind of conversation. I employ several voices in many of my poems—sometimes several of my own and several borrowed ones. I remember that when I was working on *Answer Back* I was experimenting with a tape recorder, and in the process I often ended up having conversations with myself. I'd play back tapes of notes I'd made, or drafts of passages I'd written, and respond to them, or elaborate on them. I found in that way I could avoid sententiousness, one of the besetting sins of goal-oriented poetry.

POETRY MISCELLANY: This notion of the poem as conversation is intriguing. There's also an interesting relation in your poems to what we might call the "Other." In "Morning Song," you say, "more and more / we become one another." In "Wow Shaft," there is a sort of animal self who comes out when you sleep. I've always been fascinated by the ways your poems find to fuse assorted voices. It seems to occur in a very moving way in "The Wheelchair Poet," where the "You" who is being addressed tends to become the "I."

DONALD FINKEL: I think it all begins with the fact that when we are writing we are alone. The meditation in solitude is interrupted, and this interruption leads to conversation. The writer moves from an awareness of himself toward points of view outside himself. In solitude you can begin to comprehend your own complex relationships to people close to you as well as people very distant from you. For example, in this new sequence on interspecies communication, I find myself moving from a third-person to a first-person point of view. It seems to me easier to understand the chimpanzee's point of view than the "technician's"—and it occurred to me just yesterday that the only way I'm going to be able to deal with the technicians is to put myself in their position. I often find this kind of shift illuminating because it allows me to understand things I hadn't understood previously. The technique extends beyond irony. It allows me to feel shame, guilt, embarrassment, or disgust without becoming trapped in any one of them.

POETRY MISCELLANY: This raises the problem of the relation of the finished poem to its sources—all the material you interpolate to explore different points of view. What do the poems do to the sources you transcribe? How would you conceive of the poem altering our reading of the sources? Could this be a way in which poems and sources converse?

DONALD FINKEL: I'm not sure. I know that very often I quite consciously distort sources by taking them out of context. Sometimes I've actually felt guilty about it. It's so easy for me to select fragments out of research, say, from my research on the Lana Project, and to mock the people who conducted the experiments by altering the context, by leaving out some of the more sensible things they said.

POETRY MISCELLANY: Yet, if we are to believe Foucault or Derrida, this sort of wrenching from context is a very acceptable way of exploring the possible relations in scientific discourse or a way of uncovering what is implicit in that discourse.

DONALD FINKEL: I guess the problem arises when I think of someone misreading me, or, rather, misreading my sources. I don't wholeheartedly embrace the New Critical idea that intention is irrelevant—it can't be entirely ignored. You can distort something so much by simply removing it from its context that it no longer bears any relation to the source. What I want to do is to uncover some layer of unconscious or subliminal intention not immediately apparent in the original. Clearly, when someone starts out with the notion that any conversation must be goal-oriented he's expressing a much deeper attitude toward life than he may imagine. I may want to use his statements about conversation to illuminate some other area of experience. I think that's fair, and that's what I usually attempt to do. I just want to avoid using material of this kind to construct playing-card houses, where it doesn't matter in the end whether I used a king or a deuce to make the roof.

POETRY MISCELLANY: In "The Stranger" you say, "here at last / I can say what I mean without fear / of being understood." How do you relate this view of yourself to your views about sources?

DONALD FINKEL: Perhaps those lines are a bit too facile. I was struck at the time by the resemblance between the situation of a stranger in a foreign land with that of the poet in our time. There's a certain perverse pleasure one can take in such circumstances. There are even certain merits in the predicament. I think I was contemplating the dangers inherent in being only partially understood—or even in being too neatly understood. To be understood is often to be misunderstood. Any poem is in that sense a lie.

POETRY MISCELLANY: Language becomes a very material thing for you in some poems. Words for you can "push in unison," they can be scooped out of people, consonants can fall like pebbles. In "Remarkable Light Effects," there is a passage that is only barely coherent because there is the illusion of a ripped page. In "Item," part of the theme is the way the line ends are justified. "To think is to thingify," Coleridge once wrote. How do you see this aspect of language in the contexts you've been describing here?

DONALD FINKEL: Probably what I'm doing is treating the elements of language exactly the same way I treat other elements or sources given to me. They are all to some extent arbitrary, all have some life of their own, though they have the potential to be organized. For me, this is true when you look at language as it is broken down into arbitrary syllables, consonants, vowels. In "Remarkable Light Effects," I found myself staring at a collage my daughter had made in kindergarten which included a scrap torn from a catalog, which intrigued me as much by virtue of what was missing as by virtue of what remained.

POETRY MISCELLANY: Jacques Lacan has a passage in his *Écrits* that says in Kafkalike terms, "If Cleopatra's nose changed the course of the world, it was because it entered the world's discourse, for to change it in the long or short term, it was enough, indeed, it was necessary, for it to be a speaking nose." Can poems, in your view, contribute to such change? Can writing be a form of action in any way?

DONALD FINKEL: That's a complicated issue, and I have ambivalent views on it. I guess I've always been satisfied with Auden's idea that poetry makes nothing happen. I remember a formal gathering where a number of politicians and poets were present and someone spoke about political poetry— some line Washington was supposed to have recited while crossing the

Delaware. Well, all the poets sank down in their chairs trying to dredge up some such appropriate line of their own. Then Robert Frost got up, a little old and tremulous, and said, "a poem—is a little thing." A great sigh arose from the beleaguered poets.

I think, though, that poets do have some effect upon the way some people see themselves and conceive of history. I entertain some hopes that poetry might modify the narrow views most people take toward human experience and behavior. There is a tendency in all of us to oversimplify history in terms of superficial cause and effect. If my view of history as sheer blunder is correct, we should be attempting to appreciate its complexity, the ambiguity and ambivalence of all human motivation. I think the *bricolage* technique attempts to do just this. If you're continually conscious of ambivalence in your attitudes, then political action is difficult at best.

But your question really deals with the way poetry might enter general discourse. I think that fiction might be more relevant here. A work of fiction might provide a clearer sense of what is already happening. It might lead people to start focusing their attention on something—say, a form of sexual behavior—that they were not conscious of up until that moment. It might allow them a language in which to define themselves and their society. They would then begin to reinforce tendencies of which they had not previously been aware. Here again we encounter the question of beginnings. Does the fiction merely assist a tendency already under way, or actually initiate it? I suspect the writer is describing something already present in his environment, but the effect on his readers may be incalculable.

POETRY MISCELLANY: I sense behind many of your poems, despite the spatial strategies about time, a pessimism about history. There's a lurking linear view of time in *Adequate Earth*. As you suggest, the tourists and the commercial aspects of society will eventually pollute Antarctica. A similar muted pessimism informs "Water Music." Would you agree?

DONALD FINKEL: I guess in some ways I have a pessimistic view. But what's really reflected there is the expectation that something like what has happened in the past is bound to happen in the future—sooner or later. I know we're going to make the same mistakes, but I'm so much caught up in the present, in our well-intentioned blundering, that I can still delight in it—or become fascinated by it. We begin again and again. As with Gahuku-Gama, there's no way of winning, but there is always the chance to try again. The process is endless. Our conclusions are provisional. And I think there's a source of optimism in that.

Fred Chappell, 1980

On the Margins of Dreams

POETRY MISCELLANY: In a poem, "The Father," in *The World Between the Eyes*, you have the line, "One moment informs every moment." The statement seems to me an accurate description of your work; there's a sense of what Shelley called "interpenetration." I think of the simultaneous visions of the child in the house and the soldiers in "The World Between the Eyes" and then the linking of that poem with "The Father" through the phrases uttered by the soldiers. In *Midquest* this procedure is intensified; the structure is both simultaneous by its echoes of phrase and image and by the fact that the four books that make the poem take place in one day and progressive in the sense that there are gradual discoveries and modulations of phrase and image. In a way, *Midquest* glances back to rewrite part of *The World* in the sense that some images link the two; "Cleaning the Well" builds upon "The Father," for example. But in *Midquest* itself, I think of an image like the bell image (which also appeared in *The World*, in "Sunday"), which is used in several poems in *River, Wind Mountain*, and *Earthsleep*, climaxing in "My Grandmother's Dream of Plowing," where the bell becomes gold becomes child, then goblin, and then is associated with death and quiet in her dream, which is also a dream of her transformations. The way that image echoes and also progresses describes the way the whole poem moves. Perhaps, then, we could begin to talk about this sense of interpenetration and of the problems of writing the long poem today.

FRED CHAPPELL: I made several attempts to write a long poem in my first book, which I don't think is very successful, but I wasn't able to chain fragments together as I was able to do in the quartet, *Midquest*. I don't think I knew what I was doing; it was an experiment. The long poem is a way to contain fragments, as you perceptively pointed out, to tell a story that goes forward in time and yet is still a whole poem. Yes, all four books are one poem—they begin at the same moment in time; they end at the same moment in time.

I'm very conscious of the images and the way they reverberate. Actually, the bell image first appears in a poem called "Cleaning the Well" in *River*. A boy is sent down to clean a well and thinks he may find the bell that has been lost. The speaker's great-grandfather built a church, and when the church burned down the bell was lost. The bell, then, links several generations and appears in several other poems, as you've noticed; it is probably the main thing that pushes time forward in the poem.

Now, images like the bell image grow through their associations throughout the four books. You know, there's something you learn about the lyric poem, and that is that it is a narrative poem. There's a narrative in the background though by and large the lyric itself doesn't tell a story. That is why you hear lyric poets begin a reading of a poem by telling you the story behind the poem. Well, I wanted *Midquest* to be the kind of poem where I wouldn't have to go outside the text to explain anything; it would include its own backgrounds within it. The long poem, I guess, needs this narrative thrust if it's not going to be an arbitrary collection of lyric moments.

POETRY MISCELLANY: Poe, I think, has influenced the fate of the long poem, at least in America, by suggesting that poems should be short, expressive lyrics rather than longer and discursive. He wanted a poetry of pure moments.

FRED CHAPPELL: You do not make a poem by leaving out "nonpoetic" stuff. What you do is absorb as much of the world as you can into the poem. There's no way to do this by "poetic sensibility." You have to do it by shifting techniques. *Midquest* uses lyric and narrative modes, private and public voices, different forms, levels of rhetoric. The long poem is going to include some parts that are connectives, that have to be written, and you have to make those as good as possible, but there are obviously more chances to be taken.

POETRY MISCELLANY: The lyrics that open and close each book are like still moments that explode with all the narratives and images within the books.

FRED CHAPPELL: I think of the opening lyrics as overtures. That is, they give the themes, images, and a little bit of the narrative element that will come later. I'm not sure how they work as independent lyrics because they were written after the other poems in each volume. Each book also contains a central poem that is a long, kind of crazy monologue that counterbalances the lyrics. In these poems I wanted to articulate a number of different things. The model here was John Coltrane's jazz techniques; the question was how much I could include without disintegrating the poem. The important thing, not just in these rambling poems, but throughout *Midquest*, in any poem, is to give a portrait of the mind, the way it works and feels. I try to suggest a whole milieu of life through the stories, through the persona of a narrator.

POETRY MISCELLANY: Let's talk a bit about your sense of narrative, about what makes a good story. In *Midquest* there are at least three kinds of narrative. First, there's the movement of images, a pacing, a rhythm, the undercurrent, which is the rate at which the reader discovers things. Second, there's the repetition of narratives within a poem, the story lines themselves, the plots. Third, there's the whole poetic narrative of the self, a biography of sorts. But for any of these to work there always, it seems, has to be a sense that the story is suggesting more than it could say. I think of poems like "My Grandmother's Dream of Plowing" and her change, not fully understood at the end.

FRED CHAPPELL: Well, the persona, "ole Fred," and it is important to follow the movement of his mind, the pacing of perceptions, as you described it. Though he has some things in common with me, he's not me. But he likes stories, not just the context but the telling of them, that process. Any story has to be entertaining and also infinite in its implications, in its complexity. The trouble with the story, as with a painting or a piece of music, is that it is very hard to talk about a story purely in its own terms. It is very hard to pin down the meaning you want out of it. The hard part about the quartet was getting the stories. In the lyrics, I generally knew what I wanted to say. But the stories were hard because you can't fake a story like you can a lyric. You have to be very true to the storyteller's art, have to make a good story, and yet it has to have something to do with the other concerns of the poem. I don't think I'll be able to do that kind of poem again.

POETRY MISCELLANY: In what sense would you say your narratives are like the tall tales that are so famous in these hills? You include some tall tales — "My Father's Hurricane" is an outrageously funny example — in *Midquest*, but how do they relate to the more somber narrative?

FRED CHAPPELL: The stories try to get at what it is like to live in this part of the country, in the North Carolina hills. But stories do this in a special way. What is *Moby Dick* but a big lie, a tall tale? The trick is to tell a lie that means something. Take the poem about the boy who thinks he saw a man shoot a bridge and kill it; he doesn't recognize that the bridge fell coincidentally. And by the way, I actually saw that. But anyway, the boy can make a whole world out of that. There's no difference between what we imagine and what happens. Whatever we imagine is what happens in the world. The trouble is we always give in to our cheaper imaginations; look at the way Asheville has developed over the years, the kinds of establishments that have come in.

POETRY MISCELLANY: It's curious, in this context, that one reviewer criticized your poems for not posing final answers to questions. This is an attitude that is still apparent in some criticism. Some critics don't want questionings, unsolvable problems, relative or provisional solutions. I think that in "Firewood" the problematics of meaning have become the subject.

FRED CHAPPELL: How about that! I honest to God doubt that you'll get any answer from Tolstoy, Chaucer, Shakespeare, whoever. If you look for answers you'll get something reductive like: "Life is real, life is earnest, and life is not an empty dream." What's the meaning? You miss the point when you take that approach. You have to celebrate life. Everybody who proposes a solution is suspect. What you learn from a poem is the way somebody's mind works, the ways he feels, recollects, talks, hurts, laughs.

POETRY MISCELLANY: I think that is evident in the way you use language. In your "Science Fiction Letter" in *River*, the narrator says how he likes "any story in unknown languages and codes." Then he goes on to make a comic myth about the origins of the world from language. That principle is at work in some of your poems that literalize metaphors or figures of speech. For example, in "Three Sheets in the Wind," the character, drunk, is literally wrapped in sheets; in "My Mother Shoots the Breeze," she, in a way, literally does in shooting down the kite; "Second Wind" and "My Mother's Hard Row to Hoe" are similar poems. Stories emerge out of the expressions.

FRED CHAPPELL: I wanted to write a poem about my people, as I was saying earlier. We wouldn't have said those expressions if they hadn't had some genesis in the experiences of the area. Now, the whole poem, *Midquest*, is about rebirth. I try to get reborn through some of the most familiar things I can think of and in the process let them be reborn. I wanted to choose the most familiar, burned-out material in the world and make it fresh. That's why I chose Louis Armstrong rather than Coltrane or Charlie Parker for the jazz poem—he's more familiar.

POETRY MISCELLANY: As in the poem, "Second Wind," where the woman can't stand the commotion at her husband's funeral, then goes out, experiences a literal rebirth, a second wind in religious terms, herself?

FRED CHAPPELL: Yes. If you've ever seen a mountain funeral, you'd know that one of the troubles is that it's usually summer, very hot, there's fried chicken, all kinds of people crowding in, including relatives who haven't seen the dead person in years but hope they've been left some corn crib or something. Then someone wants to sing. So the woman goes out to escape all this and makes a discovery on her own. I think now that I'd cut the poem toward the beginning. It might be too wordy and too sentimental. I took a chance like many of those poems.

POETRY MISCELLANY: The poem also points out a tension, which I think you've hinted at here today, between the communal aspects of poetry, that is, the stories, the world of the country funeral, and the private aspects of poetry, that is, the lyrics, the world the girl discovers when she goes outside. I think "Susan's Morning Dream of Her Garden" confronts this problem, and the incremental build-up of *Midquest* as a whole seems to be toward community. There is an absence, an emptiness, a nothingness that always threatens the self, say, in poems like "Remembering Wind Mountain," and it has to be filled, populated.

FRED CHAPPELL: I don't try in *Midquest* for an insight that is indubitably mine, but I want one that is correct in a public sense, and it may not be communicable in any one poem. A poet like James Wright has to be reborn each time he writes a poem; each poem has a unique vision. But I don't think most of us live like that. I knew what I was giving up in trying to write a more public poem—intensity, special insights. I suppose in a way that I've written a reactionary poem, an unfashionable one. But my first three novels have hard, tough, private things, and I wanted to get away from that.

I think there is something gregarious about iambic pentameter too. It's not an inward meter. I've often thought that Hamlet's "To Be or Not To Be" soliloquy fails because it can't be inward enough. You get a stage suicide. The verse seems too padded—the "bare bodkin"—he's talking about putting a hatpin in the back of his brain, not stabbing himself in the heart. The speech is too public in its meter for such an inward struggle. Now, Edward Arlington Robinson writes inward poems in that meter, but they're always spoken to another character, and Wordsworth's *Prelude*, after all, is spoken to Coleridge. In *Midquest*, I tried to vary the meter in the more private sections, the more lyrical sections like in "How to Build Earthly Paradise: Letter to George Garrett," but even there, you see, there's a public dimension because the poem is a letter.

Linda Pastan, 1979

Unbreakable Codes

POETRY MISCELLANY: In her essay "Against Interpretation," Susan Sontag writes against a mimetic or referential approach to art, "against interpretation that strives to find some hidden meaning." What she's against is the way most critics have tried to explicate a poem at the expense of the sense of a poem's energy: "Real art has the capacity to make us nervous. By reducing the work of art to its content and then interpreting that, one tames the work of art. Interpretation makes art manageable, comfortable." What she would strive for, she says, is "transparence"—experiencing the luminousness of the thing itself, of things being what they are. Finally, she says, instead of overintellectualized theories, we need an "erotics of art." Who would you perceive as your ideal critic, assuming that critics are needed for some readers at least?

LINDA PASTAN: I do believe that in teaching, particularly in high school and college, it's necessary to interpret the poem, to learn how to read, and I think a good poem can survive that. A student can analyze it, then he can come back to it and try to read it as if for the first time and actually get much more out of it. Though you can never duplicate the pure reaction of a first reading, I don't think a good poem ever really loses its energy and freshness for having been analyzed. The remembered pleasure of the first, more pure, response will make the student want to go back into the poem again, this time for a richer yield—fuller than that afforded by the impact of surface clarity. I'm not necessarily talking about layers of meaning, though; it could just as well be layers of feeling.

As for ideal readers or critics, they should have a receptivity to the work of art. But I don't feel you can think in terms of an audience while you are actually writing the poem.

Interpretation is interesting for the poet, though, too. People have pointed out things in my poems that I hadn't noticed or thought about before. Occasionally these things can be very farfetched and even ridiculous, but sometimes they remind you of what William Stafford once said: that you learn by writing. I do think there is more in a poem than I realize was there as I wrote it. Often a reader will be able to pinpoint it in a way that the author couldn't or didn't think to.

POETRY MISCELLANY: There's a kind of transparence to your poems. They rely a good deal on description to evoke mood and provide movement. And very often there is a powerful description that's so complex yet so simply put, so calm yet so terrifying, as to create that quality of nervousness that Sontag describes. In your poem "Short Story," you talk about everything fading—even as you write—and say:

> ...And though
> there's room for a brief
> descriptive passage (perhaps
> a snowfall, some
> stiffening of the weather)
> already
> it is dark
> on the other side
> of the page.

Although the description would in some ways support the sense of loss, it would also be temporalizing, holding off of darkness. There is the sense that as long as something can be described, something can be said. Could we talk a little about the tensions you feel in those poems that achieve that "nervousness" as a playing off between graceful description and fearful subject and, more generally, about description itself—what kind of things you tend to describe, what kind of descriptions these are, and what you like them to do in your poems?

LINDA PASTAN: A "holding off of darkness," as you say, is interesting, though I don't really find the natural world to be menacing. And I don't think of it as being indifferent, although clearly it is. But outside of its more dangerous manifestations, it can be the greatest source of metaphor for me, and it also helps to put things in a perspective that makes life more manageable. I live in an oak forest in Maryland and spend a lot of my time alone there, and I spend the summers on Nantucket, so my life is naturally focused on the out-of-doors, not in the sense of jogging or swimming or doing much, but in a more visual sense. It will always surprise me how one thing, like a changing leaf, can feel at times comforting and at times threatening, depending on how you are looking at it.

I've found, though, that it isn't enough just to have a series of the kind of descriptions you would ordinarily find in your daily rounds of the natural world. There needs to be more complexity to it than that. The detail, the concrete, needs to be worked up. My poem about the apples, for instance, began as just a long list describing apples in every possible way I could think of. It struck me at that stage, however, as being a little too much like a still life. I felt it wasn't doing anything. It needed another dimension, another focus. I finally used voice to accomplish this. Instead of a list of descriptions, it became a symposium of voices or attitudes: Eve's, Gabriel's, the serpent's, Adam's.

POETRY MISCELLANY: Howard Nemerov speaks of poetry as a "speaking silence" — "a means of seeing invisible things and saying unspeakable things about them." For him, poetry "attempts to catch the first evanescent flickerings of thought across the surface of things." There's a sense, then, that there is always some incalculable, impossible-to-reach center that a poem can only hint at. Do you feel this way about your own poems? I think, for example, of your recent poem in the *Georgia Review*, "When the Moment Is Over," which ends:

> And we listen for echoes
> from the buried chambers
> of the heart
> whose messages are tapped out
> in unbreakable code,
> whose fires are stolen secretly
> even as we sleep.

Perhaps we could be talking about the role of the unconscious? Is it that, for the poet or the critic, trying to reach the center in the unconscious is like progressing through your poem, "Arithmetic Lesson: Infinity" — one keeps taking half steps toward a destination that cannot be reached?

LINDA PASTAN: The center of the poem for me is that part of it that is in some mysterious but literal way "given." I mean this in the sense that we use the term when we say that someone is "gifted." If there is a definite history of where the poem comes from, I will never understand it. (I always feel that each poem I finish will be the last I will ever be given.) Sometimes I find myself at a point where a page full of things that wouldn't look like anything but a mess to anybody else will look like "the given" to me, the possibility of a new poem. I will just have to put in a few months working on it. I don't know where this first chaos comes from, but I know it is the mystery it carries with it that will keep the poem from being paraphrasable.

I do recognize these things as coming from somewhere inside my head. I think of the unconscious as a kind of depository of everything: all sensual and intellectual experience that one has picked up since birth, all jumbled up in one place. But, as I say, these things come out in a formless, chaotic way. I will usually begin a poem with a visual image (my imagination being very visual) or sometimes with a line that has just come into my head, and I suppose I proceed in the way a sculptor might. He is given a large chunk of marble which is his raw material. He chisels away at that with no final form in mind. The form comes quite late in the process. In poetry, it imposes itself by the way the language goes. I spend enormous amounts of time on things like line breaks, stanzas (and things like that), but I come to those things very late in the working of the poem. The poem will suggest its own form to me, and if I keep myself receptive to it, I will eventually get it into the proper shape.

POETRY MISCELLANY: Recently I've been reading, for another project, Gaston Bachelard and Mallarmé. Both place metaphor at the very center of poetry. Bachelard feels that examining a poet's or a culture's central metaphors can give a feel for that poet or that culture. In one passage, Mallarmé talks about poetic language, symbolic and metaphoric language, as being like a worn coin—the "meaning" of images, as we discussed before, might be lost, but it nevertheless gets passed around from hand to hand, there's some exchange—or to continue the analogy, there's an investment, an appreciation in value precisely because of the blurring. Perhaps I've wrenched Mallarmé out of context here for my purpose, but the notion of money and language is interesting. Do you ascribe a similar central place to metaphor in your own poems? What qualities make for a good metaphor?

LINDA PASTAN: Well, I think the primary function of the metaphor is to order the world through language. Its function on philosophical terms is to link disparate entities and compare unlike things, even if this has to be done in an intellectually or emotionally violent way. You find similarities where it might not look like there are any. You impose an order—or you discover it really—in the process of dealing with the things in a seemingly very chaotic universe. But a metaphor also has the function of providing pleasure. It makes you see something that is abstract in a sensual way, and this has its own value. If the poet has made you see something in terms of something else—in a way that you would not ordinarily have thought of putting two things together—then you have learned to see something as if for the first time, and you will see in a fuller way. After all, what the poet tries to make you do is look freshly at the world.

POETRY MISCELLANY: There are a couple of central metaphors in your poems that keep surfacing. One is enclosures of various sorts. This is particularly evident in *A Perfect Circle of Sun*, where the speaker sits in a room without lights, at a distance from the world:

> And here in the center of this house
> deep under shingles, under tar paper,
> under plaster pale as unsunned flesh
> I see through one round skylight the real world
> held up to the sun by its heels and moving—
> it is like candling eggs.

In "Elevation 700 Feet" a few pages later, the lack of boundaries seems a threat. In *Aspects of Eve* you have the poem "To Consider a House," in which the same sort of safety in boundaries is suggested. But in *Aspects* another problem surfaces, as in "Inner Storms," where the dangers seem to come from inside. In "Night," there is an attempt to move out, beyond the skin, the boundary, into dream. I wonder how aware of this you are in retrospect, and how you feel this sort of tension. Perhaps the poem itself can be seen as a boundary, a means of defense by ordering?

LINDA PASTAN: It could be a part of some mystical instinct that women have of trying to find a safe place in an unsafe universe. Maybe that is part of my intention—especially with houses and with building houses in real life, which I always seem to be doing—and then with writing about that sort of thing. It's a way of making a safe place for my family. I relate this to a woman's point of view at this time probably because this issue is fresh in my mind. My lecture at Bread Loaf will be on the notion of women's subjects in poetry. It will be an exploration of what other people's attitudes have been about sex roles in poetry. Some theories have it that only women can get to the heart of the world and that women have to give back to the male his feeling. That women have the job of teaching men how to feel is a notion that, while I don't really believe it, interests me. I use Randall Jarrell's poem about the supermarket in the lecture because I don't think anyone could have guessed that a man could capture those concerns so beautifully and feelingly. And I read Anne Sexton's poem "At Forty," which is about menstruation, and Donald Justice's poem "Men at Forty," which is about shaving and show that they are, after all, in many ways the same poem. I discuss a kind of sexual ventriloquism: Jarrell speaking in a woman's voice, speaking in the persona of a soldier of the first World War, and discuss how well it seems to work. I use some of the categories from Patricia Meyer Spacks's *The Female Imagination* and read some poems that deal with women's bodies, childbirth, and the relationship with the mother. But I conclude that there are only really a few subjects in poetry: growing old, dying, intellectual or physical passion, the search for self or identity. The smaller subjects we might write about are just ways to get into those basic things. A good poet writes out of everyday life and, right now, a good part of what a woman might write may be domestic in nature simply because women have been more involved in the domestic. As a woman changes, her poetry will change. The same will be true of men who do already occasionally write so-called "men's poems" on domestic subjects.

POETRY MISCELLANY: Can we talk about the structures of your books—how you plan them, how they evolve, for example, the seasonal structure in *A Perfect Circle* or incremental structure in *The Five Stages*? Are many poems left out? Does the sense of forming a book help to generate poems?

LINDA PASTAN: If you are going to the trouble of having a book, it shouldn't just be a hodgepodge of poems written since the last book. I think that one owes the reader a kind of total experience. But I don't start thinking about structure until I have a lot of poems. I like a book to be about fifty-five to sixty pages—something you can comfortably read in one sitting. I think too many poets publish everything that they have written, particularly when they have reached the point where they have a reputation. I think it is damaging to them to publish their bad poems with their good poems, and I think that it is unfair to new writers who are having a hell of a time trying to get published. I try to have four or five years between book manuscripts. I write something like twenty-five poems a year and maybe only fifteen of those will appear in a book, so that when I have about seventy-five poems I will set them down and read them over and over again and think of various ways in which I might organize them. With *Perfect Circle of Sun*, I was writing many more poems that were dependent on the seasons. With *Aspects of Eve*, I was writing a lot more about women's concerns, and I knew that I wanted the title to be what it is, but I didn't know how to organize the book. I read *Paradise Lost* about five times in those months because I was trying to find some kind of organizing principle from Milton. Then someone pointed out Archibald MacLeish's "Eve's Exile." When I saw his little stanza, it gave me the structure. Then I did something I never did before or since. The book needed a few poems that hadn't been written yet. I wanted to end each section with an Eve poem, and I didn't have "Symposium: Apples" yet, so I wrote the poem for the book. I don't do that often.

I had no idea that *The Five Stages of Grief* would be able to be organized around specific stages. Perhaps the explanation is that all of us are always going through these stages, coming to terms with death over and over again, even as we are writing seemingly unrelated poems.

Robert Creeley, 1981

Projecting the Literal Word

POETRY MISCELLANY: Let's begin with a question about language. There has always been a directness, a forcefulness about your language which comes from, among other things, its avoidance of metaphor and simile and some other figures in favor of definition. In an essay, "To Define," you say: "The process of definition is the intent of the poem." I think of Whitman's distrust of simile and his emphasis on simplicity in the 1855 "Preface" — "nothing is better than simplicity...nothing can make up for excess or for the lack of definitiveness....The greatest poet has less a marked style and is more the channel of thoughts and things without increase or diminution, and is free of the channel of himself." W. C. Williams's linking, in *The Wedge*, of particular speech and a particular form of poetry it "engenders" is also pertinent here. I suppose the poem of yours I think most of in this context is the untitled one in *Pieces* in which you say, "I Hate the metaphors. / I want you." Perhaps you could begin, then, by sketching out a sense of what you feel is your relationship to your language, what characterizes it, and how it has developed over the years.

ROBERT CREELEY: I don't know that I've avoided metaphor. It's simile, as Charles Olson said, drags the feet. It sets up a comparison, largely defined by "difference," curiously enough, and distracts the attention to consider something else rather than the primary term of focus. Metaphor seems more an instance of transformation — "I'll eat my words," as the dictionary says, whether literally or not. In the poem you note, I suppose it's that I can't—at least at that moment—stand any transformation of the literal, because it's a specific situation in which one wants love, presence, to be literal. It proves a very claustrophobic situation of feeling.

In any case, it's very hard to objectify, to qualify, one's own "relationship to...language, what characterizes it, and how it has developed over the years." I don't know that I'd be capable of such hindsight or definition more than to say, I believe in Wittgenstein's "Wörte sind auch Taten." They are certainly *words* also but, as such, they *act*, they have reality as *acts*. Therefore—coming from New England this probably goes without saying—one wants them free to be as directly to the purpose, the possibility, as one can have them. In other words, I'm displaced by the demands of an ulterior rhetoric I have also to think about in saying, for instance, "please pass the peas." So I've spoken, written, directly in my own habit of saying things without much consciousness of alternatives—as either Ed Dorn or Robert Duncan might actively define them. I've said what I had to, as I could. And I've very much liked the ability to do that, always.

POETRY MISCELLANY: Yet on a more basic level there is a way in which you are always trying to subvert language or decenter it from its traditional norms and concerns. I think of the increased attention you give to articles, prepositions, and conjunctions. There's the direct emphasis on "and," for example, in "For W.C.W." And there's the emphasis on pauses, silences in the line breaks that seem to place the texture of the language somewhere between natural speech and artifice, which seems to call attention to itself as an object and as an instrument. In "trees" from *A Day Book*, things, words, actions, places come together in those twelve lines to create a "resonance, of experience, // all words are a vi- / bration," that last line break enacting the vibration, the being of language. I suppose in a way that this decentering or subversion is part of the defining process.

ROBERT CREELEY: I'd meant to give the example of Louis Zukofsky's *80 Flowers* as what I'd so dearly wish to have the ability of, put it. The poems certainly "subvert" usual senses of language, and yet they are almost homely, comfortably familiar, in their literal words,

> still livid tulip to leaf
> green blue pointed heart valentines....
> ["Tulip"]

It's the so-called syntax makes one have (!) to think. Anyhow, he was terrific, as a model, as was also William Carlos Williams, so dear to my heart always. Zukofsky said, "A case can be made out for the poet giving some of his life to the use of the words *the* and *a*: both of which are weighted with as much epos and historical density as one man can perhaps resolve."

That's from "Poetry," written in 1946 and easily found in *Prepositions*—and it's a very useful musing on what poetry is. Two years before that (1944) Williams had written that very provocative note for *The Wedge*—I can quote much of it to this day—and that text was edited by Zukofsky at Williams's request. You'll note the book is dedicated to Zukofsky, a fact which gets sadly lost in *The Collected Later Poems*.

Well, to return more directly to your question—I haven't really been concerned with "decentering" or "subversion," but my preoccupation has without question been, in Williams's statement: "How shall we get said what must be said? // Only the poem..." Etc. That's early on in "The Desert Music," and I'm interested that those two words, "subversion," "decentering," have each a strong political flavor. And I would feel "political" as Williams is in this poem. He felt, of course, that "the government of the words," the poet's responsibility, was absolutely a political act, "for which many have been beaten and sent into exile."

Elsewise, that sense of line breaks, "silence," is happily engaged in a note from an old friend, Gil Sorrentino, recently: "I was telling my class last night of how you run line-end pauses against the internal metres of your poems for the sake of counter-rhythms, and I think, by Jesus, that they understood it. Will wonders never cease?"

POETRY MISCELLANY: In poetry, as you say in "Notes for a New Prose," "reality is just that which is believed, just as long as it is, believed. Poets are more used to this thing: reality as variants round the center, or, simply, what has been left us." In "There Is," your talk about the way language comes together leads to the line, "a graph of undeterminate feeling." I think that perhaps the tension in your poetry is between the definitive aspect of your poetry and this indeterminacy. This sense of things probably also defines the leaps, retracings, subversion of forms, and so forth in your language. Even the quick little leap you get in a poem like the early "Like They Say" projects a certain chance, gladly accepted, because "why / not?" One's position is always unstable in this world view, and so such leaps seem crucial for living in it and dealing with it.

ROBERT CREELEY: I do stick with that disposition you quote from "Notes for a New Prose" that reality is what's believed in, for as long as it is. That's what I'd presume being human is all about, what, humanly, is felt, known. That's the "world," so to speak, a human imagination. You'll recall, again, Williams's emphasis on this point:

> ...A new world
> is only a new mind.
> And the mind and the poem
> are all apiece.
>
> ["To Daphne and Virginia"]

That's what I take him also to mean in saying, "Only the imagination is real."

Anyhow, it really has nothing to do with whether or not I like to take chances—sometimes I do, and sometimes I don't. But there is no human way to guarantee the proposed world for more than a factual moment. There is no *one* we all live in *in* imagination, only the literal, "biological" "event" we so begrudgingly admit we are forced to "share." When anyone appeals to "one world" these days, you can be sure it's one he believes himself to have bought and paid for. In short, its theirs. Myself, I'd far rather someone just cut the cards, and deal, I'll do what I can with what I get.

POETRY MISCELLANY: Would you agree with Duncan's notion that poetry is a revelation of language rather than of personality? Your own poetry is obviously less mythic than his, less historical than Olson's, but it is not at all confessional in a simplistic way; one gets a sense of a hidden history of language, an archaeology of language in your poems that tends to provide a context that goes beyond the self, that makes an object or symbol of the self. In *A Day Book*, the "I" is certainly prominent, but sort of objectified, made an object, a function of language perhaps. How do you conceive of the role of the "I" and of the other pronouns?

ROBERT CREELEY: Olson has a great phrase, like they say, for "personality"—"that seal of a mealy justice." Something like that. And he works it over, usefully, in "Human Universe." It's not good enough, as a content or qualification. Too much like old-time Dale Carnegie. So, absolutely, I'd agree with Duncan's "a revelation of language." A revelation *in* language, I want to say, as I read him. He once put it charmingly, "I tell the truth the way the words lie." Fair enough! I love the fact that words are precedent, antecedent, free—no matter how hard one may have to work to earn them.

Thinking, then, of pronouns—just that they are supposed to "stand for" nouns makes me want to substantiate them, make them "real" in themselves, including "I." Look what happens to "I" in Ed Dorn's *Gunslinger*. You've got to be careful these days!

His statement in *New American Story*, which Donald Allen and I edited in 1965, is much to the point—that "limited presence" is the seeming dilemma of this pronoun. For my own part, the one play I ever wrote, a radio play I simply "told" to a tape recorder, is dense with pronominal interplay and has also a great quote from Wittgenstein, be it said, on the mysteriousness of this first person. Did you ever think, incidentally, why those numerical tags, and don't they make a peculiar judgment? They are certainly apt enough, albeit they preempt the world! Anyhow, the title of the play is *Listen*, and another relevant text is "Numbers." Then read the stories, where everyone is he/she/it sooner or later, and that's it. "As soon as / I speak, I / speaks...."

POETRY MISCELLANY: In "Notes Apropos 'Free Verse,'" you express your hope that contemporary criticism might develop "a vocabulary and method more sensitive to the basic *activity* of poetry and less dependent upon assumed senses of literary style." You mention, in particular, Roman Jacobson's terms, "contiguity" and "parallelism," which might provide better "modes of linguistic coherence." You also mention what you call "grammartology" as a way of examining "syntactical environment." Now, curiously, some contemporary critics, the deconstructionists, work by a technique called "Grammatology." These critics are trying to find a better way to discuss texts by deconstructing old forms of speaking about them and by seeing how these texts themselves deconstruct old assumptions. I wonder, then, if you think that current criticism is getting a better sense of the process of poetry. And perhaps you might comment on the relation of poetry to its criticism.

ROBERT CREELEY: Sadly, I've found that subsequent criticism has proved even less interesting than that which I was then speaking of. It's the more bitter just that the skills and information I presumed might requalify the activity gave it, seemingly, an even more diffuse "attention." In fact, your way of putting it— "These critics are trying to find a better way to discuss texts by deconstructing old forms of speaking about them, etc."—makes clear how very insular and self-reflecting a process it's become. Not since the 1940s have specific texts (poems, stories, novels, plays, et al.) been given such a meager, "occasional" situation as either something to read or to write. One seems an "excuse" at best for these people.

I think the dilemma is that they're *partial* "philosophers"—certainly the structuralists are—they're not professionals of either situation. And then when one considers a critic like Helen Vendler *or* Harold Bloom, be it said, how argue their relevance at all? At best (as Joshua Whatmough would say), it's only an exchange of opinion—and since the range of the information is so determinedly narrow (would *that* be "taste"?), who cares—except, of course, the people battered by such ill-tempered obtuseness.

Therefore, I depend always on those Pound long ago said would be the likely source for intelligent proposal—other writers. For instance, I've just got a copy of *Language, Volume Four*, edited by Bruce Andrews and Charles Bernstein—and it's to the point that the collection is published by writers in turn, Open Letter (which very much pleases me just that three old students and friends are involved with its editing, Frank Davey, Fred Wah, and George Bowering—*and* it's Canadian, another very useful extension. I'd hate to think we had to live and die with Northrup Frye, however catchy that might be as a slogan.).

Anyhow, do check that out. There are *thirty-two* writers on the job—and that ought to keep anyone busy for awhile. You know, something to *think* about? It's amazing what pleasure it can be, after that greasy kid stuff, as they used to say. I hate it when criticism simply becomes another manipulation of consumer goods.

POETRY MISCELLANY: In *Pieces*, there are some lines to the effect that what you'll say is "Nothing but / comes and goes / in a moment." There is a sense of the moment in your poems that seems to focus on isolated, discontinuous bits, definitions, and yet there is also a sense of movement, "neither seen nor / felt but endlessly, / heard." The double sense of time as moment and movement seems to lead to other doublings or blendings of time as in "A Sight," where you say "the place *is* / *was* / not ever enough." The expanding or opening up leads, sometimes, to a circular or repetitive motion—"Again and / again and again, how // insistent," you say near the end of *A Day Book*. Could you talk about your sense of time? of timing? of the self as time?

ROBERT CREELEY: Perhaps I should make clear that we're not sitting "here" talking with one another—that I am, in fact, now writing answers to questions you had sent me by mail some two weeks ago. In any case, as I first read them, I made occasional notes in the margin, to attempt to stimulate some active reply. So, as answer to this question, let me quote the notes directly:

> Time is subjective measure—
>   in self-preoccupation.
> Otherwise, it "happens"
>   Akin to "temperature"—"to measure
>   is all we know"—the beat, rhythm
>   —what one "dances to." One *is* a rhythm,
>   with determinant period.

POETRY MISCELLANY: In the Introduction to *The New Writing in the USA* you talk about place, how one presences a place not through description but through the "activation of a man who is under its spell." Then, again, you talk about form as "simply the presence of any thing." Could you discuss this notion of presencing and perhaps how the notion of place might be related to Olson's idea of the "field." This might be productively related to Heidegger's notion of a "site," which is a context where someone is becoming. All this could be discussed in terms of your poems "Place" and "Here," which combine several of the aspects of site and activation. Perhaps also I should mention "The Language," where the sense of "location" is in parts of the body and in the language itself as a sort of site for everything.

ROBERT CREELEY: *Presences* is the title of a book I did with the sculptor Marisol, incidentally, with this quote as motto: "Classicism is based on presence. It does not consider that it has come or that it will go away; it merely proposes to be there where it is." That's a very bright remark by *one* critic I much admire, Donald Sutherland. He did the first substantial work on Gertrude Stein, and no one as yet has done better. Anyhow, you can see his point—it's like it's home, the old folks, it's just where we live—like they say. He's using it as against romanticism (it comes from a book of his, *On, Romanticism*) where everything's on the move, being hustled along—*get out of here*! As an old romantic, I'm very familiar with that particular invocation.

I guess I'm loath to spell out what Olson said so much about, not just the projective verse piece, but the endless demonstration and variation his texts provide—and the *range* of the criticism, say, in *Poetry and Truth* and *Additional Prose*. That sure is a *field*!

Then, thinking of Olson, there's Ed Dorn's very useful piece, "What I See in the Maximus Poems"—which you can now find in a great collection of his critical work, *Views*. The first part says a lot about "place" especially.

Well, think of it as what Olson called "habits" and "haunts"—which terms are familiar in New England, be it said. They take time, they're not, as he says, easy to have. He's saying this, by the way, on page four of *Mythologos, Vol. II*—so that one can easily get to.

POETRY MISCELLANY: Your prose, and I say this in light of *Was That a Real Poem and Other Essays*, seems to assume a contextualism that melds together fiction, art, poetry, criticism, music—all the arts—and one of the watermarks of any context, whether it be poem or painting, seems to be its refusal to come to conclusions in a classical sense. The end is always another experience that needs to be supplemented, perhaps from another one of the arts, or from another poem. Could you discuss your opinion about the relationships among the arts, especially from the point of view of poetry? And this sense of an ending that does not end? Perhaps a beginning point would be the kinds of definition, narrative, extension one gets in these contexts?

ROBERT CREELEY: You may have read the same generous review I did of that book by Ron Sukenick, a prose writer incidentally, who also did an early bright book on Stevens. He notes, usefully, that I think of art as a *various* measure and response to the world. There isn't one way only. And back of it all, presumably, is the fact of being human. So I "meld" with the best of them.

Otherwise one gets stuck with an "I only work here" sense of things, a very small imagination of place and function. Far better to think of it as Duncan: "I make poetry as other men make war or make love or make states or revolutions: to exercise my faculties at large." One is proposing to live in the *whole* world—"Come into the world," as Olson says. The "subjects" are divisive, distracting. The arts are not antagonistic to one another. Only the manipulators of their "product" have that relation. Art is a primary information, *any* art—again, as Duncan might say, and *in-forming*. It's Pound's "news that stays news." Any "news." So one doesn't depend on or admit even to categories. They prove a useless distraction.

As to why no "conclusions"—I guess that it's just the fact I'm not done yet.

POETRY MISCELLANY: Most poets have a curious relationship between the occasions for poems and the poems themselves. I believe that many of your poems are done right on the typewriter so there is a confluence of two moments—one that you refer to and one that you write in; and perhaps the point is to make these two, one, or have one emerge from the other. I do know that for you the text is what it refers to, or at least it seems that way, but I wonder if you could explore a little further the relationship between composing and the final thing that's said, or between words and the whole poem, or the materials—emotional, psychological, linguistic—and the shape of the poem.

ROBERT CREELEY: Actually, I haven't written poems directly on the typewriter for years and years—since sometime around 1963, in fact. If you know a collection of interviews with me called *Contexts of Poetry*, you'll find out what happened in the title one. Thanks to Allen Ginsberg, who gave me a little notebook to get started with! I'd chained myself to the damned machine up to then. At first, I liked the "objectifying" of what I was saying that the typewriter seemed to provide—like real-life print, etc., etc. But one couldn't haul it around everywhere, so it proved a useless instrument for getting stuff down on the spot. And I couldn't keep it in my head for very long unlike the great poets of the oral tradition. So since the mid-1960s—the shift begins toward the end of *Words*—I've written usually in a notebook of some kind, with ball point pen. Voila.

The philosophical, psychological concerns of your question are more difficult to answer. Briefly, I always seem to myself in writing to be where I am, writing. Since I revise rarely, there is usually no second "vision," no chance to be "here" again. At least not more than reading then makes, which is, for me, something else. I can sit here thinking of a lot of things, people, that aren't here, say, and they will come into what I'm saying—as, now, my sister, Helen, who lives in Maine, or our mother, who's dead. But they are *here*—in the sense I recall first meeting in a quote of Mencius, I think it was, by I. A. Richards: "How is it far if you think it?" Like Wittgenstein's "A point in space is a place for an argument"—first found in Zukofsky's *Bottom: On Shakespeare* section printed in *The Black Mountain Review*, Spring 1956. So that's the point, and that's what any of us get. Fair enough.

David Ignatow, 1978

Answering the Dark

POETRY MISCELLANY: In your *Notebooks* you talk about "seeing everything as a flat surface," referring both to a style and a perceptual mode. You say, "I look back on my style of work and realize that there is only brightness and a certain hardness that comes from light shining on a thing constantly from all sides." Over the years, the notion of darkness has entered your poems more frequently, and you still retain much of the flat style, what Barthes calls "neutral writing," so that the darkness, too, seems to be a surface. The title of your last book, *Tread the Dark*, suggests this. But sometimes, as in the poem "For Stephen Mooney," the darkness seems more murky, less substantial, less a surface thing.

DAVID IGNATOW: In one way, of course, the darkness is a surface. I also think of it as a hard object which you have to go through—it's penetrable. It is the environment that surrounds you, and you are in its depths. So you are right in seeing the duality. Sometimes the dark is set off against light, suggesting something like, say, the physical as opposed to the nonphysical. Now, in the poem you refer to, the physical presence of the man in the universe is a light since he is a conscious being, but he could also be the dark generating itself as a conscious object. In a sense, we are an emergent factor from the dark; and what is beyond our consciousness is the unknown, the dark. That doesn't mean the dark is something fearful; it can be something very exciting, the sense of the unexpected. It is our existence; we are perpetually in the dark. Even now, here, we don't even know what we are going to say next.

In my own poetry I can only speak for my own consciousness. It may be that my subconscious rises to a conscious state in writing. I feel myself always in touch with impulses and unformed ideas within me, and when they are framed, articulated, I consider them as breaking to the surface. I don't deliberately search for an unconscious stream; I want everything finally to be on a surface. To bring things to the surface is what it means to live in a consciousness about things.

POETRY MISCELLANY: There's a dialectic of light and dark, then, a balance of inner and outer?

DAVID IGNATOW: Yes, one doesn't exist without the other; that is true on the level of physics as well as metaphysics. I've thought of myself as mediating the two. I try to reflect simultaneously in my work both the light and the dark. I think there is a quality of ambiguity in the work, an openness. That is, there can be no ending; the light and the dark are constantly merging into one another. And so the poem can't just come to a stop, a finality.

POETRY MISCELLANY: I think a good deal of the open-ended quality of your work is particularly evident in the prose poems in *Tread the Dark*. They seem to be more interrogative in mood. In Number 9 you end, "I want to call all this the reality. And I must settle for a question." That pretty much seems to define their mode for me.

DAVID IGNATOW: That's fairly accurate, though at their centers they are very skeptical questions. It is curious how they have developed. About ten years ago the free verse lyric was becoming a mannerism, becoming part of "traditional" poetry as it could not have been called twenty years ago. The short poem method was producing a metaphoric free verse poem focusing on an image. It was becoming too easy, too automatic, and finally too restricting. So I broke away into the prose poem to give more emphasis to the intellect, to the search, to the mind, to thought rather than only feeling, only the image. I couldn't say enough in the short poem; I didn't want to be locked into a metaphor or image, but to go beyond them. I wanted the metaphors to be under my control, I wanted to be in control of the form, to play with the possibilities without having to observe line lengths. The emphasis now fell on developing the metaphor along with an analysis of the metaphor. The point was to analyze the metaphor for what it could give beyond its simple statement. So, yes, that gives it the nature of an inquiry; it is constant inquiry.

POETRY MISCELLANY: How have these and the "traditional" poems developed? What has the inquiry led you to recently?

DAVID IGNATOW: A review of the last book called the poems "lyrical meditations," and I think that is accurate. They combine the analytic and the lyrical. But to me, that is already something I don't want to do. I can't raise questions any more. I want to answer them.

POETRY MISCELLANY: In *Tread the Dark* you have a poem that begins, "To look for meaning is as foolish as to find it." It describes a seashell found on the shore, and the process of examining it for a moment is compared to thinking, "So / that thought itself must pause, / holding the shell lightly, / letting it go lightly." Even back fifteen years ago in the *Notebooks* you say, "It's wrong to read into nature meanings that are not there. All nature should be treated simply as phenomena, happenings, and all happenings treated simply as to their movements." So I want to ask about the nature of "answers" that you would find, the nature of meaning, really. Is it momentary, like the dropped shell? To what degree is it separate from, or part of, our own subjectivity?

DAVID IGNATOW: Meaning changes with circumstance. You can read Spinoza today with a meaning he never intended. We produce Shakespeare today in a way he never could have conceived. Meaning is totally relevant. As long as language retains its basis in contemporary reality, it is a changing thing. The meanings of things, then, become lost in this change. A friend of mine, a Chinese scholar, will translate from Chinese poems that cannot be translated into their original meanings any longer. The problem is not just with the language because, though he's lucky to know Mandarin, there are still nuances, inflections, intimacies, peculiar details of the historical period that do not cross over. They don't exist. But he has his own reality that the poem must adapt to.

POETRY MISCELLANY: I think of Shelley's statement in the *Defense*: "All high poetry is infinite; it is as the first acorn, which contained all oaks potentially. Veil after veil may be undrawn...and after one person of one age has exhausted all its diverse effluence which their peculiar relations enable them to share, another and another succeeds, and new relations are ever developed."

DAVID IGNATOW: I have a good example. I recently saw a show at the Museum of Natural History about some people who were living thirty thousand years ago. Their images, artifacts, drawings of men and women are amazingly like ours and with a degree of sophistication amazingly like Picasso's. But these things have different meanings for us than they did for them. We have applied another view, an aesthetic one. Perhaps for them the meaning was cultural or religious, or perhaps they did combine an aesthetic with other meanings.

POETRY MISCELLANY: Are there limits to what things can mean? I'm thinking of your poem, "The Question," where you ask as you dream you are flying above the city, "if I say the people are bacteria / who will deny it?" And you commented elsewhere that you liked Jackson Maclow's experiments with a poetry of meaninglessness.

DAVID IGNATOW: Well, the character in "The Question" is creating his own reality, but he still has to come down sometime, as the end of the poem suggests. The reality is what we all participate in, our culture that we draw from. Even when you withdraw from it there is an emotional and mental attachment. In the background is our culture with its different thought habits. Reality according to the poem is that which you are in at the moment. By meaninglessness I meant in relation to a single meaning, a single reality. I don't mean that an object has no meaning, but that the meaning we give it is of the moment, while we are in communication with it.

POETRY MISCELLANY: Related to what we have been discussing is a certain primacy you give to the "moment," the "now." In the *Notebooks* you say, "The Highest poetry recreates the reality of the moment and in recreating assures itself of immortality, because it is in the process of recreating that poetry is most akin to reality."

DAVID IGNATOW: Time is the body, the body is the poem. I don't see time in a classical sense. Recent scientific theory is correct—time and space are the same thing, and space is physical. We're space. Space lengthens, time lengthens. If time is the body, then the body is of every moment, a constant process. So I try analogously in my poems to create the moment as a bodily thing, as a moment of the body. Now, I don't think of the body as merely physical; isolated from intelligence and feelings, it is not human. The poem is a consciousness of the author, which also involves a sense of the body within his total meaning for the poem. The lines, the language, the rhythm, the syntax, should recreate the physicality of the body at the same time they are being employed to create an insight, an idea.

POETRY MISCELLANY: And so, as you say in another *Notebook* entry, "No ideas but in things and things die, with their ideas" in a parodic extension of Williams's statement. The poem, you suggest, is like an echo, a footprint— "the voice of a bird echoing after its silence and even death." How is this sort of echo through time related to the moment?

DAVID IGNATOW: The poems that I write are really episodes or parts of an ongoing long poem that will never end. It can't end because the body of the universe doesn't end. To establish a sense of the physical in language is to identify with everything that is around you that will always go on, will always be physical. In everything I write I try to celebrate the physical. It's the idea that changes more than the physical. That's where meaning is so relative, to go back to what we were saying before.

POETRY MISCELLANY: How does this notion of celebration relate to the dark, to the "tragic" vision you have identified in your own work? I remember a stunning passage in the *Notebooks* that describes the way the universe is expanding, creating greater distances, more emptiness, more nothingness. Ironically, it is as if Emerson's transcendent circles were being hollowed out.

DAVID IGNATOW: I think I'll have to go back to my feelings about Whitman. I have a lengthy article, written sometime ago, where I talk about my total faith in the ability of Whitman's work to turn people around and give them fellowship and perhaps ameliorate some of the harsh conditions we live in. It took me a long time to realize this whole need for fellowship was not going to be brought about by his poetry and prose. Still, you don't want to give up on such an idea. And so I said, if it is not going to work out in the affirmative, at least let us communicate that we can't have fellowship. At least that is a human and civilizing thing to do. That's the tragic aspect of the vision. Everything I've gained from Whitman can be seen in this negative sense. That is, I'm reflecting his concept of transcendence, his sense of progress toward man's total communal society. What I retain from him is his ability to remain open to everything and therefore reflecting given forms in poetry and living. His idea is to make life for yourself rather than have life make you, and that is enough to gain from any poet.

POETRY MISCELLANY: Sometimes that self you are trying to make seems threatened with an inwardness in *Tread the Dark* that leads to terror. In poem 51 you confront a door behind which may stand some other fearful self. "The Two Selves" also seems to deal with the problem, though in a different way. But by the end of the book these selves, even the whole problem, seem to have been shucked off. The dark has become light, to use the earlier metaphor.

DAVID IGNATOW: It's that I've gone past that stage. It seems to me now to be basically a middle-class problem, the problem of the person who serves himself through society, remains isolated, and then, maybe, finally confronts himself as isolated even from himself. We have to serve society through ourselves. This is what the poet should do, however limited that service is in our present society. We define ourselves through others. So I don't personally have a sense of loss of identity. If I do question my identity, it is to question myself as a human being in relation to a tree, or the sea—it's to know myself as a human being, as a being in life, and to communicate that to others. In "The Two Selves," I meant the question in a physical sense—what was I before and after I was born? Did I ever know myself at the time of my birth? The poem, as we said earlier, brings these things to the surface, to communicate them to others, to share our identity with others, to have a sense of community.

POETRY MISCELLANY: Would you say your vision has become more optimistic? Certainly it is at least more stoical. In the poem "Explorer," using the metaphor of mountain climbing, you say, "I am about to begin," and then, "My joy is in the trees and grass...," and "My joy is skyward," and finally end the poem with "I am the joyful man."

DAVID IGNATOW: I think I'm going in a direction that is ironically the opposite of what Robert Bly, a poet I have tremendous respect for, is recently doing. From my conversations with him, I begin to sense he feels that transcendence has its own limitation: he's starting to go below the surface where the quirkiness of individuals lies, not their general human consciousness. I want to see if there's a possibility of transcendence, though certainly not in any Emersonian sense. I hope to do something different in the next book, to say "yes" to a lot of things. Perhaps I've been saying "no" too long.

Marge Piercy, 1980

Shaping Our Choices

POETRY MISCELLANY: Let's begin by talking about the problematics of language. In your poem, "Lies," you say, "I give too much importance to words / and my words define me. / I am always becoming words / that walk off as strangers." In several other poems the possible duplicity of language is encountered. In "Some Collisions Bring Luck," the relationship seems in trouble at one point because "We coalesced in the false chemistry of words / rather than truly touching." And in "Doing It Differently," you have the lines, "a mistrust of the rhetoric of tenderness / thickens your tongue." Perhaps we could talk about your consciousness of the difficulties of saying things right in language and of the poet's role in this context.

MARGE PIERCY: I think that probably anyone who works with language is very conscious of the state of it. In one poem I say, "Words live, words die in the mouths of everybody." We all make language; we all use language; and we live in a society in which the language is constantly debased by the power system that attempts to control us and by the commercial uses to which it is put. Now, in a lot of poems I'm not talking about the deliberate debasing of language, as in the lies a government will tell, but about more specific and everyday experiences—the false chemistry of words, the social lies people say when they think they agree but don't. These are personal relationships where the other person fails to recognize conflicting wishes, wills, and so forth. Sometimes people just aren't aware of what this or that word or expression might mean to someone else. The more the language becomes debased generally, the tougher all these problems become.

As a writer, I entrust my life's work to language. It is my tool, and as with any tool you have to be constantly aware where it fails you and where you fail it. This doesn't mean that the poet should "purify" the language, as some people suggest. There's been an argument going on in poetry for a couple of hundred years at least between those poets who want to refine the language of poetry, take it out of the daily ferment it undergoes, take it toward a level of greater artifice, and the poets, with whom I would align myself, that want to use the language of everyday in a heightened, intensified way. You can use the language of the everyday without using a debased language; it requires care and an awareness of how language works.

POETRY MISCELLANY: Some of your poems are written in a different voice, such as "Postcard from the Garden"—"I sit on a rock on the border and call and call / in voice of cricket and coyote, of fox and mouse, / in my voice that rocks smash back on me. / The wings of the hawk beat overhead as he hovers, / baffled by waiting, on the warm neck of my flesh." In other poems, it's a modulation of voice, sometimes a metamorphic change of tone, that produces the great range that characterizes your best work.

MARGE PIERCY: Occasionally there are poems in a different voice or persona, but there are relatively few. There's "Another Country," where the character goes down and swims with the dolphins, a sort of transparent character, a fictional character who speaks for me. In terms of what we were just saying, the character says: "All conversation is a singing, / all telling alludes to and embodies / minute displacements." And there is a way in which voice provides a sense of range, but I would talk about range more in the sense of subject matter, type of lens. For example, I write very imagistic poems; I write very lush poems; I write very simple, stark poems; I write with long lines, short lines, poems with stanzas, poems without stanzas.

POETRY MISCELLANY: Many of the poems are written in sections, and shifts of the type you're talking about occur within a single poem. These poems have a more encompassing gesture, as do the various sequences you've written. The movement is described in a poem like "The Perpetual Migration," where you say, "We remember / backwards a little and sometimes forwards, / but mostly we think in the ebbing circles / a rock makes on the water." It puts you in the school of Whitman and Muriel Rukeyser. But there is also "Season of Hard Wind," which is much smaller, but is a quest poem ranging from a phone to Antarctica in its references.

MARGE PIERCY: Well, I'm not really conscious of that sort of encompassing gesture. In fact, I think of "Season of Hard Wind" as a very tight poem; I think I could argue why the images are appropriate to the poem. The telephone, for example, appears in several poems to represent the difficulty of communication. In other words, there is always an underlying argument, and I try to censor out images that divert too much, that are too bizarre. On the other hand, there are shifts in the poems—a longer poem, especially, might shift from comic to tragic, not to denigrate the emotions, but to show their complexity in these turns. These are shifts in tone; I associate them with some techniques in modern art. What is really important to me is that the poems have an emotional context. There should be a strong emotional coherence that can carry a lot of jumps of meaning and images. If there is not that emotional coherence, the poem will fall apart. Sometimes a poem will, in a sense, say more than I know, take me *past* what I know, especially in a long sequence. The images take me to a different level, but the controlling emotion keeps it coherent.

POETRY MISCELLANY: I think of Susan Sontag who, in "Against Interpretation," wrote that what we need is an "erotics of art." She says, "Real art has the capacity to make us nervous. By reducing the work of art to its context and then interpreting *that*, one tames the work of art."

MARGE PIERCY: It's difficult to learn how poems work because of how they're taught in school. There's not enough emphasis on feeling and emotion. When I went to college at Michigan the emphasis was very much on criticism, as much at least as on the primary works. It seemed that the point of writing a poem was to fit it into a vast critical superstructure. Later, at another school, the approach I encountered was more biographical. It was refreshing to hear about someone's life because that seemed more human, and poetry, after all, is a human activity. Perhaps the best thing a literature teacher could do is not teach interpretation. What you have to do is teach a passion for literature. Literature has to speak to you when you're in trouble or in pain, when you're happy. It gives you images of what you feel and what you want to feel, what you are and what you want to be, gives you strength and courage. People seem to need poems. There is a rise in amateurism. Many people, many who occasionally write poems, know one book of poetry; they have one book of poetry which they read, and it becomes their book of poetry which they'll wear out.

POETRY MISCELLANY: Tess Gallagher, in a recent issue of *APR*, talks about "woman-time." She worries that women haven't written enough poems that are more open, longer, take more into account a woman's sense of rhythm. I think you do so in your longer poems and sequences, which we talked about. "The Lunar Cycle," for example, does this. In "Cutting the Grapes Free," you say, "I do not seek to leap free from the wheel / of change but to dance in that turning." And in "Twelve-Spoked Wheel," you measure time by "the turn of the wheel" and say, "I have tried to forge my life whole, / round, integral as the earth spinning." Seasonal structures are important in *Twelve-Spoked Wheel* and in other poems. Could you sketch out your sense of the way you sense time?

MARGE PIERCY: There are three kinds of time. The first is clock time, the everyday world of deadlines. The second involves being conscious of yourself in history, a political sense of time. For example, I am conscious of myself as a creature upon whom certain historical forces act. This is a sense of history as process, but it is a process which the individual can participate in and help create, in which you can affect other people. That is, you recreate the past and try to sense implications for the future. The third kind of time is a presence as opposed to this process. There's that poem, for example, where I am like my grandmother who's like my mother; there is a sense of continuity established here. This third kind involves cycles, too, and this perhaps relates to the way we were talking about how poems move, gather their images, talk about them, come back to them.

POETRY MISCELLANY: "Tumbled and Tangled Mane" describes an immersion in a physical, dynamic world, but also searches for moments of clarity. The world for the poem becomes "as in the eye of a hurricane / when the waves roll cascading in undiminished / but for a moment and in that place the air / is still, the moment of clarity out / of time at the center of an act." These moments seem very important for your poetry, sometimes almost prophetic, as in "September Afternoon at Four O'Clock"—"In the perfect / moment the future coils, / a tree inside a pit." They are moments of stillness and recognition that give an act direction, that is, do not actually take it out of the flow of time.

MARGE PIERCY: I guess that what I would add is that there's no way of holding on to those moments. The perspective changes. Even though there's a sense of repetition and cycles, there's also a uniqueness and difference. And yet, unless you can apply the knowledge of that whole structure back into your life, then things will remain merely discreet, discontinuous. Feminism has provided such a structure for me, for it provides a way of holding on to and assimilating insights.

POETRY MISCELLANY: The moments bring into focus questions of will, perhaps. In "For Sohshana—Pat Swinton" you say, "No, I am not a soldier in your / history, I live in my own tale / with others I choose." In the introduction to "Laying Down the Tower" in *To Be of Use*, you talk about the need to "break through the old roles to encounter our own meanings in the symbols we experience in dreams, in songs, in vision, in meditation." You go on to say, "The myths we imagine we are living...shape our choices." The sequence attempts to "reconcile" you to the various histories around you, including the women's movement.

MARGE PIERCY: Yes, that's one of a series of poems in which I've been concerned about the nature of choice, what it means as a woman to be able to choose. These are difficult issues today in general and especially for women on a political and social level. Feminism provides a point of view through which to understand problems, but I wouldn't say everything should be reduced to that. Racism is very real; the class struggle is very real. Feminism involves a strong sense of history, a strong sense of ourselves in nature, in natural cycles, and a sense of responsibility to each other whenever we need aid.

POETRY MISCELLANY: The question of political and sociological poetry is arising once again, and its defenders have become more articulate and their poetry better perhaps than a few years ago. I'm thinking of Philip Levine and AI in particular. And yet there really aren't many good political poets today. This, of course, is an important dimension in your own poetry, say, the poem about radiation in *The Moon Is Always Female* or the poems against the military establishment in *Hard Loving*. I think, too, of "Heavy as in Being Squashed," where you combat "The vast incomprehensible / inertia of what is," which summarizes a stance against injustices.

MARGE PIERCY: First of all, on a personal level, we are all social beings. There are social dimensions to poetry, political dimensions, as well as all the other rational and irrational meanings and structures that poetry, like any human activity, participates in. It is as absurd, though, to reduce poems to political statements as it is to deny they have a political dimension. Any attempt to reduce poetry to one thing is always doomed to fail. Poets in the past have always understood this; poets like Chaucer, Pope, Dryden, Byron, Shelley, and Wordsworth understood it. But there is an attitude that has developed since about the 1890s that attempts to cast all politics and sociology out of poetry. I don't understand how anyone can seriously maintain this attitude. Actually, the attitude is itself political. Art which embodies the ideals of the ruling class in society isn't conceived of as being political and is simply judged by how well it is done. Art which contains ideas which threaten the position of that ruling class is silenced by critics; it is political, they say, and not art. This is what happens, for example, to feminist poetry. It's absurd.

Michael S. Harper, 1978

Magic: Power: Activation: Transformation

POETRY MISCELLANY: With respect to many of your poems, perhaps all of them, it can be said that you are an interpreter of the past, a historical poet. I mean this the way Gadamer does when he says that the "interpreter" is always an interpreter of history in the sense that he must account for his own present as an extension, however modified, of a past. That is, one cannot simply uncover what was, but must "fuse his own horizons," his own present, with that past. I think of this in connection with the notion of "modality" that appears so often in your work. For example, in "Corrected Review" you say, "Our mode is our jam session / of tradition, / past in this present moment / articulated."

MICHAEL HARPER: I think I am a lyrical poet, but being a lyrical poet becomes absorbed in the difficulties of what it means to be historically responsible, and to become historically responsible means to open yourself up to options not immediately available. There is a historical perspective that you can bring to add perspective.

I think it will be useful to focus on the idea of modality. Though the idea can have a musical reference, it really comes from a spiritual context. It has cosmological references. The primary forces of men are life forces. Modality is always about relationships. It is also about energy, true only unto itself, which means that a mode is perceived in a noncomparative context. The Cartesian analogical way of looking at the world will not do for modality. A mode is true only unto itself and can be understood only inside the modality. So that when one gets into a heavy schizophrenic method of analysis, that is, discursive thought, the Western orientation of division between denotation-connotation, body-soul, life-spirit, soul-body, mind-heart—that is a way of misunderstanding what modality is. Modality is always about unity.

The point that I want to make is oneness, unity. That's why the lines in one poem go: "modality: we are one; a man is another / man's face, modality, in continuum, / from man, to man, *contact-high*, to man, / *contact-high*, to man, high modes, oneness." This is a practical application of modality. The poem is a summing up of my relationship or kinship with another man. At the experiential level, that's all there is; but then in the process of writing a poem dimensions are provided which are larger than that. That's where the historical comes in.

POETRY MISCELLANY: When you talk about modes as rejuvenating sources, I think of your new sequence, "Uplift from a Dark Tower," where you relate to Etienne, to Washington, to Du Bois's analysis of Washington, your own personal situation. In a sense, this modal view allows you to have a conversation with the past—I mean with other people and perspectives.

MICHAEL HARPER: The context is Yaddo. The Trask family who owned the building had a private history drawn up, much of which is a rationale for their doing what they did. Now, what I have done is go into that place, occupied it, walked over the thresholds Etienne and the others did, and revivified the context, and not only that, but have taken energy from it. From a linguistic point of view, from a point of view of the images, I have tried to revitalize it so as to put it in a proper and more open-ended type of focus. It talks about the role of the artist, about relationships between blacks and whites, property and money, ownership, and the difference between ownership of body and ownership of soul, about landscape as peopled by people and as peopled by what we call nature, and it questions the Western philosophic tradition in doing so. It's about ways of knowing. There are ways of knowing that don't necessarily presuppose experience, something we call symbolic geography, a symbiotic relation between the way we ascertain experience and the way we ascertain information. Information is full of symbolism that we have to manipulate.

POETRY MISCELLANY: This open-ended aspect is crucial for modality, for the way both ideas and techniques interact, isn't it? Take the title of the poem you quoted from before, "High Modes: Vision as Ritual: Confirmation." It progresses by modes. Things are always beginning, setting out, but the poem is also controlled as the colons control or modulate the parts of the title.

MICHAEL HARPER: Let me talk about architecture; let me talk about orchestration. Poems come to me as wholes though they work themselves out individually. Now, there are some grammatical premises that are associated with this. The use of colons is careful and important, as you pointed out—sometimes they provide an equal sign which cues before and after, and this is standard grammatical practice though the emphasis on colons is part of the orchestration of the poem. Sometimes stanzas will have the same relationship to each other as the parts on either side of the colon, and poems in a whole book can be related in that way.

Now, in terms of the manner in which composition is open-ended, if you take the two concepts, centrifugal and centripetal, and put them together from a linguistic point of view, then I think you'll have some idea of the forces I'm trying to control. In "Corrected Review," a response to Leon Forest's book, *There Is a Tree More Ancient Than Eden*, the form is improvisational or open-ended. But it is also a philosophical and artistic statement about a way of seeing and a way of living. It is a black jazz man's improvisational world view, and the assumption is that what he takes and what he makes, in the specific, is kind of accidental. I want to point out that there are values in the process of being articulated, values that are often lost when people only pay attention to a particular form. We also have to remember that for the poet, the craftsman, there has to be some sort of design. You have to know where you might be going at the same time you remain open-ended. If there's a need for a map, you can make one if you don't have one, or you can transcend the map when you get into areas where the map won't help you.

POETRY MISCELLANY: In connection with this open-ended view, I think there is an increasing tendency among contemporary thinkers to follow through a method of what Nietzsche calls "Effective History." I think it is in this tradition that Du Bois writes: history becomes a kind of "striving." The focus is not upon larger traditional patterns, but upon singular, often smaller events that are often sentiments, loves, aspects of consciousness in individuals and groups, deep-rooted instincts. These things might chart a group of images, a reserve of archetypal images, an "index" as you say, that contains implications people were not aware of at the time of an action, and the meanings have to be drawn out later. I think here of the chapters on Crummell and Jones in *The Souls of the Black Folk* and the way Du Bois can infuse great meaning into those lines in the light of his own time. You do something like that, say, when you write about Brown or Washington—or your mythical-historical "John Henry Louis." In *Debridement*, you say, "When there is no history / there is no metaphor." And in "Eve," you have the saying, "tall tales to larger truths." What is the relation between fact and truth or history and metaphor? And are there certain ways in which indexes of images operate in that relation?

MICHAEL HARPER: Du Bois is vastly misunderstood. *The Souls of the Black Folk* is organized and orchestrated in a very prescriptive manner. There are fourteen chapters: the four that come last are most important for blacks and whites to see simultaneously; the first ten are primarily for white people. The book ends with the sorrow songs, true repositories of experience translated into song; the whole book attempts to transform values. Du Bois tells the short story about John that you refer to in order to show how a certain amount of information fails by definition. There are nuances and modes of expression that are lost simply because they have not been apprehended, because the inclination of the age is not to apprehend. The stated agenda is different from the real one. He is worried about black people, but who don't understand the parameters of leadership, don't even understand the nuances of language their own people use. How can they go on planting seeds, yeasts?—there, I've used some of my images you refer to in order to describe the issue.

The Crummell section of the book is most important to me in this respect because it is the story of failed leadership. In terms of the prescriptive ways of measurement, Crummell ought to have succeeded. He had the audience, the respect, but failed to do what he intended, and failed in his own analysis of himself. I have great admiration for Du Bois, with all his great and enigmatic contradictions, but we have different artistic points of view.

Poetry Miscellany: If "Nightmare Begins Responsibility," then, of course, history and art do, too. But, then, what responsibilities, specifically, does the poet have?

Michael Harper: The artist's responsibility is to activate. Activation is done by craft. You must put your materials together in a way that produces power. If it has power, then it can transform.

What I love about *The Tempest* is that it's about magic. That's another way of saying it's about power. If you have the power to transform, you have the chance to dominate reality. And if you can dominate reality you can change the way people see things: magic, power, activation, transformation. A poet takes people out of themselves; they have no reference points that are easily translatable in terms they expect. If you are allowed to negotiate with what is supposed to transform you, then you will never understand what was supposed to happen to you. You'll be negotiating, not experiencing. That's why seduction is so very important in art. To be seduced is to be taken out of self. That's what interests me about Jean Toomer. He writes a book called *Cane*, which talks about cosmic violation. You are disarmed at the time you are being penetrated. The reality is slavery and its aftermath, but the way that it is written is so beautiful that you are disarmed. That's what I mean by seduction.

So what interests me is this potential to activate. To be able to dominate your reality by the word, and to get all its nuances—that is the real battle. I see this as a both/and situation. We have to be good magicians, manipulators of the various provinces of the word in all their dimensions, and this can involve complexities and contradictions— "In the beginning was the word—and the denial of the word." There are centrifugal and centripetal forces to contend with.

An artist by definition has to be a good craftsman, conversable in his medium, and he has to be moral. By morality I mean he has to be true to the components he is using; he has to understand the attributes of the materials that are being orchestrated. Like a composer, he has to know what his instruments can do, what the force field will be like when they are placed together—or displaced. But the artist shouldn't be intimidated by prescriptive notions about how things can be put together—he shouldn't be afraid to experiment. To improvise you have to have the skills that ensure you against thinking only in terms of what might be workable. I think artists themselves must be pulled out of self so that they can begin to examine from another point of view their own premises.

POETRY MISCELLANY: This business about the artist as magician, about the morality of art and the power of language is roughly akin to some of Freud's theoretical views in *Moses and Monotheism*, a radical history on one level. Though his discussion is in a different context—a different mode—his notion of the duality and struggle within a tradition and the violent displacement of one religion by another—and the linguistic basis of this displacement—seems instructive here.

MICHAEL HARPER: Ah, yes, well, Moses against Pharaoh is a cosmic war. Both are perfect men, though Moses is of a higher order. That is, in terms of the cosmology involved, Pharaoh is not an imposter. When he brings forth his magicians, they are real magicians. They bring lots of power to the situation. In cosmological terms, we know the Egyptians knew more about the world, the universe, than anybody. When Pharaoh brings these magicians to bear, his cosmological perspective is a correct one; for him to be overcome by Moses shows there's a new day. Now, the fact that Moses is an interloper, that it is revealed he is going to come, that it is prescriptive that he come, and the fact that he bests Pharaoh means that normal events are way out of scale. From my point of view, the Western-Hebraic perspective for exploring that phenomenon is inadequate. When I talk about the perfect man, in "Corrected Review" for example, I'm talking about value and principle. What are these things supposed to mean? How do you make them concrete? When you speak of sacred traditions, let's use the Bible as an example, you have to decode that tradition. You have to understand what its premises are—and for me there are too many things undone in discussions of Moses. I like the idea of Moses as a man who had to make choices— choices that must have seemed blasphemous. And I want to know what higher laws were given to him by which he could make those choices. You used the phrase "violent displacement," and I'd say a reordering of priorities.

POETRY MISCELLANY: Let's follow this problem of doubleness and the need for unity or wholeness a bit further. Of course, in several poems you refer to Du Bois's double consciousness and the veil. He talks about black history as the "history of strife—longing to attain self-conscious manhood, to merge his double self into a better and truer self." Whether he succeeds in this enterprise is, as you suggested, perhaps a different matter. I think your poems do achieve a wholeness—your entire vision does. One of the most powerful images you use is, I think, the image of photographs—in fact, the whole context of photography. In "Smoke," the images of making bread and developing pictures come together to form a complex and unified perspective. In *Song: I Want a Witness*, there are numerous references to photography, especially in one section. To see your own or someone else's image as a negative, for example, is a perfect way of casting your philosophy. And you even carry the uses of the image further into transformational ideas. For example, in "Trays: A Portfolio," you do a typically rich thing—an image as such becomes the reality; cranberries like drops of blood are modulated into the image of being "bedded with Blood" as the final thrust of the poem changes dramatically in tone. The basis of such transformations always seems a doubleness transcended.

MICHAEL HARPER: "Smoke" on one level deals with enlargement in various senses; it deals with the difference between static reality and ongoing essential reality—and the spiritual aspects of both. The magic of naming, or taking a picture, does not obliterate who occupies the terrain. Du Bois, remember, in *The Souls of the Black Folk*, gets on a train, supposedly sees Indians through the window. What he's doing is conjuring. His mode of operation is a Jim Crow car. The train is a vehicle, but also an image, a metaphor about a condition. When I was living in Massachusetts, I discovered that we were in fact on an Indian burying ground. That had a lot to do with my sense of responsibility to redress the injury that I'd seen. I had to understand that the cranberry bogs and all the rest were connected to burial grounds. All these things come together in the poem, are frozen in it. I'm interested in the difference between taking a picture—freezing a dimension of reality—and at the same time being able to ascertain and go beyond the image one has in one's mind and one's being.

This whole business of photographs is magical. When I was in South Africa, I had to have a passbook, be subject to that whole process of experiences, the images of the different cultures frozen together. The "Militance of the Photograph in the Passbook of a Bantu under Detention" makes use of family background. My grandfather was a missionary in the AME church from 1908 to 1916, and I saw the first building he'd built in Wilberforce Institute, forty-five to fifty miles from Johannesburg.

POETRY MISCELLANY: History truly does become your own heartbeat. It seems that in these new poems and in the newer poems in *Images of Kin* you've built on the wholeness you earned earlier. One of the turning points in your vision seems to me to be "Nightmare Begins Responsibility."

MICHAEL HARPER: I had been carrying it around with me for years. I wanted to come to grips with my own loss of children. I also knew there were things I wanted to resolve with myself. I knew I had been victimized by some reality and some fantasy in science. I myself was an image when I presented myself as a father, and some in the profession had a predisposition to see me in a certain way. To understand that we have a racial history is a prerequisite for understanding what I had to do. Love has to do with doing as well as being. What you do under pressure often gives you clarity about what you have to do as a person, and what I wanted that poem to do was take me on as a principal in the action as well as an artist. I had to look at myself carefully before anyone could be blamed. Now, the poem is also a larger statement than just my own personal situation. It has to do with the culture we live in, the idiom we use to express ourselves, our own contexts, our genealogy.

POETRY MISCELLANY: Some of those forces and contexts you mention—that you've mentioned in other places as well—are pretty bleak, and not just in theoretical terms, but in raw, physical terms, as many of your poems show and feel. Michel Foucault says that history is the "analysis of a descent"; its aim is "to expose a body totally imprisoned by history and the process of history's destruction of the body." *History Is Your Own Heartbeat*, for example, is filled with references to assaults of various kinds on the body. Pain throughout your poems becomes almost a metaphysical idea—the notion of a cost of history.

MICHAEL HARPER: The body is obviously an important image for me. What I don't like about the whole Cartesian way of seeing things is the separation of the body and soul, and this idea seems to reverse it somewhat. Now, one of the reasons I'm preoccupied with pain is because there is a cost to the vision. The body is always in a state of dissolution, and therefore one's premises about the material world are evanescent. They're always passing. They might be imperceptible. We have to understand that what is indestructible about us has to do with qualitative things. That which you are likely to undergo, the beatings you take in physical or psychic terms are limited to the context you are operating in. My hope is that my readers will feel it is more important to have clarity and resolve than it is to buffer yourself against the realities of things; you are able to endure anything if you know that you have the spiritual underpinnings to know that even in dissolution you are indestructible.

Obviously, Du Bois and Douglass understood there was no contradiction in being black and being American. The history of race relations, the Declaration of Independence, the Bill of Rights, the Constitution—these are watermarks in the discourse with reality. That offers a semblance of reality for me for it shows the degree of intention needed to transcend a condition. When I talk about transcendence, I'm not talking about leaping out of the body and leaving the fight. I'm talking about dealing with problems in very precise ways—political, sociological, historical. We have to endure and demand clarity. You can't just attempt to fortify yourself; you have to be able to be taken out of yourself. The best self-protection is the capacity to endure and insist on clarity at any price. We all have our little filmstrips in our heads about how we want things to come out. What did Caliban say about language? And how is he going to rest upon it? Is that a paradigm of the world?

Donald Hall, 1979

On the Periphery of Time

POETRY MISCELLANY: This past spring I read a book titled *The Origin of Consciousness in the Breakdown of the Bicameral Mind* by Julian Jaynes, which suggests that consciousness is not necessary for human thought, that consciousness, in fact, is a relatively recent development in human history. According to him, early minds listened to auditory hallucinations that originated in one side of the brain, a bicameral brain half conscious, half unconscious, or preconscious. The wonderful thing about all this is that Jaynes has shown a genuine source for poetry outside the conscious mind; he's given us a "scientific" means of accounting for inspiration, the voice of the muse—or what you call the "vatic voice." What we have to do, you say in an essay, is let that voice sing or speak to us. We have to listen. It's like some lost potential, isn't it? A loss that's made us less than human?

DONALD HALL: To me the act of writing the poem is an enormous and almost unequaled collaboration of conscious and unconscious processes. The vatic voice is for listening: to stories, songs, puns, all sorts of things inside yourself; the tendency of the world, for a couple of thousand years, probably longer, has been to suppress. Various things that I have read about the development of consciousness have suggested that planning—the kind of planning necessary for agriculture—required development of consciousness. But a complete person must use both consciousness and unconsciousness.

Many contemporary theorists concentrate on the unconscious contents as Freud does in "The Relation of the Poet to Daydreaming." Therefore, they don't deal with the finished poem; they do not speak of what shapes and organizes unconscious contents into a poem, into that formality which in itself is a kind of singing. I think there are two ideas of singing; one is metaphorical, as Jaynes probably intended—songs as opposed to discourse, emotion and expression as opposed to reason; but on the other hand, there is the resolution of assonance, or the resolution that shapes metaphorical coherence. Language is a development of consciousness. Poetry is *not* a primitive form of language, but a sophisticated form of language—because of its control.

There is a part of us that is always dreaming, whether we are awake or asleep; at times one has access to this part. But this dreaming seldom provides materials of resolution, materials of formal wholeness. The unconscious *does* give us the rabbit which disappears down the hole; we have only a glimpse of that rabbit, a vanishing message. I work on poems over a long time, and the first draft may be very intuitive; I write without knowing what I write *about*. Later drafts involve more consciousness, but there are always excursions back into the unconscious. One cannot say that the unconscious provides all the content, the conscious all the form. On the one hand, writing a poem is organizing language, an act of the consciousness. On the other hand, much of the act is *immediately* intuitive: I write something as I am revising, and I do not know why I do it. I do it because it *sounds* good. Then a day later or a week later I may understand what I have done.

POETRY MISCELLANY: I'm also very curious about your notion of "peripheral vision," where frequently the important things are glimpsed as if out of the corner of the eye, not by a conscious focus on the object. Oddly enough, I was reading Jacques Lacan's *The Four Fundamental Concepts of Psychoanalysis* at the same time I was rereading for this chat. Lacan talks about what he calls the gaze—a condition of perceiving through which we can be surprised: "What I look at is never what I see," he says. He even goes so far as to provide an illustration—two concentric circles, one inside the other. "Reality is marginal," he says; it exists along the outer band, the periphery. It made me think of how your poems, particularly the later, longer ones, proceed by an associative movement, an encompassing.

DONALD HALL: Sometimes a dream is vivid. It nibbles away at the edges of my mind. Then, after a while, I begin to *see* something about it, associations, as when a rock tossed in a pond ripples out, the circles getting larger and longer. The image of the pig in "Eating the Pig" was like that. In the poem "Flies," there is the line, "The blow of the axe resides in the acorn." The line came one morning, and I staggered out of bed to write it down. I woke up later thinking I dreamed a line and I wrote it down. When I looked at what I had written I could barely read it, but I carried it around with me, repeating it until finally I saw what it meant. Sometimes there are important things that you haven't yet quite understood—you shouldn't be so quick to edit them out just because they seem to be peripheral.

POETRY MISCELLANY: Very often, though, it seems that the center is critical, too, as in the essay "Goatfoot, Milktongue, Twinbird: The Psychic Origins of Poetic Form," where you "come to the end of the trail" and meet your three psychic and mythic characters (four later) who remember things further back than we can reach—there's what Freud calls the knot, Lacan the gap. In your poem, "The Stump"—"It is a door into the underground of old summers, / but if I bend down to it, I am lost / in crags and buttes of harsh landscape / that goes on forever."

DONALD HALL: Yes. Frequently I feel I can go so far and then I get stuck. It is frustrating, but a true record of the poem. In the "Town of Hill," there is a screen door at the end of the poem. Robert Bly asked once, "What's behind the screen door?" I don't *know* what's behind the screen door.

I want to emphasize the struggle of consciousness to make a true record. Many of my poems from several years ago did not pursue with diligence and patience the implications of things. I was too willing to follow the poem to a point where something exciting happened, where there was a momentary lighting up of a landscape. If I could make something out in that flash, I'd end the poem. Now I'm concerned to pursue these images further, to struggle with these "knots," as you call them.

POETRY MISCELLANY: Let's talk a little about the language of that pursuit, a language of sensual sounds. I think of Stevens's poem, "The Creation of Sound," where he says, "We say ourselves in syllables that rise / From the floor, rising in speech we do not speak." One strives, does he not, to recover the "vowels of bright desire" ("Kicking the Leaves"), the "village / of little sounds" ("Stone Walls")? Don't we search for what you call in your brief essay, "Words without Bodies," the "dark mouth of the vowel by which the image tells its sensual rune." And isn't this Coleridge's desire at the end of "Kubla Khan"?

DONALD HALL: One of the notions that Coleridge suggested is the hypnotic effect of meter. The preverbal sources that I discuss in "Goatfoot, Milktongue, Twinbird" are brought into consciousness by rhythm. When I move into Twinbird in that essay I begin to talk about form, but form includes forms of thinking. The movement of human thought is formally embodied in the shape of the poem, in rhyme and in the resolutions of assonance, in rhythm and the unfolding of metaphors. I don't mind saying what I've said before: when I have discovered how to make a new noise I have discovered a new content.

POETRY MISCELLANY: And obviously there's a new rhythm in your longer lines. The rhythm is more incantatory and more orchestrated.

DONALD HALL: That longer line developed in the fall of 1974 with the beginnings of "Eating the Pig" and "Kicking the Leaves." That line with its many pauses and its possibilities for asymmetry opened up a great deal for me. Whitman and Roethke and Kinnell have made their mark on me. The longer line makes you push forward, be more inclusive, more extensive than intensive.

POETRY MISCELLANY: This inclusive gesture informs the sense of time in your poems, particularly your sense of the moment in "Kicking the Leaves," a moment that is constituted, as Husserl would say, by retentions and protentions. We've already discussed how "Eating the Pig" and "Stone Walls" use references that cross several types of time and several periods of time while they focus on particular acts. In a way, the very bareness of autumn allows the old stone walls to be seen, and the stone walls themselves, "emerging" each autumn, are man's counterpart to the "unperishing hills," to the cyclic nature of the seasons. You remember in the poem the way your grandfather spoke: "riding home from hayfields, he handed me the past." This handing over of the past is possible because of the intuition of the nature of the moment, isn't it? It makes time, in a sense, available?

DONALD HALL: I have a special access to time here on the family farm. There are pictures on the wall, and old clothing upstairs, and the graves down the road—the presence of the dead, not just an abstract, but the dead. Past and present are here together, and a dimmer sense of the future.

I think this sense of the availability of time, as you put it, explains my liking for specific detail. They make time's texture. They may be also important as peripheral details, to refer back to what we were saying earlier.

POETRY MISCELLANY: Yes, the handing over of the past is not transcendental in an Emersonian sense, but more rooted in Thoreau's sense. If you say in one poem that you wish to "return" to "the world that lives in the air," you also want to "walk on the earth of the present." There's a balanced perspective, isn't there? All things seem to interpenetrate, seem to be layered in this physical sense of time. I think of "Maple Syrup," where your dead grandfather's syrup, found later, gives "from his lost grave the gift of sweetness."

DONALD HALL: This sense of the past is like strata of rock, or perhaps like the layers archaeologists uncover that show several historical periods in a simultaneous cut-away. Also I emphasize moments of disconnection, detachment from the self and its past, and so from time. Freud refers to this as the oceanic experience. It's like floating out in space, or on the sea, severed from any temporal orientation. This oceanic experience suggests something about the absolute coextension of various times. In fact, the extension of space in such an experience is a metaphor for the simultaneity of all time.

When I was a boy, and living here on the farm, I would interrupt my morning reading by going out into a field, into a kind of hollow hidden from the road, and lie on my back, look up at the clouds, and practice floating out of myself into that world that lived in the air.

Time and space, then, are closely related for me. I think of the moment as the axis of a cross. There is a sideways movement which is space, the coexistence of, say, Calcutta and Danbury, New Hampshire, of everything possible in the world. But that linear spatial plane is insufficient to live in. There is also a vertical, temporal line that connects, say, a cathedral with the generations it took to build it. The present is most alive in the place where these two movements cross.

POETRY MISCELLANY: The moment, of course, always perishes, as the "moment of roses" does in "Old Roses." But "Kicking the Leaves" as a whole transcends this loss, for the handing over of the past extends toward the future as you replace father and grandfather. It's like Heidegger's "retrieve" of the past—a return to retrieve past possibilities. In the poem, when you kick the leaves, those "lids of graves," it also seems to be an act of prefiguring—"kicking the leaves, / Autumn 1955 in Massachusetts knowing / my father would die when the leaves were gone." In a similar way, watching your own son and daughter grow old and distance themselves as they create their own lives, you project: "I / diminish, not them, as I go first / into the leaves, taking / the steps they will follow, Octobers and years from now." Finally, you see yourself as "building / the house of dying," as "taking a place / in the story of the leaves."

DONALD HALL: Without the past there is no future. It is imperative to understand the future. When we retrieve the past, in the Heideggerian sense you mentioned, we have the opportunity to understand the possibilities of *difference* from the past, and this leads us to the knowledge that there can be change; this makes the future thinkable. Handing over the past is, then, a form of reconstruction, not just of the past but of possible futures. It is not an act of simple repetition, but an opening up of the self to the whole dimension of time. It is important to remember that the present extends to past and future this way; they are coextensive and form the unity of the present moment.

John Hollander, 1978

The Candle in the Pitcher

POETRY MISCELLANY: In the Notes to "Spectral Emanations," you refer the reader to Kierkegaard's *Either/Or*, specifically, I assume, to the chapter entitled "The Rotation Method," as a source for the title of your poem, "Rotation of Crops." It seems to me that Kierkegaard places the source of action in a boredom, which is itself the "result of the Nothingness that pervades reality." The method for overcoming this boredom—a moral and metaphysical ennui—is this Rotation Method. It is based on a principle of limit that involves a balance between remembering and forgetting, tradition and freedom. For Kierkegaard, the crucial thing is self-limitation, which can include a subversion of hope, and achieving results intensively rather than extensively.

JOHN HOLLANDER: The turning around of what was there and turning it into something else—in those two senses of turning into, that is, conversion and inversion—I suppose now that you mention it, I'd have to say it is very basic.

What I was doing in that poem was substituting for the erotic methodology of the first part of *Either/Or* a poetical one. I was very unhappy when I wrote the poem, very unhappy with my work. It was written just after *The Night Mirror*, which had been badly received, and the "tedium" in the poem concerns my discontent with what I had previously written. So it is a poem about farming my own work—I use the definite article as in the phrase "the Farmer John" to refer to part of myself.

The nursery rhyme that is referred to in the poem—"Neither you nor I can know / why oats, peas, beans, and barley grows"—is probably a crop rotation formula. There would be a sequence: oats, peas, beans, barley, fallow. Now, the meaning may be lost, but we have the formula. (Remember Shirley Jackson's "The Lottery"— "Lottery in June, corn ripe soon"?) There's a kind of magic, a mystery involved in all this that has always been present, as least in my own poetry.

Actually, "Rotation of Crops" is a poem that perhaps knew a little more about my life than I did at the time. (This phenomenon has been happening increasingly the last six or seven years.) I'm very grateful for it because the poems of mine that matter most to me now are those I didn't fully understand when I wrote them. The first poem of this kind was "The Night Mirror." Part of it included material from a childhood dream, and it was about a certain kind of fear of an image of myself. I knew it had to be just the way it was written, but I couldn't explain why everything was in it, or why some things were left out. I suppose the best example of this is "The Head of the Bed." I knew it had to occur in a certain sequence that is not quite the sequence of composition, especially in the first half, but I couldn't produce a paraphrase of the poem that would explain this. I understand "The Head of the Bed" better now, partly because some people have written about it. For example, Harold Bloom once wrote that the two figures at the end were really the same, and at the time I thought it was nonsense, but I've come to realize he was probably right, and the poem knew more about itself than I did.

POETRY MISCELLANY: This is a "turning around" of your own attitude toward or understanding of your work, then. How does it affect your sense of your own development?

JOHN HOLLANDER: Well, there is a problem of innovation in art. I've always felt that the most radical gesture of innovation is already contained, limited. That is, after a certain age I didn't try to do avante garde–looking things because that way seemed just to follow another tradition. The problem is in moving on—how to get to the next thing without writing forgeries of what you have been doing. Now, the oeuvres of Picasso and Stravinsky are models for phased careers, and I think that the programmatic quality there is as bad as staying in a rut. I've always liked to think of the problem in terms of setting new tasks too difficult for myself. In some ways, perhaps, *Visions from the Ramble* was difficult even by these standards at the time I was doing it, but I learned a lot from doing it. I wasn't able to do what I really wanted to until "Spectral Emanations." There is a price, of course; it is not an easy poem, and it depends on the relation of the parts to the whole.

POETRY MISCELLANY: We might focus this notion of difficulty, the setting of a goal really, and the notion of "turning" or rotation more specifically on technique for a few moments. There's the struggle, in *An Entertainment for*

Elizabeth, between Variety, who becomes Chance, and Pattern; they are two modes of composing. In "Violet," you have the lines, "At the song's beginning / Even as our voices / Rise we know the last words." It seems to me there is always a tension in your work between an incredibly playful wit and the often elaborate structure that houses it. What is the relation between chance and teleology?

JOHN HOLLANDER: Sometimes the difficulty of a task may act as a starting point. "Fireworks" was written as an accentual and perfectly matched Pindaric Ode. It was, for me, a poem of fireworks, a pyrotechnic display, and it involved several mythological patterns. Fireworks were to be poetry, and this was to be a Fourth of July poem, and it was to lead to the section about the ninth of July, which I took to be a crucial moment of the American imagination, as midway between the fourth and the fourteenth. It starts out, "Fire is worst, and fires of artifice thirst after more than / Water does." Now, this is a private allusion for me and not necessary for the reader to know. It is the complete reverse of the opening of one of Pindar's Odes, which begins, "Water is best," and "fires of artifice" is a mistranslation of the French for "fireworks" (*feux d'artifice*). I was mistranslating to make something else: instead of calling for the muse or waiting for light to strike, what I was doing, and what I have frequently done, is to begin with something else.

Even though there is an opposition in *An Entertainment* between chance and structure, it is obvious that they are symbiotic with each other. There is always a great risk in plotting something beforehand, as I did in "Spectral Emanations." A valuable experience I had was in doing shaped poems. They came after *Visions from the Ramble*, which I felt was too prolix. I wanted to write something tighter, more epigrammatic. I was in England at the time and owed the harpsichordist Ralph Kirkpatrick a letter, so I wrote that poem, half as a joke, in the shape of a harpsichord. I simply drew it and typed out the dummy with x's. I had done a poem in the shape of an hourglass before, but that was a rhymed sonnet I worked into the shape, and this was done for the typewriter character by character. Then I did one in the shape of a cup and found I had a way of generating poems. Very often I would type out the shape, then tack it up on the wall, sometimes for months, before I knew what the poem was going to be. I always wanted to do a picture book; but I can't draw, and these poems make a nice book of emblems.

So the notion of a certain limit as a means of freedom is important for me. I suppose what frees me is the chance to do some problem-solving. I don't think this aspect of poetry is central, but it can enable some people to open up various possibilities, as I've explained, in my case, about the "Fireworks" poem. You know, I've discovered that when you do something for the sake of a rhyme it is imaginatively dead, but if you do something for the sake of rhythm you often uncover something that is more true. Changing a rhyme might produce something witty, but changing a rhythm might cause you to discover what something really meant. There's a certain magic to it, as I mentioned before. By diverting your attention from certain things, the rhythm might clear a way for other things to occur. The pattern might produce a chance discovery.

POETRY MISCELLANY: I think there's an important philosophical context to this play between chance and discovery, and it has to do with the notion of the moment—how the moment relates to a longer structure of time. In *Either/Or,* Kierkegaard says that moments can't be given so much significance that they can never be forgotten, but enough to be recollected at will. These moments, he says, if they cannot be determined by the self, can at least be seized. I think that many of your poems are such opportunistic seizures of significance. For example, at one such moment in "Fireworks" you say, "This is the time most real: for unreeling time there are no / Moments, there are no points, but only the lines of memory / Streaking across the black film of the mind's night." Such moments for you seem always to be threshold ones, as in "Tales Told of the Fathers," where the character stands waiting at the beginning "Moment," as the section is called. But if a moment usually passes quickly, the poems seem often to be able to create deferred moments. In "Yellow," you have the lines, "To have been kept, to have reached this season, / Is to have eternized, for a moment, / The time when promise and fulfillment feed / Upon each other." And in "Humming" you describe singing, poetry in a sense: "This is the business of being. To have heard / these undying cicadas, immortal while yet they live, is to burn / For a time in the moment itself."

JOHN HOLLANDER: I'm fascinated by your observation because, though I love to read, say, Proust, time is not something I brood about conceptually. These lines you've quoted to me I would not have thought to put together, but of course they do reflect something, and now you make me ask myself, "what do I mean?"

Let me try this: It may all have to do with the way my memory works. I can remember thousands of details, but often in a fragmented and reconstructed way. Perhaps there is something about my memory that tries to defeat continuity. To remember fully and perfectly would be to unreel a long stretch of time, and perhaps the implication is of movement toward an end, toward death.

Now, I don't mean to suggest that one simply writes discontinuous poems. Some poems, particularly by younger poets, employ a visual montage technique with only the thinnest narrative or abstract wiring holding the poem together. When you finish those poems, you just wonder where you are. Collage has to have a very careful structure; the moments have to fit into a larger pattern.

POETRY MISCELLANY: Sometimes that larger pattern or shape of time seems pessimistic. I'm thinking of the way the notion of fading seems to inform many of your poems. At the end of "The Head of the Bed," the image of death, some terrible end to things, invades the force of myth and life that wants to be asserted. Kierkegaard talks about a man who comes across a letter containing information about his life's happiness, but the writing is pale and fine—and fading. He tries to read, making out a word at a time, hoping like Cupcake that if he could figure out one word the next would follow. But he never does, and the whole thing crumbles into uncertainties. I see many of your characters, not just Cupcake, facing the same problem.

JOHN HOLLANDER: Yes, I suppose many of the poems are melancholy in that sense. A very important experience for me was my youthful love for and contemplation of "dissolves" in films. A fading in would occur contrapuntally with a fading out so that you would get not a crude ironic montage—not, say, where a clock on the wall dissolves into a prisoner's face as he waits to be executed—but more subtle and random ones. I used to love to try to remember the image that had faded out at the beginning of the scene. It was a natural experience for me, as important as regarding sunsets. "Movie Going," which I began as an Horatian didactic poem (in what is now Naples Pizza in New Haven) concerns this technique. It's a poem I can't read aloud anymore—it simply became a forerunner of journalistic kitsch nostalgia. I didn't know how important the idea was for me back at that time.

POETRY MISCELLANY: Isn't this in a sense one of the problems, or tasks as you've called them, that "Spectral Emanations" must solve? I mean, here is this complex poem that concerns the meaning of different colors—how they blend and blur—and, taken at one final moment when they are all together, make up the color white. But "white" isn't a title, only an unreached sum, for the poem has to present the colors sequentially, temporally. Is that really the problem of all poetry?

JOHN HOLLANDER: That's absolutely right. It is also the problem of any fiction that takes as its pattern anything like what Alastair Fowler calls "Triumphal Forms," that is, an array—pattern rather than a temporal, musical form. And when you add some kind of development or growth and have a poem that goes on for a long time, then the problems multiply. The problem of middles is very important, isn't it? How do you know when you are precisely at the middle of something spontaneous? Beginnings and endings are easy—they are the first things we learn. The question of the middle is a question of pace, of timing, of rhythm.

POETRY MISCELLANY: This notion of the middle appears directly in "Green," the middle section of the poem and the lamp. "Only at the moment of green is there time for a story, for only that branch is vertical, the other supports being parabolic," you say.

JOHN HOLLANDER: Yes, well, that's it. Also, the "Green" part is the fullest and richest, and most optimistic of the colors. The "Red" poem is the most essayistic and is about the primitive kinds of thoughts and feelings. The obvious things we say about red are that it is blood and earth and clay: the "Red" poem is the crudest about its interpretation of what a color is, though the prose commentary that goes with it is the purest prose poem in the sequence. The "Green" is that mock narrative which is in some ways a residue of the Cupcake narrative. It is highly organized: all of the conspirators have the names of the colors in different languages. The whole thing is a kind of caper; that caper is the way by which the poem disposes of the most trivial aspects of its fiction. If you take the notion literally, that perhaps this lamp has been buried all this time, then the obvious thing to do is dig it up so the rest of the poem can deal with more important things.

POETRY MISCELLANY: How did the poem originate? How, in a sense, was it dug up?

JOHN HOLLANDER: In the early 1970s I had contemplated a science fiction quest romance. I lived the fiction of there being a planet with seven satellites—what would it be like to have several moons illuminating in their different ways, with their different shades of color? And what about the order of elements changing? I remember I had a note that said, "a place where gold is as common as lead." I didn't know I was actually going to do anything like the present poem until I came across a passage in Hawthorne's *The Marble Faun* in the summer of 1972 in Rome. There is a section that comes after the one I quoted about the idea for "a mystic story or parable" that suggests that several American poets do several different poems that would make up "The Recovery of the Sacred Candlestick." I said to myself, "I'll do it," and it became a question of identity, a difficult task. I began to brood about what it could mean.

By the fall of 1973 I had started it. During the Middle East War I started the "Red" section. I had written the "Blue" section previously as an attempt to do a poem of pure imagination. It is a playful poem; the reason the "Blue" commentary developed earlier was because my scheme had to have Mercury, a force of destruction, somewhere in it. I was beginning to discover the meaning of my self-imposed mythology. The "Blue" prose commentary is a grotesque and amusing thing about doing away with one's predecessors, and the comic machine, the "contraption," is a parody of a person. But then there was the "Red," more serious and dismal, and I was stalled. I knew the next one I wanted to do was "Orange," and then "Yellow," but I couldn't do them. I knew what the "Indigo" would be like even when I hadn't written it yet, because indigo, before my school days, vanished from the spectrum, and it had to be about that. But I didn't know what "Orange" and "Yellow" would be about.

POETRY MISCELLANY: In the note you use, Hawthorne suggests something "full of poetry, art, philosophy, and religion."

JOHN HOLLANDER: Yes, of course, what else after all? I carefully set out in the beginning by deciding Hilda would be the Muse of the poem. That's why "The Muse in the Monkey Tower" was originally the proem. That particular poem is dedicated to James Wright because he lived in the same room in Rome the year after I had, and we exchanged notes. It was right across from the tower where Hilda lived, in *The Marble Faun*. But as the "Spectral Emanations" unfolded it was obvious that the Muse was Miriam as well. That is, the poem that set out to be an American poem had also to be a Jewish one. Perhaps this dooms the poem to one terrible kind of split because the heroines are so different; one is dark, dismal, evil and Jewish, the other is bright, glowing, Protestant, and American. But I think the way they work together is mutually supportive.

POETRY MISCELLANY: This whole question of the genesis of the thing, the idea of "turning into" that you described earlier is fascinating.

JOHN HOLLANDER: Well, you know, when I was stalled I began to send out the Cupcake messages, and after I had completed *Reflections on Espionage* I knew what the relation of "Orange" and "Yellow" was going to be. "Green" and "Violet" were the last ones. They were done in the summer of 1975, but by then everything had fallen into place.

It is interesting that—in terms of the idea of imposing a difficulty in order to discover meaning that we discussed earlier—the scheme I imposed on myself was something that was not arbitrary, was not something I was fighting against; it was something whose meaning I had to determine. This is the way I think about form now, not in technical terms. Before I had written any of "Spectral Emanations" I had to ask myself what the poem was going to look like. I had to determine its scale, given that it would be somewhat long. I knew it all involved seven—the seven branches of the menorah determine that, as well as the seven colors. Well, seven could give you all sorts of things, but I finally tried factorial seven (7!), which gave me the length, and then dividing 504 by 7 would give seventy-two lines per poem. But then they couldn't be all the same length. The longest lines would be in the middle, so it developed in the pattern of 6-8-10-12-10-8-6 syllables for the line lengths in the seven successive sections of the symmetrical lamp. Now all this evolved from my *sense* of the architecture of the poem, but it was before I knew what the poem was going to be about.

Then the task was to determine first, what does a color mean, and second, what does the boundary *between* two colors mean, for that, in a sense is what defines them. What happens when you pass from one to the other? (The solar spectrum does not have lines on it.) Where do you draw the line? The poem had to be able to draw the line, and that was like drawing the boundaries of a myth or the boundaries of a concept. For example, the general task of my fable seems to have turned out to be a questioning of the possibilities for nobility and beauty. Ordinarily, it just doesn't look like there are going to be any. Now, that could be associated with the quest for "where does red end and orange begin?" And in this case it moves from blood to orange juice, to a poem of waking up and starting out, of enterprise, of gold. Then the relation of orange to yellow is the difference between gold and *golden*, the metaphorical or vegetable gold that is real worth. In moving from "Orange" to "Yellow"—and this is a miniature of what the "Green" prose does— I had to invent that funny fellow Roy G. Biv to mock the gold out of existence. The whole process is summarized section by section in a moment in the prose of "Indigo." The possibilities of heroism and antiheroism are equally discounted. I'm still coming to understand the poem now myself. What I had understood from the beginning was something about the construction, but what I hadn't known was what it could do, and then what it had done. I realize that it is a difficult and puzzling poem, but it won't be puzzling forever.

POETRY MISCELLANY: The whole poem ends on a kind of balance— "a gathering of what had been half heard among the trees," a sense of death and ashes, but also a phoenixlike growth out of the ashes.

JOHN HOLLANDER: Oh, yes, it's dialectical. That's why the image at the end of the last section of poetry is so important. Lighting the candle in the pitcher as some families did in northern Portugal combines a Jewish symbol with a tradition preserved in their Catholic families. They were unaware of its meaning; they were probably converted Jews from the fifteenth century. But the Jewish and Christian aspects I discussed earlier are momentarily synthesized here.

POETRY MISCELLANY: The whole poem is about an economics of motion, too, isn't it? I'm thinking of "Mount Blank"—the man falls and the sun rises. You use the word "restitution," and the whole poem participates in an economics of restitution. In "Green" you have a conspirator say, "I would gaze at the ruins and contemplate not reconstruction, not restoration, but restitution."

JOHN HOLLANDER: Yes, there is a paying back for many things: patriotism, religion, neither of which is readily available. Now, this may be obviously Emersonian. I find I am constantly rediscovering roots, and one is the very idea of America. Understanding America is analogous to understanding mythology, understanding tropes. It always surprises me in this respect that most of the people who read Whitman read him literally; they are only talking about free verse. Williams often tends to read him somewhat literally, whereas Stevens understands Whitman much better and reads him as a poet.

POETRY MISCELLANY: This is a problem in contemporary poetry criticism generally, isn't it?

JOHN HOLLANDER: Yes, it's endemic. But some people are not capable of understanding Milton either. There are two problems. First, many readers have no problem with incoherence, but coherence gives them great trouble. A poem whose organization is based on fragmentation with a loose or trivial structure, as I described earlier, provides no problem of "understanding" for them. Yet when a poem does have a deep structure, one that is complex but coherent, they cannot handle it. Second, the problem is especially acute in American criticism. Think of Poe, for example, who is interested (in his essays) only in how those boring and terrible poets were misplacing iambs. Pound did some damage, too, though he is careful to talk about "writing" as distinct from poetry. These critics rarely talk about the relation of fiction to life, never about what being figurative means, never about being figurative and living in the knowledge that you are going to die.

POETRY MISCELLANY: This seems to be a perfect summary of Cupcake's problem in *Reflections*. "Which is the work and which is the life, which is the cipher of the other," he asks. His problem is confusion, and so, boredom. Sometimes things seem to mean too much and he wants things simplified.

JOHN HOLLANDER: That's very interesting, and I think it's quite true. I hadn't really noticed it, but one of the things he does suffer from is too much meaning. That's very good.

POETRY MISCELLANY: You suggested earlier, by the way, that working on *Reflections* helped with your writing of "Spectral Emanations."

JOHN HOLLANDER: Sending out the Cupcake messages actually enabled me to finish the other poem. The two poems have a strange relation to each other. There was a complete shift of ground. I had written a small poem years earlier, the Cupcake entry in which he is sitting, doing a picture puzzle. But it was done independently. I had been reading Sir John Masterman's book on the double-cross system where German spies in England were turned into double agents. I loved the names of the spies so much that I imagined a spy called Cupcake. I had him write to his control, Lyrebird, a Muse of sorts. The spy who couldn't do his work became the poet who couldn't write. Later, when I looked at it again, one phrase struck me, the phrase about "daily twilight messages," and that seemed a very beautiful condition—to have to send out messages every day lest they get you. I just sat down and wrote that first Cupcake entry. The others are arranged chronologically through the first half, and I altered some in the second half to provide a narrative structure. I had been sending them to one person, then started sending them to another without telling either that the other was receiving messages also. The fiction itself started to shape everything. That's why I refer to project Orange and project Yellow—they are the parts of "Spectral Emanations" I couldn't do.

POETRY MISCELLANY: And project White, too, which is associated with the final cipher? Hilda's reference—the white light?

JOHN HOLLANDER: Yes, and there are overtones of the symbolist notion— what is *the* way to write. Certain great poets seem to find the final cipher early, as Stevens and that blank pentameter line he could always count on. The interesting thing in *Reflections* was using that eleven-syllable line, the grid, the code. But, yes, to complete project White would be to finish "Spectral Emanations."

POETRY MISCELLANY: You've talked a great deal about a process of discovery. I like to think of it as a bringing to light. In "The Shades," you have the notion that where there are no shadows of shades, there are "no / Flickering images of soul, no soul— / The body's pale nightmare of mind, faded." In *Either/Or*, if we can turn to Kierkegaard for one last moment, the narrator talks about his "Shadowgraph" method of revealing characters. The inward picture doesn't become perceptible until he sees it through the external, the outer shadow on the wall.

JOHN HOLLANDER: *Either/Or* is filled with little passages like that. Possibly it came back to me while I was writing "The Shades." I love the poem because I got my two cats into it. The problem in the poem is one of wondering: is the gray one the shadow of the black or the black one the shadow of the gray? Finally, I decided to dispense with that and put them both in. The poem deals with shades as a problem of meaning—shades of color. I took the phrase in a lot of its various meanings and did a version of each one. It goes back to a youthful curiosity about how shadow didn't mean just cast a shadow. In the King James Bible and Shakespeare it meant a phenomenon that did not have a physical basis—specter. Then I learned "shade" from that; it opened up a whole array of possibilities. The poem is a journey through possible meanings of this darkening, a journey of discovery. It ends hopefully, with the image of God walking in the garden in the cool of day, and the others "Acknowledging light under chestnut leaves." They are waking as the sun is ducking under the shades.

Selected Bibliography

This listing includes the major books of poetry written by each of the poets interviewed (disregarding chapbooks) and, for the reader who wishes to explore further the concerns of the interviews, a short selection of critical books or major essays about the poets. As yet, no books or major essays have been written about several poets, especially the younger ones. For them, the reader should refer to reviews in various journals, which are indexed in *Contemporary Poets* (New York: St. Martins's Press); *Contemporary Authors* (Detroit: Gale Research Co.); the excellent bibliographies in *PMLA*, *Contemporary Literary Criticism*, *Journal of Modern Literature*, and *An Index to Book Reviews in the Humanities;* and the book-length bibliographies that have been published for several of the poets included here. The reader should also be aware of *American Poets since World War II*, 2 vols. (Detroit: Gale Research Co., 1980), edited by Donald Grenier, which includes excellent introductory essays on more than half of the poets interviewed and for which a second part is planned to include poets not covered in the first two volumes. The reader may also consult Kirby Congdon's *Contemporary Poets in American Anthologies, 1960–1977* (Metuchen: Scarecrow Press, 1978), and the two standard bibliographies of contemporary poetry, Charles Altieri's *Modern Poetry* (Arlington Heights, Ill.: AHM, Goldentree, 1979) and Karl Malkoff's *Crowell's Handbook of Contemporary American Poetry* (New York: Crowell, 1973). In addition, informative essays on several of the poets interviewed appear in Charles Altieri, *Enlarging the Temple: New Directions in American Poetry of the Sixties* (Cranberry, N.J.: Bucknell University Press, 1979); Robert Boyers, ed., *Contemporary Poetry in America: Essays and Interviews* (New York: Schocken Books, 1974); Richard Howard, *Alone with America*, 2d enlarged ed. (New York: Atheneum, 1980); Lawrence Lieberman, *Unassigned Frequencies: American Poetry in Review* (Urbana: University of Illinois Press, 1977); Helen Vendler, *Part of Nature, Part of Us* (Cambridge: Harvard University Press, 1980). Finally, Alberta Turner's *50 Contemporary Poets: The Creative Process* (New York: David McKay Co., 1977), contains essays by several of the poets on their own poems.

A. R. AMMONS, b. 1926, Whiteville, North Carolina; teaches at Cornell University. POETRY: *Ommateum, with Doxology* (Philadelphia: Dorrance, 1955); *Expressions of Sea Level* (Columbus: Ohio State University Press, 1964); *Corsons Inlet* (Ithaca: Cornell University Press, 1965); *Tape for the Turn of the Year* (Ithaca: Cornell University Press, 1965); *Northfield Poems* (Ithaca: Cornell University Press, 1966); *Selected Poems* (Ithaca: Cornell University Press, 1968); *Uplands* (New York: Norton, 1970); *Briefings: Poems Small and Easy* (New York: Norton, 1971); *Collected Poems, 1951–1971* (New York: Norton, 1972); *Sphere: The Form of a Motion* (New York: Norton, 1974); *Diversifications* (New York: Norton, 1975); *The Snow Poems* (New York: Norton, 1977); *The Selected*

Poems, 1951–1977 (New York: Norton, 1977); *A Coast of Trees* (New York: Norton, 1981). CRITICISM: Thomas Wolf, "A. R. Ammons and William Carlos Williams: A Study in Style and Meaning," *Contemporary Poetry* 2, no. 3 (1977): 1–16; Harold Bloom, "When You Consider the Radiance," in *The Ringers in the Tower* (Chicago: University of Chicago Press, 1971); *Diacritics* 3, no. 4 (1973): special issue on Ammons.

JOHN ASHBERY, b. 1927, Rochester, New York; teaches at Brooklyn College. POETRY: *Turandot and Other Poems* (New York: Tibor de Nagy, 1953); *Some Trees* (New Haven: Yale University Press, 1956; reprint, New York: Corinth, 1970); *The Tennis Court Oath* (Middletown: Wesleyan University Press, 1962); *Rivers and Mountains* (New York: Holt, Rinehart and Winston, 1966; reprint, New York: Ecco, 1977); *The Double Dream of Spring* (New York: Dutton, 1970; reprint, New York: Ecco, 1976); *Three Poems* (New York: Viking, 1972; reprint, New York: Penguin, 1977); *The Vermont Journal* (Los Angeles: Black Sparrow, 1975); *Self-Portrait in a Convex Mirror* (New York: Viking, 1975; reprint, New York: Penguin, 1976); *Houseboat Days* (New York: Viking/Penquin, 1977); *As We Know* (New York: Viking/Penguin, 1979); *Shadow Train* (New York: Viking/Penguin, 1981). CRITICISM: David Shapiro, *John Ashbery: An Introduction to the Poetry* (New York: Columbia University Press, 1979); David Lehman, ed., *Beyond Amazement: New Essays on John Ashbery* (Ithaca: Cornell University Press, 1980); Charles Altieri, "Motives in Metaphor: John Ashbery and the Modernist Long Poem," *Genre* 11 (1978): 653–87.

MARVIN BELL, b. 1937, New York City; teaches at University of Iowa. POETRY: *A Probable Volume of Dreams* (New York: Atheneum, 1969); *The Escape into You* (New York: Atheneum, 1971); *Residue of Song* (New York: Atheneum, 1974); *Stars Which See, Stars Which Do Not See* (New York: Atheneum, 1977); *These Green-Going-to-Yellow* (New York: Atheneum, 1981). CRITICISM: Arthur Ober, "Marvin Bell: 'Time's Detriment. / Once I knew You,'" *American Poetry Review* 5 (1976): 4–8.

PHILIP BOOTH, b. 1925, Hanover, New Hampshire; teaches at Syracuse University; also lives in Castile, Maine. POETRY: *Letter from a Distant Land* (New York: Viking, 1956); *The Islanders* (New York: Viking, 1960); *Weathers and Edges* (New York: Viking, 1966); *Margins* (New York: Viking, 1970); *Available Light* (New York: Viking, 1976); *Before Sleep* (New York: Viking, 1980).

FRED CHAPPELL, b. 1936, Canton, North Carolina; teaches at University of North Carolina–Greensboro. POETRY: *The World Between the Eyes* (Baton Rouge: Louisiana State University Press, 1981); *Midquest* (Baton Rouge: Louisiana State University Press, 1981; a quartet of books also published separately by Louisiana State University Press: *River*, 1975; *Bloodfire*, 1978; *Wind Mountain*, 1979; *Earthsleep*, 1980).

ROBERT CREELEY, b. 1926, Arlington, Massachusetts; teaches at SUNY-Buffalo. POETRY: *Le Fou* (Columbus, Ohio: Golden Goose, 1952); *The Kind of Act of* (Majorca: Divers, 1953); *The Immoral Proposition* (Highlands, N.C.: Jonathan Williams, 1953); *All That Is Lovely in Men* (Highlands, N.C.: Jargon, 1955); *A Form of Women* (New York: Jargon-Corinth, 1959); *For Love: Poems, 1950–1960* (New York: Scribner's, 1962);

Words (New York: Scribner's, 1967); *The Charm: Early and Uncollected Poems* (Madison, Wisc.: Perishable Press, 1967; reprint, San Francisco: Four Seasons, 1969); *The Finger* (with Bobbie Creeley) (Los Angeles: Black Sparrow, 1968); *Pieces* (Los Angeles: Black Sparrow, 1968); *St. Martin's* (with Bobbie Creeley) (Los Angeles: Black Sparrow, 1971); *1-2-3-4-5-6-7-8-9-0* (with Arthur Okamura) (Berkeley: Mudra, 1971); *A Day Book* (New York: Scribner's, 1972); *Thirty Things* (with Bobbie Creeley) (Los Angeles: Black Sparrow, 1974); *Away* (with Bobbie Creeley) (Santa Barbara: Black Sparrow, 1976); *Presences* (with Marisol) (Santa Barbara: Black Sparrow, 1976); *Selected Poems* (New York: Scribner's, 1976); *Hello* (New York: New Directions, 1978); *Later* (New York: New Directions, 1979); *The Collected Poems of Robert Creeley, 1945–1975* (Berkeley and Los Angeles: University of California Press, 1982). CRITICISM: Cynthia Edelberg, *Robert Creeley's Poetry: A Critical Introduction* (Albuquerque: University of New Mexico Press, 1978); Arthur Ford, *Robert Creeley* (Boston: Twayne, 1978); Robert Kern, "Composition as Recognition: Robert Creeley and Postmodern Poetics," *Boundary 2* 6/7 (Spring/Fall 1978): 211–30.

DANIEL MARK EPSTEIN, b. 1948, Washington, D.C.; teaches at Johns Hopkins University. POETRY: *No Vacancies in Hell* (New York: Liveright, 1973); *The Follies* (Woodstock, N.Y.: Overlook Press, 1978); *Young Men's Gold* (Woodstock, N.Y.: Overlook Press, 1977); *The Book of Fortune* (Woodstock, N.Y.: Overlook Press, 1982).

DONALD FINKEL, b. 1929, New York City; teaches at Washington University in St. Louis. POETRY: *Simeon* (New York: Atheneum, 1964); *A Joyful Noise* (New York: Atheneum, 1966); *Answer Back* (New York: Atheneum, 1968); *The Garbage Wars* (New York: Atheneum, 1970); *Adequate Earth* (New York: Atheneum, 1972); *A Mote in Heaven's Eye* (New York: Atheneum, 1975); *Going Under* and *Endurance* (New York: Atheneum, 1978); *What Manner of Beast* (New York: Atheneum, 1981).

DONALD HALL, b. 1928, New Haven, Connecticut; lives in Danbury, New Hampshire. POETRY: *(Poems)* (Oxford, England: Fantasy, 1952); *Exiles and Marriages* (New York: Viking, 1955); *The Dark Houses* (New York: Viking, 1958); *A Roof of Tiger Lilies: Poems* (New York: Viking, 1964); *The Alligator Bride: Poems New and Selected* (New York: Harper & Row, 1969); *The Yellow Room: Love Poems* (New York: Harper & Row, 1971); *Kicking the Leaves* (New York: Harper & Row, 1978); *The Toy Bone* (Brockport, N.Y.: BOA Editions, 1979). CRITICISM: Ralph Mills, "Donald Hall's Poetry," *Iowa Review* 2 (Winter 1971): 82–123; *Tennessee Poetry Journal* 4, no. 2 (1971): special issue on Hall.

MICHAEL S. HARPER, b. 1938, Brooklyn; teaches at Brown University. POETRY: *Dear John, Dear Coltrane* (Pittsburgh: University of Pittsburgh Press, 1970); *History Is Your Own Heartbeat* (Urbana: University of Illinois Press, 1971); *Song: I Want a Witness* (Pittsburgh: University of Pittsburgh Press, 1972); *Debridement* (New York: Doubleday, 1973); *Nightmare Begins Responsibility* (Urbana: University of Illinois Press, 1975); *Images of Kin: New and Selected Poems* (Urbana: University of Illinois Press, 1977).

JOHN HOLLANDER, b. 1929, New York City; teaches at Yale University. POETRY: *A Crackling of Thorns* (New Haven: Yale University Press, 1958); *Movie Going* (New York: Atheneum, 1962); *Visions from the Ramble* (New York: Atheneum, 1965); *Types of Shape* (New York: Atheneum, 1969); *The Night Mirror* (New York: Atheneum, 1971); *Tales Told of the Fathers* (New York: Atheneum, 1975); *Reflections on Espionage* (New York: Atheneum, 1976); *Spectral Emanations: New and Selected Poems* (New York: Atheneum, 1978); *Blue Wine and Other Poems* (Baltimore: Johns Hopkins University Press, 1979). CRITICISM: Harold Bloom, "The White Light of Trope: An Essay on John Hollander's *Spectral Emanations*," *Kenyon Review* n.s., no. 1 (Winter 1979): 95–113.

DAVID IGNATOW, b. 1914, Brooklyn; teaches at York College-CUNY and the School of Arts at Columbia. POETRY: *Say Pardon* (Middletown: Wesleyan University Press, 1962); *Figures of the Human* (Middletown: Wesleyan University Press, 1964); *Rescue the Dead* (Middletown: Wesleyan University Press, 1968); *Poems: 1934–1969* (Middletown: Wesleyan University Press, 1970); *Facing the Tree: New Poems* (Boston: Atlantic–Little, Brown, 1975); *Selected Poems* (Middletown: Wesleyan University Press, 1975); *Tread the Dark: New Poems* (Boston: Atlantic–Little, Brown, 1978); *Sunlight: A Sequence for My Daughter* (Brockport, N.Y.: BOA Editions, 1979); *Whisper to the Earth* (Boston: Atlantic–Little, Brown, 1982). CRITICISM: Ralph Mills, Jr., "Earth Hard: The Poetry of David Ignatow," *Boundary 2* 2 (1974): 373–429.

MAXINE KUMIN, b. 1925, Philadelphia; lives in Warner, New Hampshire. POETRY: *Halfway* (New York: Holt, Rinehart and Winston, 1961); *The Privilege* (New York: Harper & Row, 1965); *The Nightmare Factory* (New York: Harper & Row, 1970); *Up Country* (New York: Harper & Row, 1972); *House, Bridge, Fountain, Gate* (New York: Viking, 1975); *The Retrieval System* (New York: Viking, 1978); *Our Ground Time Here Will Be Brief: New and Selected Poems* (New York: Penguin Books, 1982).

STANLEY KUNITZ, b. 1905, Worcester, Massachusetts; lives in Provincetown, Massachusetts. POETRY: *Intellectual Things* (New York: Doubleday, 1930); *Passport to the War: A Selection of Poems* (New York: Holt, Rinehart and Winston, 1944); *Selected Poems, 1928–1958* (Boston: Little, Brown, 1958); *The Testing-Tree: Poems* (Boston: Atlantic–Little, Brown, 1971), *The Poems of Stanley Kunitz 1928–1978* (Boston: Atlantic–Little, Brown, 1979). CRITICISM: Marie Hinault, *Stanley Kunitz* (Boston: Twayne, 1980); Robert Weisberg, "Stanley Kunitz: The Stubborn Middle Way," *Modern Poetry Studies* 6 (1975): 49–73.

HEATHER McHUGH, b. 1948, California; teaches at Warren Wilson and SUNY Binghamton. POETRY: *Dangers* (Boston: Houghton Mifflin, 1977); *A World of Difference* (Boston: Houghton Mifflin, 1981).

W. S. MERWIN, b. 1927, New York City; lives in Haiku, Hawaii. POETRY: *A Mask for Janus* (New Haven: Yale University Press, 1952); *The Dancing Bears* (New Haven: Yale University Press, 1954); *Green with Beasts* (New York: Knopf, 1956); *The Drunk in the Furnace* (New York: Macmillan, 1960); *The Moving Target* (New York: Atheneum, 1963); *The Lice* (New York: Atheneum, 1967); *The Carrier of Ladders* (New York:

Atheneum, 1970); *Asian Figures* (New York: Atheneum, 1972); *Writings to an Unfinished Accompaniment* (New York: Atheneum, 1974); *The First Four Books of Poems* (New York: Atheneum, 1975); *The Compass Flower* (New York: Atheneum, 1977). PROSE: *The Miner's Pale Children* (New York: Atheneum, 1970); *Houses and Travellers* (New York: Atheneum, 1977). CRITICISM: Cheri Davis, "Time and Timelessness in the Poetry of W. S. Merwin," *Modern Poetry Studies* 6 (1975): 224–36; Cary Nelson, "The Resources of Failure: W. S. Merwin's Deconstructive Career," *Boundary 2* 5 (1977): 573–98.

CAROL MUSKE, b. 1945, St. Paul, Minnesota; lives in New York City. POETRY: *Camouflage* (Pittsburgh: University of Pittsburgh Press, 1975); *Skylight* (New York: Doubleday, 1981).

ROBERT PACK, b. 1929, New York City; teaches at Middlebury College. POETRY: *The Irony of Joy* (New York: Scribner's, 1955); *A Stranger's Privilege* (New York: Macmillan, 1959); *Guarded by Women* (New York: Random House, 1963); *Selected Poems* (London: Chatto & Windus, 1964); *Home from the Cemetery* (New Brunswick: Rutgers University Press, 1969); *Nothing but Light* (New Brunswick: Rutgers University Press, 1972); *Keeping Watch* (New Brunswick: Rutgers University Press, 1976); *Waking to My Name: New and Selected Poems* (Baltimore: Johns Hopkins University Press, 1980). CRITICISM: Lawrence Raab, "Art's Will, 'The Last Will and Testament of Art Evergreen' by Robert Pack" in *A Book of Rereadings*, ed. Greg Kuzma (Lincoln, Neb.: Best Cellar Press, 1979), pp. 112–26.

LINDA PASTAN, b. 1932, New York City; lives in Bethesda, Maryland. POETRY: *A Perfect Circle of Sun* (Chicago: Swallow, 1971); *Aspects of Eve* (New York: Liveright, 1975); *The Five Stages of Grief* (New York: Norton, 1978); *Selected Poems* (New York: Norton, 1980); *Waiting for My Life* (New York: Norton, 1981).

MARGE PIERCY, b. 1934, Detroit; lives in Wellfleet, Massachusetts. POETRY: *Breaking Camp* (Middletown: Wesleyan University Press, 1968); *Hard Loving* (Middletown: Wesleyan University Press, 1969); *To Be of Use* (New York: Doubleday, 1973); *Living in the Open* (New York: Knopf, 1976); *The Twelve Spoked Wheel Flashing* (New York: Knopf, 1978); *The Moon Is Always Female* (New York: Knopf, 1980); *Stone, Paper, Knife* (New York: Knopf, 1982); *Circles of the Water: Selected Poems* (New York: Knopf, 1982). CRITICISM: Joyce Landenson, "Marge Piercy's Revolutionary Feminism," *Society for the Study of Midwestern Literature Newsletter* 10, no. 2 (1980): 24–31.

STANLEY PLUMLY, b. 1939, Barnesville, Ohio; teaches at University of Houston. POETRY: *In the Outer Dark* (Baton Rouge: Louisiana State University Press, 1970); *Giraffe* (Baton Rouge: Louisiana State University Press, 1973); *Out-of-the-Body Travel* (New York: Ecco, 1976). CRITICISM: Peter Stitt, "On Stanley Plumly: That Enduring Essence," *American Poetry Review* 9, no. 2 (1980): 16–17.

DAVID ST. JOHN, b. 1949, California; teaches at Johns Hopkins University. POETRY: *Hush* (Boston: Houghton Mifflin, 1976); *The Olive Grove* (Syracuse: W. D. Hoffstadt & Sons, 1980); *The Shore* (Boston: Houghton Mifflin, 1980).

CHARLES SIMIC, b. 1938, Yugoslavia; teaches at University of New Hampshire. POETRY: *Dismantling the Silence* (New York: George Braziller, 1971); *Return to a Place Lit by a Glass of Milk* (New York: George Braziller, 1974); *Charon's Cosmology* (New York: George Braziller, 1977); *White: A New Version* (Durango, Colo.: Logbridge-Rhodes, 1980); *Austerities* (New York: George Braziller, 1982). CRITICISM: Victor Contoski, "Charles Simic: Language at the Stone's Heart," *Chicago Review* 28, no. 6 (1977): 145–57; *Manassas Review: Essays on Contemporary American Poetry* 1, no. 2 (Winter 1978): special issue on Simic.

WILLIAM STAFFORD, b. 1914, Hutchinson, Kansas; teaches at Lewis and Clark College. POETRY: *West of Your City* (Georgetown, Calif.: Talisman Press, 1960); *The Rescued Year* (New York: Harper & Row, 1966); *Allegiances* (New York: Harper & Row, 1970); *Someday, Maybe* (New York: Harper & Row, 1973); *Stories That Could Be True: New and Selected Poems* (New York: Harper & Row, 1977); *Things That Happen When There Aren't Any People* (Brockport, N.Y.: BOA Editions, 1980); *A Glass Face in the Rain* (New York: Harper & Row, 1982). CRITICISM: Jonathan Holden, *The Mark to Turn: A Reading of William Stafford's Poetry* (Lawrence: University of Kansas Press, 1975); Linda Wagner, "William Stafford's Plain Style," *Modern Poetry Studies* 6 (1975): 19–30.

MARK STRAND, b. 1934, Prince Edward Island, Canada; teaches at University of Utah. POETRY: *Reasons for Moving* (New York: Atheneum, 1968); *Darker* (New York: Atheneum, 1970); *The Story of Our Lives* (New York: Atheneum, 1973); *The Late Hour* (New York: Atheneum, 1978); *The Monument* (prose) (New York: Ecco, 1978); *Selected Poems* (New York: Atheneum, 1980). CRITICISM: Harold Bloom, "Dark and Radiant Peripheries: Mark Strand and A. R. Ammons," *Southern Review*, n.s. 8 (Winter 1972): 133–41.

JEAN VALENTINE, b. 1934, Chicago; teaches at Sarah Lawrence College. POETRY: *Dream Barker* (New Haven: Yale University Press, 1965); *Pilgrims* (New York: Farrar, 1969); *Ordinary Things (New York: Farrar, 1974); The Messenger* (New York: Farrar, 1979). CRITICISM: Philip Booth, "On Jean Valentine's Poetry: A Continuum of Turning," *American Poetry Review* 9, no. 1 (1980): 4–6.

ROBERT PENN WARREN, b. 1905, Guthrie, Kentucky; lives in Farmington, Connecticut. POETRY: *Thirty-Six Poems* (New York: Alcestis Press, 1935); *Eleven Poems on the Same Theme* (Norfolk: New Directions, 1942); *Selected Poems: 1923–1943* (New York: Harcourt Brace, 1944); *Brother to Dragons* (New York: Random House, 1953, revised 1979); *Promises: Poems, 1954–1956* (New York: Random House, 1957); *You, Emperors, and Others: Poems, 1957–1960* (New York: Random House, 1960); *Selected Poems, New and Old: 1923–1966* (New York: Random House, 1966); *Incarnations: Poems, 1966–1968* (New York: Random House, 1968); *Audubon: A Vision* (New York: Random

House, 1969); *Or Else: Poem/Poems, 1968–1974* (New York: Random House, 1974); *Selected Poems, 1923–1975* (New York: Random House, 1977); *Now and Then: Poems, 1976–1978* (New York: Random House, 1978); *Being Here: Poetry, 1977–1980* (New York: Random House, 1980); *Rumor Verified: Poems, 1979–1980* (New York: Random House, 1981). CRITICISM: Victor Strandberg, *The Poetic Vision of Robert Penn Warren* (Lexington: University of Kentucky Press, 1977); Charles Bohrer, *Robert Penn Warren* (New York: Twayne 1964); Leonard Casper, *Robert Penn Warren: The Dark and Bloody Ground* (Seattle: University of Washington Press, 1960); Richard Jackson, "The Generous Time: Robert Penn Warren and the Phenomenology of the Moment," *Boundary 2* 9 (Winter 1981): 1–30.

DARA WIER, b. 1949, New Orleans; teaches at The University of Alabama. POETRY: *Blood, Hook & Eye* (Austin: University of Texas Press, 1977); *The 8-Step Grapevine* (Pittsburgh: Carnegie Mellon University Press, 1980).

RICHARD WILBUR, b. 1921, New York City; lives in Cummington, Massachusetts. POETRY: *The Beautiful Changes and Other Poems* (New York: Reynal & Hitchcock, 1947); *Ceremony and Other Poems* (New York: Harcourt, Brace, 1950); *Things of This World: Poems* (New York: Harcourt, Brace, 1956); *Advice to a Prophet and Other Poems* (New York: Harcourt, Brace & World, 1961); *The Poems of Richard Wilbur* (New York: Harcourt, Brace & World, 1963); *Walking to Sleep: New Poems and Translations* (New York: Harcourt Brace Jovanovich, 1969); *The Mind Reader: New Poems* (New York: Harcourt Brace Jovanovich, 1976). CRITICISM: Paul Cummins, *Richard Wilbur* (Grand Rapids: Eerdmans, 1971); Donald Hill, *Richard Wilbur* (New York: Twayne, 1967); Ejner Jensen, "Encounters with Experience: The Poems of Richard Wilbur," *New England Review* 2 (1980): 594–613.

MILLER WILLIAMS, b. 1930, Hoxie, Arkansas; directs the press and teaches at University of Arkansas. POETRY: *A Circle of Stone* (Baton Rouge: Louisiana State University Press, 1964); *So Long at the Fair* (New York: Dutton, 1968); *The Only World There Is* (New York: Dutton, 1971); *Halfway from Hoxie: New and Selected Poems* (Baton Rouge: Louisiana State University Press, 1976); *Why God Permits Evil* (Baton Rouge: Louisiana State University Press, 1977); *Distractions* (Baton Rouge: Louisiana State University Press, 1981).

Index